A SHORT LIFE OF CHRIST

Other Books by Everett F. Harrison

INTRODUCTION TO THE NEW TESTAMENT
THE SON OF GOD AMONG THE SONS OF MEN
BAKER'S DICTIONARY OF THEOLOGY *(Editor)*
THE WYCLIFFE BIBLE COMMENTARY *(Co-editor)*

A SHORT
LIFE OF CHRIST

by

EVERETT F. HARRISON

Senior Professor of New Testament
Fuller Theological Seminary

WM. B. EERDMANS PUBLISHING COMPANY
GRAND RAPIDS, MICHIGAN

ISBN 0-8028-3333-0

First printing, December 1968
Second printing, July 1973
Third printing, October 1975

To
Arline
whose love and companionship reflect His
of whom this book is written

PREFACE

In our day scholars are no longer attempting to write a full-length life of Christ that takes account of every incident and every movement involved in the story. There are reasons for their reluctance. One is the vast accumulation of information made available by research, much of it tucked away in the learned journals. To weave it all together would be a difficult and delicate task. Men prefer to write on a single facet of the story where they can hope to blaze a new trail or at least supplement earlier investigation.

Heavily influential also has been the development known as form criticism, which for more than a generation has been the accepted methodology of a considerable number of scholars. The tendency of this approach to the Gospels is to emphasize that the tradition lying back of the Gospel records has been greatly affected by the outlook and situation of the early church, so that the stamp of the church's life and faith is on the narratives to a degree that makes the objectively historical material, as distinct from what is ecclesiastically motivated, almost impossible to ferret out. Along with this goes the contention that the tradition existed for the most part in rather brief fragments, from which the writers, who were basically editors, put together the various Gospel accounts. Since the links in the narrative are regarded as editorially supplied, no confidence can be placed in the chronological sequence of the narrated events. So the writing of a comprehensive life of Christ seems futile.

Furthermore, it has come to be widely recognized that the Gospels are not biographies, since they leave out much that would be of biographical interest. Rather, they are what the titles indicate, Gospels. To use Mark's phrase, they are accounts of the beginning of the gospel. There was no intention of providing the necessary ingredients for a "scientific" history of Jesus of Nazareth.

More recently the conviction is gaining ground that the units of gospel tradition are not arbitrarily put together, without rhyme or reason, but are to be regarded as the work of men with an artistic and theological conception of their task, who wrote out of a definite purpose that can only be appreciated as one studies the whole Gospel as a unit. This is a definite gain, for which all should be grateful.

The present volume has been produced under the conviction that in spite of all obstacles in dealing with the text, there is still room for a treatment of the life of Christ that concerns itself with the leading events that carry us along in a fairly obvious sequence from the beginning to the end. Some aspects have been included that are quite independent of chronological problems, such as the teaching, miracles, character, and claims of Jesus. Here the considerations of sequence are either absent or are minimal in their importance.

Some readers may be disappointed that there is no review of the quest of the historical Jesus, especially in its more recent aspects. After due consideration it was felt that even a cursory review of these developments would unwarrantably extend the length of the book, and would not make a sufficient contribution to the whole to make the addition worthwhile. For those who wish to pursue this branch of study for themselves a few titles have been provided in the bibliography under Chapter One.

It should be recognized that since entire books have been written on each one of the subjects treated here, the handling of each theme has of necessity been in the nature of a summary rather than an exhaustive treatment.

EVERETT F. HARRISON

CONTENTS

ABBREVIATIONS

CBQ — *Catholic Biblical Quarterly*
CQR — *Church Quarterly Review*
EQ — *Evangelical Quarterly*
ET — *Expository Times*
HDB — Hastings' *Dictionary of the Bible* (1899)
HDCG — Hastings' *Dictionary of Christ and the Gospels* (1924)
ICC — *International Critical Commentary*, ed. C. A. Briggs, S. R. Driver, *et al.* (1895ff.)
ISBE — *International Standard Bible Encyclopaedia*, ed. J. Orr, *et al.* (1929, 1939)
JBL — *Journal of Biblical Literature*
JTS — *Journal of Theological Studies*
KJV — King James Version
RB—*Revue Biblique*
*RSV — Revised Standard Version
SBK — *Kommentar zum Neuen Testament aus Talmud und Midrasch*, by Strack and Billerbeck (1922)
TDNT — *Theological Dictionary of the New Testament*, ed. G. Kittel and G. Friedrich (1933ff.), trans. G. Bromiley (1964ff.)

---

* Unless otherwise indicated, the biblical quotations in this book are taken from the Revised Standard Version.

CHAPTER I

THE HISTORICITY OF JESUS

> *"Jesus is God lived by man."*
>
> —F. Godet

> *"To the two questions: What does God offer to man? and What does God require of man? the New Testament returns one answer: the Life of Christ."*
>
> —T. W. Manson

> *"The man who can read the first three Gospels . . . without being sensible that a mighty personality is at work in them—a personality swaying the hearts of men and far beyond the power of men to invent—must be denied the capacity to distinguish between fiction and the documentary evidence to a historical and personal life."*
>
> —Adolf Harnack

SOME RELIGIONS, BOTH ANCIENT AND MODERN, REQUIRE NO HISTORI-cal basis, for they depend upon ideas rather than events. Christianity is not one of these. It has its roots in the Old Testament, where religion and history are inseparably joined as the expression of the purposeful activity of Israel's God.[1] Jesus Christ, the central personage of the Christian faith, came into the world "in the fulness of time." In his own preaching and in that of his followers, it is strongly insisted that he came to fulfill the promises made by God to the fathers. Jesus' career is carefully located in

---

1 Herbert Butterfield, *Christianity and History* (1949), p. 1, shows how disastrous were the effects of nature-worship upon the moral life of Israel, when the God of history was repudiated.

11

the records both as to time and place, despite the fragmentary character of the information about his life as a whole. Furthermore, the Lord seemed to be certain that his coming into the world would have a profound effect upon the course of future generations. Christianity is thus firmly yoked to history.

Until modern times, when the spirit of inquiry began to question all our traditions, no one thought of doubting that Jesus actually lived among men. Then philosophy began to join forces with comparative religion to relegate Jesus to the category of myth. Those who held that ultimate reality lies in the realm of thought without any necessary connection with historical events looked upon Christianity as valuable only in the measure in which it afforded illustration of universal truths. For example, the story of the incarnation was treasured only because it is a lovely exposition of one of the greatest truths to find lodgment in the human mind, namely, the harmonious union between God and man. Students of the history of religion were able to show that in ancient times many systems of worship were built up around figures that had no actual existence, but whose story answered to some human need or aspiration. Why should not Christianity be regarded simply as one of the mystery cults of antiquity and why should not Jesus be classed with Osiris, Adonis and others?

The drift in this direction began at the close of the eighteenth century with two Frenchmen, Volney and Dupuis, who sought to associate Jesus with astral myths of the Orient. David Strauss, in his *Life of Jesus*, though he retained a small core of factual material for the person and work of Christ, dismissed the bulk of the record in the Gospels as mythical. Around the middle of the nineteenth century Bruno Bauer undertook the task of showing that Jesus never existed except as a dramatic creation. Instead of being the founder of the church, he was the creature of the church's imagination. The Gospel records were ridiculed as abounding with contradictions and filled with alleged events that cannot be verified. Bauer assigned a second-century date for the emergence of the Gospels and disposed of the testimony of Paul to Christ by denying the authenticity of his epistles *in toto*.

Early in the present century the so-called Dutch school came into prominence, headed by Loman, van Manen, and Bolland. These men continued the radical, negative approach of Bruno Bauer and used many of the same arguments. To some extent they depended upon the theory of the existence of a Joshua cult in

Israel, playing up the identity of meaning between the names
Joshua and Jesus. But the theory suffered damage from the lack
of any evidence for such a cult in pre-Christian times.

Proponents of the mythical position continued to arise for a
time—J. M. Robertson in Britain, W. B. Smith in America, and
P. Jensen in Germany. Jensen, due to his interest in Babylonian
myth, sought to make the story of Jesus merely an edition of the
Babylonian Gilgamesh tale, despite the very great differences between it and the Gospel accounts of Jesus. Robertson counted
heavily on the nature myths and the mystery religions of the
Graeco-Roman world as the sufficient explanation for the materials of the New Testament.

The effort to link Jesus with pagan cults is doomed to failure
for several reasons. First, there is no evidence for the actual personal historical existence of any of the heroes of these cults—Attis,
Adonis, Osiris, Dionysus, and others—nor even any claim that
they had such existence. In contrast, Jesus walked the earth a
flesh-and-blood individual. He is not the dramatic embodiment
of an idea. His personality is too strongly etched, his career too
firmly embedded in a definite historic situation, his influence too
strongly impressed on those about him, to permit any such solution. Second, the cultus built up around these mythical figures
was lacking in ethical content. It is quite otherwise with the
Christian faith, which makes strenuous demands upon those who
would follow the Master. Third, any resemblance between Jesus
and the dying-rising gods of the nature cults is wholly artificial.
What was celebrated in the festivals of most of these cults was
really the annual decay of vegetation in the fall and its revival in
the spring. In the case of Jesus, death and resurrection are not
recurring phenomena, but are once-for-all in their character.
Though they are gratefully remembered by Christians, they are
not reenacted. These are events that occurred at definite times
and places, concerning which there were competent witnesses who
were able to give their testimony. This leads naturally to a fourth
consideration which is especially stressed by Guignebert, namely,
that the Scriptures represent the Christian movement to have
been established by men who were contemporary with Jesus.
Such is not the fashion with creators of myth, who regularly
place their heroes in the past "to avail themselves of the enor-
mous prestige of antiquity."[2] "It is in its attitude to history, and
to the divine purpose within history, that the Hebrew tradition,
as we can see it in the Old Testament and as it was continued in

primitive Christianity, differs both from the mystery-religions
and from the philosophy of Greece."[3]

The student of religion will naturally ask himself why Christianity survived and grew whereas the cults it is alleged to resemble so closely perished. Is this an accident of history or a
testimony to qualitative difference? Karl Holl indicts the com-
parative-religion approach when he states,

> This whole way of considering the matter, at any rate as
> regards the understanding of Christianity, is completely out
> of focus. It seeks everywhere merely the similarities, and thinks
> thereby to find the essence of Christianity. But the power of a
> religion never lies in what it has in common with others, but
> what is peculiar to itself. Christianity can have conquered only
> through what differentiated it sharply, and differentiated it as
> a religion, through something quite unique, which stamped
> with its own particular impress even what it borrowed.[4]

More recently another formidable assailant of the historical
foundation of Christianity appeared in the person of Arthur
Drews, a teacher in a German *Hochschule*. His best-known works
are *The Christ-Myth* and *Witnesses to the Historicity of Jesus*.
He included the arguments of the previously named men and
made use also of the viewpoint of Kalthoff,[5] who had claimed a
sociological basis for the origin of Christianity, the igniting of
the volcanic restlessness of the Roman masses by the messianic
hopes of the Jews. This of course does violence to the Palestinian
setting for the origin of the church. Drews' work called forth a
veritable rash of replies from contemporary scholars—Jülicher,
J. Weiss, von Soden and others. Since that time it has become
customary for those who deal with the life of Christ to give preliminary consideration to the subject of historicity.

The evidence for the historicity of Jesus Christ is threefold:
documentary, institutional, and personal. Necessarily the greatest
stress must be laid upon the documentary basis, which includes
Jewish, Roman, and Christian testimonies.

[2] Charles Guignebert, *Jesus* (1935), p. 73.
[3] J. K. Mozley, *The Doctrine of the Incarnation* (1949), p. 23.
[4] *The Distinctive Elements in Christianity* (1937), p. 14.
[5] *The Rise of Christianity* (1907).

THE JEWISH TESTIMONY

From the standpoint of earthly origin, Jesus was a Jew. His ministry was largely confined to the Jews, so much so that he scarcely left their land during his entire career. It is natural, then, to expect some evidence concerning his work from contemporaries among his own people. That Jewish literature says so little about him is due mainly to two factors. Having refused him as their Messiah, this people would naturally prefer to say as little about him as possible, even though they could not dismiss him entirely. It was the easiest way to handle an embarrassing issue. Then, too, Jewish occupation with written records became intense only after the fall of Jerusalem and the consequent breaking up of corporate national life. By the time the Talmud was written, Jewish traditions concerning Jesus tended to be vague and uncertain. Very little of the history of Israel at the time of Jesus is reflected in the Talmud anyway.[6] The important consideration is this, that in no case does the literature make any attempt to deny that he lived.

The leading passage is found in the tractate *Sanhedrin* (43a) of the Babylonian Talmud. This is not a part of the Mishnah proper, but is a *baraita* or tradition emanating from the Tannaim, teachers who flourished during the first two centuries of our era.

> On the eve of the Passover, Jesus of Nazareth was hung. During forty days a herald went before him crying aloud: "He ought to be stoned because he has practiced magic, has led Israel astray and caused them to rise in rebellion. Let him who has something to say in his defence come forward and declare it." But no one came forward, and he was hung on the eve of the Passover.

One observes here a reference to stoning as the punishment of which Jesus was worthy, yet the report of the carrying out of the sentence makes no mention of stoning but rather of hanging. The historic fact of Jesus' death by crucifixion was so well known that Jewish tradition could not well set it aside entirely.

Another item of interest is the allusion to a period of forty days (we might call them days of grace) during which Jesus was held for examination and the hearing of evidence. This is obviously an attempt to make the Jewish official proceedings appear in a

6 J. Klausner, *Jesus of Nazareth* (1925), p. 19.

more favorable light than in the Gospels, where Jesus is pictured as rushed through the semblance of a trial, then hurriedly turned over to the Roman governor.

A third element in the statement is worthy of attention. Included among the charges laid against Jesus is this one, that he practiced magic. The same charge is found in Celsus' attack on Christianity in the second century, where it is claimed that Jesus went to Egypt and there learned the secrets of the magicians, afterward returning to Palestine and deceiving the people by his quackery.[7] In both cases there is an admission of the fact that Jesus performed mighty works. The talmudic charge is a somewhat different version of the accusation brought against Jesus by the Pharisees to the effect that he was able to cast out demons because he was in league with the prince of demons.

Another talmudic reference[8] speaks of Jesus as Ben-Pandira or Ben-Panthera (Panther's son). According to Klausner, this goes back to the beginning of the second century or earlier. Several occurrences of this name may be found in *baraitas* of the period. The Jews circulated the story that Jesus was an illegitimate child born of Mary and a Roman soldier. Celsus picked up this tale and used it in his attack on Christianity. Klausner raises the question why the Roman soldier is called by this name—Pandira or Panthera. He concludes that the name Ben-Panthera is derived by simple transposition of letters in the Greek word for virgin (*parthenos*), and that the slander is an echo of the Christian belief in the virgin birth of Jesus.[9] This has not won universal acceptance. Deissmann, citing the name from an epitaph from the German frontier of the Roman empire, declares that this "shows with absolute certainty that *Panthera* was not an invention of Jewish scoffers, but a widespread name among the ancients."[10] But in any event the testimony to Jesus' existence remains unimpaired.

A further source of Jewish testimony to Jesus is Josephus the historian. After studying into the beliefs and practices of the various parties in Judaism, he became a Pharisee when still a young man. His prominence is attested by his participation in a successful embassage to Rome at the age of 26. At the outbreak

---

[7] Origen *Contra Celsum* i.38.

[8] *Aboda Zara* (Jer.) 40d.

[9] *Op. cit.*, pp. 23-24.

[10] *Light from the Ancient East*, 4th edition (1927), p. 74. Cf. W. D. Davies, *The Setting of the Sermon on the Mount*, p. 288.

of the Jewish War against Rome he did what he could to stem the tide of rebellion, but seeing that this was hopeless, accepted a military post in Galilee, thus throwing in his lot with his countrymen. Surviving the Jewish defeat, he gained the favor of Vespasian, who commanded the Roman forces, by predicting that he would be emperor. When this came to pass two years later, Josephus was given his freedom and was taken into the royal household at Rome, where he occupied himself in writing about his people for the benefit of the Romans. One of the best known of these writings is the *Antiquities of the Jews*, penned near the close of the first century. A notable passage concerning Jesus Christ reads as follows: "And there arose about this time Jesus, a wise man, if indeed we should call him a man. For he was a doer of marvelous deeds (miracles), a teacher of men who receive the truth with pleasure. He led away many Jews, and also many of the Greeks. This man was the Christ. And when Pilate had condemned him to the cross on his impeachment by the chief men among us, those who had loved him at first did not cease; for he appeared to them on the third day alive again, the divine prophets having spoken these and thousands of other wonderful things about him: and even now the tribe of Christians, so named after him, has not yet died out."[11]

It is hardly conceivable that such laudatory words could have been written about Jesus by a non-Christian Jew. Consequently, most scholars are convinced that the passage, either in whole or in part, is a Christian interpolation. Origen did not make use of this citation; and he speaks of Josephus as an unbeliever,[12] which he could hardly do if this passage represented Josephus' point of view.

On the other hand, indications are not lacking that at least part of this statement must be allowed to stand, for the references to Jesus as a wise man and to Christians as a tribe sound far more natural coming from Josephus than from some Christian source.[13]

[11] *Antiquities* xviii.3.3.

[12] *Contra Celsum* i.47.

[13] Klausner, *op. cit.*, p. 58. See also H. St. J. Thackeray, *Josephus: The Man and the Historian*, p. 137. "The evidence of language, which, on the one hand, bears marks of the author's style, and on the other is not such as a Christian would have used, appears to me decisive." F. J. Foakes Jackson, *Josephus and the Jews*, p. 279, expresses the opinion that Josephus, in order to oblige some friend or patron interested in Christianity, inserted a statement about Jesus into his own work.

Some scholars have conjectured that the laudatory items were derived by contact with Christians and are stated in sarcasm.[14]

Before final judgment can be rendered in this matter, it is expedient to consider another passage from the same author. Josephus relates that in the interval between the death of the Roman governor Festus and the arrival of his successor Albinus, the high priest Ananus hastily assembled the Sanhedrin and brought before them James the brother of Jesus, who was called Christ, and when he had accused him, with certain others, as law breakers, delivered them to be stoned.[15] It is difficult to suppose interpolation here as there is no praise of James or Jesus, and it is unlikely that a Christian writer would be content to refer to Jesus as the "so-called" Christ. Furthermore, the identifying of Jesus as the Christ without further explanation seems plainly to imply the earlier disputed passage. At any rate, there is no sound reason for ruling out the testimony of Josephus to the existence of Jesus.

Comment is scarcely needed on the medieval legends current among the Jews concerning Jesus. These are gathered up under the title *Toledoth Yeshu*. Suffice it to say that no such bitter denunciations as these could have been called forth by a mere fantasy. They are leveled at an actual person.[16]

THE ROMAN TESTIMONY

Notices by Roman writers are scanty. This is to be expected in view of the fact that Judea was but a small segment of the empire, peopled by a race whom the Romans for the most part despised. For some decades after the rise of the Christian movement Rome continued to regard Christians as a sect of Judaism, for in the early years most of them were Jews. Consequently the Christians were virtually beneath the attention of the Roman authorities. A century or more later the story was quite different, for then this faith was becoming widespread and influential.

From about the same time in the first quarter of the second century three references to Christ appear in Roman writers, though one is less certain than the others. Pliny the Younger,

---

[14] F. F. Bruce, *Are the New Testament Documents Reliable?* (1943), pp. 106-107.

[15] *Antiquities* xx.9.1.

[16] For a summary of the contents of the *Toledoth Yeshu* see Klausner, pp. 48-51.

when governor of Bithynia in Asia Minor, wrote to Emperor Trajan seeking guidance in the matter of dealing with Christians, whom he describes as coming together at fixed seasons and singing a hymn to Christ as God (or a deity). Goguel is of the opinion that the expression *Christo quasi deo* (which he prefers to render: "to Christ as to a god") "seems to indicate that, in Pliny's opinion, Christ was not a god like those which other men worshipped."[17] Goguel goes on to say, "May we not conclude that the fact which distinguished Christ from all other 'gods' was that he had lived upon the earth?"

Tacitus, in recounting the reign of Nero and the report that he was the one who set fire to the city of Rome, states that Nero sought to divert suspicion from himself by placing the blame upon the Christians and proceeded to persecute them for this offense. The record continues: "Christus, the founder of the name, had undergone the death penalty in the reign of Tiberius, by sentence of the procurator Pontius Pilate, and the pernicious superstition was checked for a moment, only to break out once more, not merely in Judaea, the home of the disease, but in the capital itself, where all things horrible or shameful in the world collect and find a vogue."[18]

The value of this testimony is well stated by C. Milo Connick.

> Tacitus did not secure his information about Jesus' death from a Christian source. If he had, he would not have treated the nationalistic outbreak in Judea (which provoked the Jewish war) and the simultaneous alleged arson activities of Christians in Rome as part and parcel of the same movement. Neither did he derive his data from a Jewish source, for it would not have called Jesus "Christus." The pagan origin of Tacitus' statements presents solid evidence for the existence of Jesus.[19]

A third Roman writer, Suetonius, has a probable allusion to Christ. He states that the Emperor Claudius expelled the Jews from Rome because of their tumults at the instigation of Chrestus.[20] This may be capable of identification with Christus. What favors it is the consideration that both the Greek and the Latin words for Christian, analogous in form, are sometimes found

[17] *The Life of Jesus* (1949), p. 94.
[18] *Annals* xv.44.
[19] *Jesus: The Man, the Mission and the Message* (1963), p. 59.
[20] *Life of Claudius* xxv.4.

spelled with an *e* rather than an *i*. In fact, all three New Testament occurrences are thus spelled in the important *Codex Sinaiticus*. It is therefore possible that Christus was also sometimes spelled Chrestus. The most probable conclusion is that the statement of Suetonius refers to Christ. Jews in Rome were divided over him as they were in other places, and the rioting caused Claudius to drive them out. This may be taken as tentative evidence that by the middle of the first century, if not before, a strong testimony to Christ was being raised in the imperial city.

THE CHRISTIAN TESTIMONY

Christian sources for the life of Christ are chiefly the four Gospels and the writings of Paul, though some testimony is scattered here and there through the remainder of the New Testament. These sources tell us not merely that Jesus lived but also what sort of person he was. Non-Christian writings come to us from those who knew that a person named Jesus Christ had been on earth; these writings, on the other hand, come ultimately from men who really knew him and have the ability to interpret him to us.

Though the Gospels stand first in the order of books in the New Testament, they were not written first. Paul's epistles have priority. They have special importance for us, too, because they contain the witness of a man who was not predisposed to believe in Jesus, but who at first resisted the claims made for him and sought by all means to suppress the growing church. Yet within two to five years after the close of Jesus' ministry this man found himself among his followers. He was not one to be swept off his feet by every wind that blows. Nevertheless this cultured, sensible, and strong-minded man, a leader in Judaism, became utterly convinced that the Christians were right and that he had been wrong.

Paul's conversion is itself a testimony to the reality of Jesus Christ. He attributes it to the intervention of the risen Savior (I Cor. 15:8-9; 9:1; Phil. 3:12; Gal. 1:1, 11-17). Whether he had ever seen Jesus in the days of his flesh is uncertain, but it cannot be ruled out as impossible. What is certain is that he was not personally acquainted with him (II Cor. 5:16). After his conversion, Paul had opportunities for contact with those who had known and followed the Lord (Gal. 1:18-19; cf. I Cor. 15:5-7). These initial meetings with Peter and James were only the beginning of an association that opened the way to learn more of the Lord's earthly life (Gal. 2:1-14; Acts 15; I Cor. 9:5). Moreover, Paul's companion during many of his missionary travels was Luke, the writer of the Third Gospel. It is inconceivable that Luke would withhold from his friend the many items of information about the life of Christ which he must have begun gathering well before the close of Paul's ministry.

Paul affirms the Davidic lineage of Jesus (Rom. 1:3), his true humanity and life under the law (Gal. 4:4), his connection with Abraham (Gal. 3:16), his institution of the Lord's Supper (I Cor. 11:23-26), his death, burial, resurrection, and appearances after the resurrection (I Cor. 15:3-8). There may also be an allusion to the transfiguration (II Cor. 3:18).

It is quite true that this is a meager list of facts as compared with the abundance of material to be found in the Gospels. Why is there not more? For one thing, more was not needed. Paul's converts had been sufficiently instructed in the facts of the life of Christ during his residence among them. The records assure us that he emphasized teaching as well as preaching. He delivered more to his churches than the account of the Supper and the leading events of the passion. The word *delivered* is used several times and suggests the passing on to others of what had been committed to him for safekeeping and communication (I Cor. 11:2, 23ff.; I Cor. 15:3ff.; II Thess. 2:15; 3:6). It is indisputable that Paul's teaching as well as his preaching (of which we have samples in the book of Acts) centered around the historic figure of Jesus of Nazareth.

The relative silence about the historic facts underlying Christianity, such as we encounter in Paul's letters, should not bother us. If such facts were continually being obtruded, we would get the impression of propaganda. As it is, there is a natural assumption of understanding between writer and reader on these items, which accounts for the rarity of reference to them.

Along with this, it is worthy of note that there is a complete absence from the epistles of any studied attempt to influence posterity. The usual point of view maintained by those who stress the "occasional" character of those documents is that there was no intention of making them normative for later times. That very fact, if true, enhances the value of the testimony they give, for the writings in question reflect in that case the actual faith and conditions of the early church and were not intended to influence future generations as to the view they should take concerning Christianity.[21]

There is another reason for the paucity of references in Paul to the earthly life of our Lord. He was more concerned with the heavenly life that followed. Valuable as the knowledge of Christ in an earthly setting may be, it is not as valuable as being "in Christ" by faith and knowing him by the Spirit (II Cor. 5:16-17). Paul's theology is built around the exalted Lord who also dwells in the hearts of believers. Yet it should be emphasized that the Christ of history and the Christ of experience are one and the same. Such they were for Paul.

We must not suppose that Paul's testimony to Christ is exhausted in the recital of the few items listed above. His epistles give indication that he was acquainted with the teaching of Jesus as well as with the events of his life. He appeals to this teaching when discussing divorce (I Cor. 7:10), and mentions in connection with the unmarried that no teaching from the Lord is available for guidance (I Cor. 7:25). A whole book could be written on the correspondences, both patent and latent, between the teaching of Christ and the pattern for Christian life set forth in the practical portions of the apostle's letters. The primacy of love, bearing one another's burdens as the fulfillment of the law of Christ, the place of sacrifice, and denial of self are only a few of the high points at which we trace the influence of the Master upon the servant Paul.

Equally striking is the impression made upon the apostle by the character of Jesus. The resemblance between Paul's delineation and the portrait in the Gospels is too exact to be a matter of chance. Paul proclaimed a Christ who was without sin (II Cor. 5:21). He was especially fond of dwelling on the humility of the Savior (Phil. 2:1-8; II Cor. 8:9; 10:1) and his selflessness (Rom. 15:3). Much should be made of the apostle's assertion that he is one who imitates Christ and is able in turn to be a model for his own converts (I Cor. 4:6; 11:1). Nothing could more strongly proclaim his concern with the character of Christ. Nothing could more clearly imply his earnest effort to know all that could be known about this matchless person.

Everything in Paul's picture of Jesus bears the stamp of fidelity. There is no hint of fanciful creation. "Is Paul's picture of Christ faithful to the facts or his own imaginative production? Men make

21 See R. H. Malden, *Problems of the New Testament Today* (1923), pp. 56-57.

their gods to resemble themselves. If Paul created the picture of
Jesus in his epistles, how does it come that it does not follow the
Pharisaic mold with which he was familiar?"[22] F. C. Porter lays
special stress upon the significance of Paul's adoption of Jesus'
term "Abba, Father" right out of the prayer life of the Master.

> This one word, used as Jesus used it and as he taught his
> disciples to use it in the "Father" prayer, carried to Paul's mind
> all the difference between his old religion and his new. . . . This
> one word "Abba" is convincing proof that Paul knew what
> Jesus was, and that the religion of Jesus was the religion of
> Paul. This one word itself disproves the common opinion that
> Paul substituted a religion about Christ for the religion of
> Christ.[23]

Paul does not attempt to prove the existence of his Lord, for
it is needless. He occupies himself rather in seeking to know him
more fully and to proclaim him to the world.

The peculiar position of Paul—lack of relationship to the
earthly career of Jesus, opposition to the infant church, dramatic
conversion and independent apostleship—only serves to throw
into sharper relief and to make more impressive the agreement
between him and the original followers of Jesus as to the person
of their common Lord.

Our primary source of information about the life of Christ,
however, must always be the Gospels, for they are concerned with
him from beginning to end. Furthermore, they are clearly intended to be taken as sober fact, for they locate Jesus Christ in
a definite historical setting and vividly trace the impact of his
person upon the national consciousness of Israel and upon individual lives.

It is true that these records are not strictly contemporaneous
accounts. The Synoptic Gospels (Matthew, Mark, and Luke)
originated three decades or more after the time of the events they
chronicle, and the Fourth Gospel is probably still later. Is it not
likely that because of this interval much unhistorical material
made its way into the record, whether by addition or falsification
or unwarranted interpretation? Hardly, because the situation
was controlled by two important factors. For one thing, many
persons who had known Christ in the days of his flesh were still
living when the Gospels were penned (I Cor. 15:6). Among them

22 David Smith, *The Historic Jesus* (n.d.), pp. 87-88.
23 F. C. Porter, *The Mind of Christ in Paul* (1930), p. 20.

were some of the most intimate and influential of Jesus' followers. No report of Jesus' life could gain the sanction of the church apart from the approval of such men. There were too many people alive who had staked everything on Christ to permit any tampering with the facts. Secondly, from the very beginning of the church, converts were placed under systematic instruction (Acts 2:42; 11:26). This teaching must have centered principally in the words and works of Jesus. It is incredible that when this oral teaching gave way to the written Gospels, or more properly speaking, was supplemented by them, contradiction existed between the oral and written forms of the tradition. Christian appeal to documents means, in effect, an appeal to history itself, for the record of the documents was valuable to the early church only as it perpetuated the reality of the historical events upon which faith rested.[24]

Much labor has been spent in recent years upon the formative period lying back of the Gospels, in the endeavor to explain how certain materials found their way into the written accounts from the oral stage. Form criticism, as it is called, seeks to reduce the materials to certain literary forms or categories that give insight into the history and life of the church. For example, it is asserted that the annual observance of Easter brought a demand for a retelling of the events connected with the death and resurrection of Christ, hence these events bulk large in the narrative. Some help can be derived from such an approach, but care must be taken lest elements are read back into the life of Christ from the life of the church in such a way that the one who created the church becomes instead its creature.[25] Fortunately, no investigation of this formative period has been able to produce a picture of Jesus that makes him less than the supernatural figure the New Testament presents throughout.[26]

So deep was the impression made by Jesus upon the minds of men that when the written period began, many attempts were made to do justice to the greatest Life (Lk. 1:1). Luke is very careful to insist that these accounts rested upon eyewitness reports (Lk. 1:2). In this way we can bridge the gap between the life of

[24] Cf. Gerhard Kittel in *Mysterium Christi*, ed. Bell and Deissmann (1930), p. 41.

[25] For a judicious appraisal of form criticism one may profitably consult E. Basil Redlich, *Form Criticism, Its Value and Limitations* (1939), or Hoskyns and Davey, *The Riddle of the New Testament* (1931).

[26] F. F. Bruce, *Are the New Testament Documents Reliable?* pp. 32-33. Also, G. S. Duncan, *Jesus, Son of Man* (1949), pp. 16-17.

Jesus as he lived it and the written accounts describing that life. Were we in possession of these narratives that Luke mentions, it is possible that we would have some materials not found in the four Gospels which have providentially survived, but it is certain that we would not encounter a radically different person at the center of the story. The church acknowledged only one Jesus, the divine Savior, Son of man and Son of God.

That we know so little about the men who have given us this information is due to a deliberate self-effacement on their part, which they must have felt to be eminently fitting in view of the superlative greatness of their Theme.

> No literary fact is more remarkable than that men, knowing what these writers knew, and feeling what they felt, should have given us chronicles so plain and calm. They have nothing to say as from themselves. Their narratives place us without preface, and keep us without comment, among external scenes, in full view of facts, and in contact with the living person whom they teach us to know. . . . Who can fail to recognize a divine provision for placing the disciples of all future ages as nearly as possible in the position of those who had been personally present at "the beginning of the Gospel of Jesus Christ the Son of God?"[27]

Our confidence in the veracity of the writers is increased by certain considerations. Aside from the fact that they were simple, sincere men who were devoted to truth, who did not shrink from reporting incidents that presented themselves in an unfavorable light, we should observe that they reported sayings of Jesus that they were incapable of inventing by reason of the very limitations imposed on them by their native ability as well as by their station and opportunities in life. "The words and the sayings of Christ emerge from the narratives, though in places it seems as though they had been imperfectly apprehended, as containing and expressing thoughts quite outside the range of the minds that recorded them; and they thus possess an authenticity, which is confirmed and proved by the immature mental grasp of those who compiled the records, in a way in which it would not have been proved, if the compilers had been obviously men of mental acuteness and far-reaching philosophical grasp."[28]

[27] T. D. Bernard, *The Progress of Doctrine in the New Testament* (1867), pp. 56-57.
[28] A. C. Benson, *From a College Window* (1907), p. 309.

A good test of the fidelity of the Evangelists is their handling of the prophetic materials of the Old Testament pertaining to the Messiah. They make fairly frequent allusion to Christ's habit of referring to the Scriptures as being fulfilled in his own person and work. In addition, they make certain observations of their own to the effect that Jesus fulfilled these ancient Scriptures at various points in his career. Many instances of this sort will occur to the reader familiar with the Gospels. The point to be noted is that the writers do not draw upon the Old Testament in wholesale fashion, building up as strong a case as possible for Jesus as Messiah by employing all possible lines of prediction. It is also true that within the areas of Old Testament prophecy that *are* utilized by the Gospel writers, not all the details are seized upon and made to apply to Jesus of Nazareth. Particularly is this observable in regard to his sufferings.[29] Such sensitive selectivity confirms the truthfulness of the narratives.

The greatest single barrier to the acceptability of the picture of Jesus portrayed in the Gospels, at least for modern man, is the unabashed supernaturalism of that portrait. Were it not for this element, it is doubtful that anyone would have questioned the historicity of the Nazarene. Much of the modern criticism of the Gospels has been directed to the task of peeling off the encrustations of theology and miracle with which, it is alleged, the early church surrounded the figure of Jesus. It was hoped that criticism could discover the "real historical Jesus," who could then be accepted for what he actually was—a great man, a sublime teacher, a dynamic spiritual leader. But it is more and more coming to be recognized that such criticism is futile, for it starts with the assumption that a Jesus thus desupernaturalized could have made the impact he made upon his generation, and that his followers, acting in his name and through faith in him, could have made the impact they in fact did make upon theirs. This is in the greatest degree improbable. Supernaturalism is so much a part of Jesus that if this is taken away, he himself is gone. It is arrogance to suppose that modern man can reconstruct the person of Jesus Christ in defiance of the testimony of those who knew him best. C. H. Dodd has well said, "The older method of criticism, in its search for bare facts, set out to eliminate whatever in the Gospels might be attributed to the faith or experience of the Church. In doing so, it deliberately neglected in them just

[29] R. V. G. Tasker, *The Old Testament in the New Testament* (1947), p. 45.

those elements which in the eyes of their authors made them worth writing."[30] Furthermore, if the supernaturalism in the Gospel portrait of Jesus be regarded as an importation, one is then faced with the difficulty of accounting for the literary miracle that is involved in successfully combining the natural and the supernatural, the human and the divine, in the artless and convincing manner that characterizes the Evangelists' records.

There is nothing so difficult as to unite in a single person attributes which experience has never seen so associated, and which thought persists in conceiving as opposites; but what would be not so much difficult as impossible would be for a writer to betray no consciousness of invention, no feeling of the abnormal; and to maintain, alike as regards nature, character, and action, the integrity and concrete unity of his hero as a rational and historical being. Yet these are the features which distinguish our canonical Gospels.[31]

The wide gulf that separates the supernaturalism of Jesus as set forth in the Gospels from that which is attributed to him in the apocryphal gospels must be given due weight in the evaluation of the Synoptic tradition. In these noncanonical writings the supernaturalism takes on a false character by its obvious exaggeration, so that by contrast the Gospel records commend themselves as grounded in sober truth.[32]

THE INSTITUTIONAL EVIDENCE

With this review of the documentary basis for the historicity of Jesus, we turn briefly to the institutional evidence. This simply means that the New Testament church is a monument to Jesus Christ, for without him it lacks adequate cause, and has no real foundation. He is represented as predicting the establishment of the church, he himself being its Founder (Mt. 16:17-19). The genuineness of this famous utterance to Peter has been challenged because it is found only in Matthew's Gospel. Yet the saying carries its own credentials. "The Semitic colouring of these verses is unmistakable. The opening beatitude, the designation of Simon

[30] History and the Gospel (1938), p. 14.

[31] A. M. Fairbairn, The Philosophy of the Christian Religion, 4th edition (1905), pp. 327-328. See also J. S. Lawton, Conflict in Christology (1947), p. 51.

[32] The best source for the examination of these documents is Edgar Hennecke, New Testament Apocrypha, Vol. I (1963).

by his father's name, the Rabbinic expression of 'binding and loosing', the eschatological struggle with the powers of the underworld—all these are indications of a primitive origin for the whole paragraph."[33]

Even if it could be demonstrated that the passage in question did not emanate from Jesus, the existence of the church would still demand an explanation, and there is none available apart from the impulse given by the historic Christ. The sacraments of baptism[34] and the Lord's Supper lose their significance if they are divorced from his person and work. Prayer offered to Christ (Acts 7:59) and worship on the first day of the week (Acts 20:7; I Cor. 16:2) in commemoration of his resurrection are highly important testimonies which cannot be ignored, especially as carried on by Jews trained in the monotheism of their ancient faith.

At the beginning, those who constituted the Christian movement were all Jews. They reverenced the same Scriptures, worshiped the same God in the same temple at the same hours of prayer, and observed the same customs as the men of Israel around them. The one thing that differentiated them from the rest was their attitude toward Jesus of Nazareth, whom they honored as Savior and Lord.

Since the nation as such had rejected him and brought about his execution under Pontius Pilate the Roman procurator, consistency demanded that the followers of Jesus be dealt with severely. But despite persecution, the Christian movement gathered strength. Obviously the leaders of the Jews would do everything in their power to preserve the unity of Judaism. If they could demonstrate that Jesus was a figment of the imagination or even that he was unworthy of the trust and devotion of his followers, they would certainly have done so. The progress of the Christian faith is evidence that they were impotent against the glowing testimony of men and women who had companied with

[33] R. N. Flew, *Jesus and His Church* (1949), p. 90. The entire chapter will repay study. See also K. L. Schmidt's article in TDNT, III, 501-536.

[34] No verbatim report of what transpired at a baptismal service is included in the records of the book of Acts. There we read of baptism in the name of Christ. It is probable that the trinitarian formula of Matt. 28:19 would be cited if such records existed, especially since the two forms are treated as equivalent in the Didache, chs. 7 and 9, a document of the early postapostolic age.

him and were persuaded that his saving mission had been certified by his resurrection from the dead.

If the inception of the church is to be traced to the powerful impact of Jesus on his followers (and to their testimony in turn to others by means of the Spirit of God), it is equally true that the continuance of the church through the succeeding centuries presupposes a living Christ. The Christian church, emerging on Jewish soil, not only claimed its thousands there, but when it spread to the Gentile world claimed its tens of thousands. Today, practically speaking, it covers the earth, having made successful appeal to men of virtually all lands and civilizations. There has been no gap in the succession of Christians. One generation has bequeathed its faith to another, so that in a very real sense the modern church has an unbroken lifeline back to the Son of God in the days of his flesh. The two primary festivals of the church, Christmas and Easter, point to the beginning and the consummation respectively of his earthly life. Christian art reaches its highest peak of perfection in portraying scenes wherein the Son of man, whether alone or in a group, claims the adoring gaze of the faithful. Christian hymnody reaches its most exalted note when it is poured out in praise of his love and grace. Every phase of investigation converges on the conclusion that Christianity is Christ.

CHRISTIAN EXPERIENCE

The third and final proof of the historicity of Jesus Christ is personal. This is simply an individualizing of the second line of proof, yet it should be given its own distinct recognition. The reality of Christian experience can only be tested, in the last analysis, in the recesses of the individual soul; and its resources can only be appropriated in individual life. Anyone who has passed through the profound transformation of conversion is in a position to say that he knows, no matter who else may doubt. We are bound to respect the integrity of the other man's consciousness of religious experience, otherwise we can expect no credence for our own. But if personal experience proclaims the *reality* of knowing Christ, the universality of essentially the same experience among Christians of every age proclaims the *validity* of such knowledge. In this way the particular and the general, the personal and the corporate, tend to complement and corroborate each other.

A final step is the recognition that the Christ who is encountered today by the believing individual and the Christian society is identical with the Christ who confronts us in history.

> The Christ of experience tallies with the Christ of the records. An ideal Christ, a creation of the imagination, could inspire to admiration, perhaps even to worship. But an ideal cannot kindle love. This can only be done by an actual person. The love of Christ both felt and in some measure returned is a potent demonstration of the truth of the ever-living Christ.[35]

Whence comes that indefinable quality known as Christlikeness? It may be fostered by emulation of devout believers; it may be deepened by the devotional exercises of Bible reading and prayer; it may be sweetened by the bitterness of suffering; but it finds its ultimate root in the sublime character of Jesus Christ himself.

BIBLIOGRAPHY

Hugh Anderson, "The Historical Jesus and the Origins of Christianity," *Scottish Journal of Theology*, 13 (June 1960), 113-136.

————. *Jesus and Christian Origins*. New York: Oxford, 1964.

C. E. Braaten and R. A. Harrisville. *The Historical Jesus and the Kerygmatic Christ*. New York: Abingdon, 1964.

F. F. Bruce. *Are the New Testament Documents Reliable?* London: IVF, 1943; Grand Rapids: Eerdmans, 1954.

S. J. Case. *The Historicity of Jesus*. Chicago: University of Chicago Press, 1912.

C. H. Dodd. *History and the Gospel*. New York: Scribners, 1938.

H. E. Fosdick. *The Man from Nazareth*. New York: Harper, 1949. Pp. 17-42.

D. P. Fuller. *Easter Faith and History*. Grand Rapids: Eerdmans, 1965.

Maurice Goguel. *The Life of Jesus*. New York: Macmillan, 1949. Pp. 37-222.

Charles Guignebert. *Jesus*. London: Kegan Paul, 1935. Pp. 63-75.

J. Jeremias, "The Present Position in the Controversy Concerning the Problem of the Historical Jesus," ET, 69:11 (Aug. 1958), 333-339.

Maurice Jones. *The New Testament in the Twentieth Century*. London: Macmillan, 1914. Pp. 60-86.

J. Klausner. *Jesus of Nazareth*. London: Allen and Unwin, 1925. Pp. 17-127.

R. J. Knowling. *The Testimony of St. Paul to Christ*. London: Hodder and Stoughton, 1911. Pp. 179-350.

35 David Smith, *op. cit.*, p. 113.

H. K. McArthur. *The Quest Through the Centuries*. Philadelphia: Fortress, 1966.

C. C. McCown. *The Search for the Real Jesus*. New York: Scribners, 1940.

C. F. D. Moule. *The Phenomenon of the New Testament*. Naperville, Ill.: Allenson, 1967.

B. Rigaux, "L' historicité de Jésus devant l'exégèse récente," RB, 65 (Oct. 1958), 481-522.

J. M. Robinson. *The New Quest of the Historical Jesus*. Naperville, Ill.: Allenson, 1959.

—————. *Kerygma und historische Jesus*. Stuttgart: Zwingli, 1960.

A. Schweitzer. *The Quest of the Historical Jesus*. London: Black, 1945.

E. F. Scott. *The Validity of the Gospel Record*. New York: Scribners, 1938.

W. L. Sperry. *Jesus Then and Now*. New York: Harper, 1949. Pp. 17-51.

B. B. Warfield. *Christology and Criticism*. New York: Oxford, 1929. Pp. 149-177.

CHAPTER II

THE BIRTH

That glorious form, that light insufferable,
And that far-beaming blaze of majesty,
Wherewith he wont at heaven's high council-table,
To sit the midst of trinal unity,
He laid aside; and here with us to be,
Forsook the courts of everlasting day,
And chose with us a darksome house of mortal clay.

—John Milton

THE FIRST BOOK OF THE OLD TESTAMENT IN THE GREEK TRANSLAtion contains the statement: "This is the book of the generation of men" (Gen. 5:1). The first book of the New Testament commences with the words: "The book of the generation of Jesus Christ" (Mt. 1:1 KJV). Whether or not the latter was intended to be the complement of the former, the parallelism is suggestive. A new beginning for the human race is being made in the person of Jesus Christ.

It is possible to describe this great event of Christ's appearance both as a birth and as a manifestation. Jesus was born; the life was manifested. The life was ageless but clothed itself now in human form. Throughout the Old Testament the persistent theme is God and man, not God alone or man alone, but God and man in their relations. Though made in the divine image, the creature man exhibits such sinful tendencies and practices that even those who are nurtured on special promises and blessed by special divine intervention reveal serious blemishes. How sadly ironical that the man after God's own heart should turn out to be an adulterer and a murderer! The passage of time reveals ever more clearly the need for the appearance of one who will demonstrate anew the primeval divine ideal for man. This occurs at the great divide of history in the coming of the God-man.

That a god might appear in human form was a commonplace of the old Greek mythology. However, it would be a mistake to see in the biblical picture of Christ a reproduction of this notion. Christianity, like Judaism, was steeled against such influence. At best this Hellenic stress upon divine immanence may have operated to create a favorable atmosphere for the reception of that phase of Christian teaching which centered in the incarnation. But the truth that God became man is Christian truth, not pagan. If the incarnation were considered repeatable this would only demonstrate that it had never occurred at all.[1]

Long before the dawn of Christianity the idea of the man-god was current. Religion had fostered it in terms of a possible absorption into deity as the goal of mystical devotion. Government had fostered it as a political device, encouraging the citizenry to honor the head of the state as divine, thus unifying the state by harnessing the loyalty of its subjects through the medium of man's most exalted interest, his religious life.

What is at stake here is not a mere matter of word order. The man-god concept means that the initiative rests with man. He aspires to deity, and the deity is of his own devising, not necessarily his own in a personal sense, but as the composite of the thoughts and longings of generations of men with whom the individual is more or less homogeneous. On the other hand, the God-man concept rests frankly upon revelation and involves the initiative of God. It is congruent with the emphasis upon the priority and supremacy of God that pervades the Scriptures. In the text: "For there is one God, and there is one Mediator between God and men, the man Christ Jesus" (I Tim. 2:5), we are quite prepared for the order of statement—"between God and men." One who moves in the stream of biblical thought would naturally phrase it that way rather than "between men and God."

George Adam Smith has drawn attention to the striking nature of what occurred at Caesarea-Philippi.[2] Here stood a temple dedicated to Caesar in which he was acclaimed as worthy of divine worship. Into this area came Jesus and his disciples, and in this

---

[1] H. H. Farmer, *The Servant of the Word* (1942), pp. 8-9.
[2] *Historical Geography of the Holy Land*, 22nd edition (n.d.), pp. 473-479.

setting one of his followers dared to confess the Messiahship of his Master and his unique position as Son of God. The one type of worship, though strongly entrenched at the moment, has long since passed away, blotted out with the passing of Rome (this is not to say that it entirely lacks modern counterpart), whereas the other has remained, and from that inconspicuous beginning has grown to a worldwide veneration.[3]

THE OLD TESTAMENT BACKGROUND

The farther back into the primitive history of man the roots of Jesus Christ can be traced, the more plausible becomes the claim of the religion which centers in him to be the universal faith, and by so much an expectation is created of the ultimate universal reception of this faith among the vast and varied populations of the earth.

Every human life has its link with the past by the simple fact of heredity. Yet the anticipation of the individual's arrival is confined to the few months prior to birth. In the case of Jesus Christ, the whole gamut of redemption history is pregnant with the promise of his coming. Beginning with the *protevangelium* (Gen. 3:15), which mysteriously yet wonderfully blends the collective and the personal reference concerning the seed that will eventually triumph over evil, the Old Testament impressively unfolds the sweep of progressive revelation. The line of messianic prediction moves to the seed of Abraham, then to the line of Isaac, then to the tribe of Judah among the numerous progeny of Jacob, and finally to the house of David among the descendants of Judah. From the time of David to the Christian era, prophecy is dominated by the covenant promise of a king from his seed who will bring Israel to a new height of glory.[4]

The Messiah is not simply a literary factor in the Old Testament, since the manifestations of God through the figure of the Angel of the Lord (he has various titles) reveal his presence and activity in the preincarnate period. Not only is the Angel identified with the Lord, whether tacitly or explicitly (Gen. 18; Judg. 6:11, 14), but his coming into the midst of Israel to judge

[3] For a treatment of Roman emperor worship, see Louis Matthews Sweet's book by that title (1919).

[4] Cf. E. W. Hengstenberg, *Christology of the Old Testament*, Vol. I (1858).

and purify is set forth in one of the last prophecies of the canon (Mal. 3:1ff.). This identification is hinted at elsewhere also, as in the case of the Angel's appearance to Manoah and his wife in the days of the Judges. The one thing that he will consent to say about his name is the fact that it is "wonderful" (Judg. 13:18). This word reappears in the great Isaianic oracle regarding the forthcoming Redeemer (Isa. 9:6). Micah, a contemporary of Isaiah, seems to gather up all the preincarnate activity of the Messiah in his majestic utterance: "Whose origin is from of old, from ancient days" (Mic. 5:2).

Examination of the nativity stories in the Gospels discloses the weighty influence of this Old Testament background. It is seen in part in the citing of explicit prophecies (Mt. 1:23; 2:6). But it is discernible also in the attitude of expectation that seems to characterize all those who come into direct contact with the babe of Bethlehem. It breathes from the *Magnificat* and the *Nunc Dimittis*, which are replete with the phraseology of the Old Testament, and appears also in the attitude of Anna the prophetess (Lk. 2:38) and even of the Magi (Mt. 2:2). It is especially evident in the genealogies of Jesus provided by Matthew and Luke. Both lists mention David and are framed with a view to attesting the royal lineage of Jesus.[5] This is in line with the popular recognition of Jesus as Son of David during his ministry, and also with the place given to his Davidic lineage in the apostolic preaching (Lk. 18:39; Acts 2:30). But Luke's table carries farther back than Matthew's, reaching all the way to Adam (Lk. 3:38). A hint may be intended here of the truth more formally developed in the writings of Paul, that Jesus is to be recognized as the Last Adam in whom the double ruin of sin and death is set aside.[6]

---

[5] Into the many difficult questions raised by the two genealogies we are unable here to enter, beyond inquiring whether both tables give the lineage of Joseph or whether Luke's is concerned with Mary. It is impossible to be dogmatic at this point, but it should be remembered that the promise to David of a seed who would be king calls for more than someone who had a legally sound title to the throne. This seed was to proceed from David's loins (II Sam. 7:12-16). Apostolic preaching emphasizes this (Acts 2:30; 13:23). So it becomes important to establish the Davidic lineage of Mary. In Luke's nativity story, Mary has greater prominence than Joseph (the reverse is true of Matthew's account), so that a genealogy of Mary would be thoroughly in accord with her position in Luke's narrative. It is granted, however, that Jewish practice was to trace descent through the male line. Hence the uncertainty regarding the intention of Luke.

[6] L. M. Sweet, *The Birth and Infancy of Jesus Christ* (1906), p. 324.

TIME AND PLACE

It is not our purpose here to retell the simple story of the birth of Jesus, which is narrated so beautifully in Luke's Gospel. But there are certain problems connected with it that require examination.

Both accounts of the nativity mention Bethlehem as the birthplace of Christ (Mt. 2:1; Lk. 2:4-7). According to Matthew, Herod the Great was still reigning over Judea (Mt. 2:1). Luke, who alone of the New Testament writers manifests a concern to place the rise of the Christian movement in the larger setting of the Graeco-Roman world, says nothing about Herod in this connection, but places the birth in conjunction with an enrollment that occurred throughout the empire during the reign of Augustus, when Quirinius was governing Syria (Lk. 2:1-7). In modern times widespread doubt of Luke's trustworthiness in this particular matter has been expressed. Corroboration for such an enrollment was lacking in extrabiblical sources. Further, there was no knowledge of Quirinius' rule at such an early period (Josephus mentions his accession as governor of Syria in A.D. 6).[7] Toward the close of the last century Sir William Ramsay felt the challenge of this situation in a peculiar way because his own research in Asia Minor had given him increasing respect for Luke as an able and accurate writer. He saw that Luke's credit as a historian was at stake in a matter of this sort, where appeal was made in a document intended for Roman eyes to facts that must have been common knowledge on the part of his contemporaries if they occurred at all.[8]

Archeology prepared the way for the investigation by the discovery of census papers in Egypt showing that under the Romans it was customary to take a count of the population every fourteen years.[9] The actual dates noted were for periods somewhat later than New Testament times, but additional papyri discoveries convinced Wilcken, as well as Grenfell and Hunt, that such

[7] *Antiquities* xviii.1.1.

[8] Ramsay's discussion of this problem is embodied in two works, *Was Christ Born at Bethlehem?* (2nd edition, 1898), and *The Bearing of Recent Discovery on the Trustworthiness of the New Testament* (4th edition, 1920), pp. 222-300. A contemporary treatment is provided by A. N. Sherwin-White in *Roman Society and Roman Law in the New Testament* (1963), pp. 162-171.

[9] *Was Christ Born at Bethlehem?* p. 132.

enrollments went back at least as far as A.D. 20.[10] Josephus mentions a still earlier one, in the year A.D. 6, just after the deposition of Archelaus as king of Judea and the incorporation of his territory into Syria, and cites the part Quirinius had in it as governor of Syria.[11] Luke's account of Gamaliel's address to the Sanhedrin includes a reference to the same enrollment and the disturbance it caused among the people (Acts 5:37). His language at this point seems designed to differentiate this from the earlier and less notable enrollment which he alone mentions (in Lk. 2:1ff.). On the basis of the fourteen-year cycle, this earlier enrollment must have occurred in 8 B.C.

The next difficulty to be faced was Quirinius' connection with Syria at such an early date. It was known that Varus governed Syria from 7-4 B.C. and Saturninus from 9-7 B.C., apparently precluding Quirinius at the time required for the census. But Ramsay found a possible line of explanation in the Tibur inscription,[12] which had been located in 1764, as it commemorated a certain official (the name is lacking due to the fragmentary character of the inscription) who had taken charge of affairs in Syria on two occasions as the representative of Augustus.[13] This official had been granted on two successive years the special honor of a triumphal recognition (*supplicatio*) in Rome for victory over a barbarian tribe. A number of authorities in Roman history and epigraphy were agreed that the official in question must have been Quirinius.[14] But it was reserved for Ramsay himself to make the discoveries that clinched the identification. These consisted of two inscriptions, one found at Pisidian Antioch, the other nearby, both in honor of the same man, a local citizen who is stated to have served in a military capacity under Quirinius.[15] Since this area was threatened by the fierce tribe of Homonadenses, it seems that Quirinius had been sent out by Augustus to subdue this tribe, which is known to have taken place at least by 6 B.C. and probably earlier.[16]

[10] Moulton and Milligan, *The Vocabulary of the Greek Testament* (1930), under *apographē*.
[11] *Loc. cit.* He is explicit that the purpose of this census was taxation.
[12] S. L. Caiger, *Archaeology and the New Testament*, 2nd edition (1948), p. 141, gives a translation of the inscription.
[13] *Was Christ Born at Bethlehem?* pp. 227-228.
[14] *Ibid.*
[15] *The Bearing of Recent Discovery*, pp. 284-292.
[16] *Bethlehem*, pp. 236-237.

It is reasonably clear, then, that Luke's statement about Quirinius has reference to his presence in Syria as a legate of Augustus charged with a special military mission. He did not displace the regular governor, whether Saturninus or Varus, who directed the ordinary affairs of state. Luke's statement indicates that Quirinius was in command or control (our word *hegemony*), which fits his position exactly. Since he was in the province for a limited time only, his name served to date the enrollment more precisely than the naming of the regular governor would have done.[17]

Ethelbert Stauffer has proposed a solution of the Quirinius problem along the following lines. The Roman census-taking for the purpose of taxation required two stages, the first, called *apographē*, being devoted to the preparation of a list of taxable persons and their property, whereas the second, called *apotimēsis*, consisted of the actual assessment of the tax.[18] The imposition of this system for the first time would naturally require a considerable interval between the two phases, running into several years. It is possible, then, that Luke 2:1ff. refers to the first census in its initial stage, whereas Acts 5:37 pertains to the concluding phase.

It is admittedly true that so far no evidence has been adduced outside the New Testament that definitely connects Quirinius with a census in the time of Herod. This evidence may someday come to light. Meanwhile, scholarship will do well to have an open mind on the subject.[19]

Though the decree of Augustus was promulgated in 8 B.C., the execution of the census in Palestine may have been considerably delayed. Ramsay argued for 6 B.C. as the date of Jesus' birth on the basis of factors pointing to such delay.[20] Others have concluded that there is no serious obstacle to holding that the birth

---

17 *Ibid.*

18 *Jesus and His Story* (1960), pp. 21-32.

19 Jack Finegan, *Light from the Ancient Past* (1946), p. 219. E. Schürer, *History of the Jewish People in the Time of Jesus Christ* (1896), took the position that Luke places the A.D. 6 enrollment under Quirinius some ten years too early. In his 3rd and 4th editions, though he took cognizance of the earlier of Ramsay's works on this subject, his attitude remained the same. M. S. Enslin, *Christian Beginnings* (1938), p. 410, ventures the opinion that Luke's account is of his own creation "in order to harmonize the two variant traditions, both of which he accepted, that Jesus' family had from the earliest years lived in Nazareth and yet that their child had been born in Bethlehem." But see G. H. Box, *The Virgin Birth of Jesus* (1916), pp. 66-67, 77.

20 *Bethlehem*, ch. 9.

occurred in the very year of the imperial decree.[21] Herod died in 4 B.C., so the birth cannot be put later without doing violence to the data in Matthew.[22]

Scripture says nothing about the time of year. The first known observance of December 25th is associated with the church at Rome about the middle of the fourth century,[23] but the practice may go back to the second century.[24] January 6 was observed in the Eastern churches. On the ground that the pasturing of flocks in the open would have been impossible at this season, many have concluded that the birth must have taken place at another time of year. But the traditional winter date is not incredible. According to Dalman, "the low-lying shepherds' plain must be taken as the place nearest to Bethlehem where scarcely any snow falls in winter, and where in the case of need flocks can remain at night in the open; for the great drop in temperature which sometimes occurs in the winter generally makes itself felt only after Christmas."[25] Edersheim judges from a passage in the Mishnah that flocks kept in the open at this time of year were those destined for temple sacrifices.[26]

The tradition that the scene of the nativity was a cave is very ancient. Justin Martyr[27] and Origen[28] affirm it. There is nothing improbable about such a cave containing a manger, and the site now pointed out in connection with the Church of the Nativity, bearing the inscription, "Here Jesus Christ was born of the Virgin Mary," however altered in appearance from early days, may well be the actual place of the Savior's birth.

One item of special interest connected with the enrollment is the fact that Mary accompanied Joseph to the ancestral city. Though Luke does not say that both were required to register,

21 John Stewart, *When Did Our Lord Actually Live?* (1935), p. 24.

22 Other dates have been proposed. S. J. Andrews, *The Life of Our Lord* (1891), argues for 5 B.C. A. T. Olmstead, *Jesus in the Light of History* (1942), pp. 1-2, champions the notion that Jesus must have been born about 20 B.C. But this can hardly be taken seriously, for the information contained in John 8:57 is obviously not intended to be used for precise dating.

23 Philip Schaff, *History of the Christian Church*, III (1867), 395.

24 W. P. Armstrong, "Chronology of the New Testament," ISBE, I, 646b.

25 G. Dalman, *Sacred Sites and Ways* (1935), pp. 48-49.

26 Alfred Edersheim, *The Life and Times of Jesus the Messiah*, 8th edition, I (1896), 186-187.

27 *Dialogue with Trypho* 78.

28 *Contra Celsum* i.51. The text reads, "There is shown at Bethlehem the cave where he was born, and the manger in the cave where he was wrapped in swaddling clothes."

this is the natural force of his statement that Joseph went up "to be enrolled with Mary who was espoused to him" (Lk. 2:5). Two centuries later Tertullian claimed that the Roman census records listed Mary as being of the house of David.[29] It is known that in Egypt the census included all members of the household, even slaves.[30] This creates a presumption that the practice in Palestine was similar.[31] Another feature was apparently common to both, namely, the requirement that everyone register at the ancestral home rather than at the place of current residence. In Egypt the purpose was to check the drift to the city on the part of tillers of the soil, to guarantee a steady supply of grain for Rome.[32] In Palestine the enrollment by tribes was probably designed to cater to Jewish sentiment, softening the edge of an imperial order that otherwise might have met serious resistance.

By way of conclusion, it can be fairly stated that modern research has gone far to relieve the biblical account of any suspicion of legendary character, as though the writers arbitrarily fixed the birth of Jesus at Bethlehem in order to satisfy a messianic requirement.[33] To the devout mind the enrollment under Augustus looms as one of the clearest indications in all history of the providential control of human affairs by an almighty hand. It is impressive to see how the administrative machinery of a vast empire was set in motion to fulfill the purpose of God in the advent of his Son (cf. Prov. 21:1).

"BORN OF THE VIRGIN MARY"

A convenient starting point for discussion of this subject is the postapostolic age. Jesus' birth of a virgin is affirmed in the Apostles' Creed, both in the form which has become standard for western Christendom and in the Old Roman Symbol, which can be traced to the latter part of the second century.[34] In view of the

29 *Against the Jews* 9.

30 Ramsay, *The Bearing of Recent Discovery*, pp. 255-274.

31 Box, *The Virgin Birth of Jesus* (1916), pp. 54-55, concludes that the purpose of this first enrollment was census-taking only.

32 Ramsay, *The Bearing of Recent Discovery*, p. 260.

33 Those who affirm such a motive for the inclusion of Bethlehem in the nativity stories (e.g. Cadoux, *The Life of Jesus* [1948], pp. 30-32) must discount Luke's claim to have traced all things accurately from the very first, and must also slight the evidence from Egyptian census-taking.

34 There is some uncertainty about the reference to the Holy Spirit's agency in the earliest form of the Creed. Tertullian includes it, Irenaeus does not. A. C. McGiffert, in declaring in favor of the shorter form, does not attempt to

brevity of the Creed, the inclusion of the virgin birth is a significant testimony to the importance the early church attached to this article of faith. Justin Martyr places it among the cardinal items of Christian belief.[35] Another apologist, Aristides, affirms it;[36] and Ignatius, who belongs to the early part of the second century, strongly insists upon it.[37] What Bishop Gore said of the testimony of Justin may also be said of the testimony of Ignatius on this subject, namely, that "his summaries of Christian belief . . . have sometimes a creed-like ring."[38]

We are thus carried back to the fringe of the apostolic age and very close to the documents setting forth the fact of the virgin birth. These, of course, are the nativity narratives of Matthew and Luke. They assert that Jesus was begotten by the Holy Spirit in the womb of the Virgin Mary, who was espoused to a man named Joseph. They also declare that before the child was born, Joseph took Mary as his lawful wife.

Did the faith of the early church spring from the recital of events contained in Matthew and Luke, or are these accounts the reflection of a tradition already current in the church? It is a fair question. If we find that the latter is true, we are brought still closer to the time of the birth itself. Luke wrote to Theophilus in order to assure him of the trustworthy character of the things he had already learned concerning the Christian faith. Since Luke proceeds to include in his account the story of the virgin birth, it is not unreasonable to suppose that this item had already come to the attention of Theophilus in the course of his instruction. He would be familiar with the central fact, if not with the details that enrich the Lukan narrative.[39] With reference

---

argue that the omission of the Spirit at this point indicates any doubt about the virgin birth (*The Apostles' Creed* [1902], p. 17). For the text of the Creed as it appears in ancient writers see Philip Schaff, *The Creeds of Christendom*, II (1877), 53.

[35] *Dialogue* 85; *Apology* 31, 46.

[36] For the text of Aristides and comment on the same, see Thorburn, *Examination of the Doctrine of the Virgin Birth* (1908), chs. 6 and 7.

[37] *Ephesians* 18:2; *Smyrnaeans* 1:1.

[38] *Dissertations on Subjects Connected with the Incarnation* (1895), p. 45.

[39] This conclusion could be set aside by showing that the infancy narrative of Luke, whether *in toto* or only the crucial passage 1:34-35, had been interpolated. But the failure of this procedure has been ably demonstrated by J. Gresham Machen, *The Virgin Birth of Christ* (1930), chs. 2 and 6. See also R. J. Knowling, *Our Lord's Virgin Birth and the Criticism of Today* (1904), p. 27.

to Matthew, it is even more obvious that the birth story is penned with a view to current Christian belief. Only in this case there is a peculiar slant to the narrative dictated by Matthew's desire to refute the slanders of unbelieving Jews respecting the origin of Jesus, which represent an attempt to twist the Christian testimony into something maliciously untrue. As Zahn remarks, "How old and how well known the Christian tradition must have been in Palestine if the Jewish caricature was so widely spread at the time Matthew's Gospel was written, that the Evangelist deemed it necessary at the beginning of his book to oppose it so decidedly!"[40] Hoskyns is probably right in thinking that this slander lies just beneath the surface in several exchanges between Jesus and Jewish opponents reported in the Fourth Gospel.[41] Note the emphatic *we* (in implied contrast to Jesus) in John 8:41.

Just when the church became the recipient of the story behind the birth of Jesus is nowhere revealed. It could have been divulged by the risen Lord during the Forty Days, or by Mary during the days of waiting for the coming of the Spirit. There may be special significance in the fact that Luke mentions Mary as being in close fellowship with the apostles during this period (Acts 1:14). The intimacy of this joyful fellowship would provide the ideal atmosphere for the disclosure of the sacred secret so full of meaning to all concerned.[42] The exclusion of the virgin birth from the preaching of the early church is no objection to this, for that preaching included nothing prior to the public ministry. C. H. Dodd has shown that there is a strong resemblance between the content of the *kerygma* or gospel preaching of the early church as set forth at various points in Acts and the main lines of the Markan delineation of the gospel.[43] One should therefore not expect to find the virgin birth referred to in Acts any more than in Mark, which begins with the public ministry.

It may be thought strange, if the virgin birth was known to the early church from the beginning, that Gospel writers speak of Joseph as Jesus' father. That they do this is evidence of their fidelity in reproducing the situation that obtained during our Lord's earthly life, when it was popularly assumed that this was actually the relationship (Lk. 4:22; Jn. 1:45; 6:42). Mary's

---

[40] T. Zahn, *The Articles of the Apostles' Creed* (1899), p. 131.

[41] E. C. Hoskyns, *The Fourth Gospel* (1940), p. 342.

[42] Ramsay argued convincingly that the ultimate authority behind Luke's nativity narrative was Mary herself (*Bethlehem*, ch. 4).

[43] ET, 43 (1931-32), 396ff.

reference to Joseph as Jesus' father (Lk. 2:48) is readily explained as pertaining to legal status. What other term could she have used?

If the knowledge of the virgin birth became the property of the church from the beginning, how is it that no mention is made of it outside Matthew and Luke? This silence, even if it were absolute, should not be regarded as warrant for questioning the accounts in these two Gospels. Nor should it be the ground for assuming that other writers did not know of the virgin birth. It is dangerous to argue from silence to ignorance.[44] Before examining this aspect of the problem, one ought to contemplate the fact that the evidence of Matthew and Luke is quite sufficient in itself to establish the event as historical. They show agreement on the central features of the supernatural conception by the Holy Spirit and the birth at Bethlehem; and the material difference in the details of their narratives means that their accounts are independent of each other, providing a double rather than a single witness.

Paul's failure to mention the virgin birth is compatible with the scantiness of his allusions to our Lord's earthly life. Some have thought they detected a reference to it in Galatians 4:4 ("born of woman"), but the tenor of the passage indicates that the apostle is underscoring the identification of the Savior with those he came to redeem. Hence he is stressing the likeness to us in terms of birth rather than the distinction from us in terms of conception. If Paul is silent about the virgin birth at this point, he is equally silent about any human paternity of Jesus, which ought to be given due weight.

The silence of John may be thought especially strange in view of the large place given to preexistence and incarnation in this Gospel. However, with the exception of the prologue, the material is regulated by the fact that the author is giving a witness to Christ based on personal observation; hence the Gospel proper begins with the ministry of John the Baptist and the contact he and his disciples had with Jesus.[45]

There is indeed a possibility that the Fourth Gospel contains a reference to the virgin birth. Though the textual testimony is meager, a reading exists for 1:13 that makes the passage refer to

44 The demonstration of this with reference to the virgin birth is the special merit of Douglas Edwards' volume, *The Virgin Birth in History and Faith* (1943).

45 Machen, *op. cit.*, p. 255.

Christ rather than believers ("who was born . . .") .[46] Harnack endorsed this reading;[47] and it gains some internal support from the consideration that the word *blood* is plural, as though to denote the commingling of male and female strains in ordinary generation (though this exegesis is not widely accepted). Furthermore, the word *man* is the term regularly employed for husband. With one exception (1:30), John reserves this word for that specialized use. Probably the safest conclusion is that John's statement is intended to be a description of the new birth of believers, but is couched in language that consciously points to the virgin birth.[48] But why should the writer seek to erect such a parallel? The answer is found by Edwards[49] in First John, where the dominant purpose seems to be the exposition of the responsibility of believers, those who have been born of God, to reflect before the world the life of the Son of God, who himself was born of God (cf. I Jn. 5:18 RSV). In the prologue of his Gospel, John is intent on stressing the parallel between Christ and believers at the point of birth, whereas in the First Epistle the comparison is drawn out to include the life lived in the flesh. The evidence is such as to warrant the conclusion that John was conversant with the virgin-birth teaching and sympathetic to it.

The fact that the early church cordially received the tidings about the virgin birth when it was first made known, and that we have no record of dissent on the subject,[50] but rather the elevation of this article of faith to a place in the creedal statements of the church, is only what should be expected in view of the harmony between this truth and all that the early Christians knew about the person of Christ from personal contact with him. The unique origin fitted perfectly the unique life.

Acceptance of the virgin-birth teaching should rest primarily upon the positive testimony in its favor. But this testimony stands in sharper relief when it is realized that all attempts to explain the origin of the virgin-birth teaching apart from the biblical accounts have failed. To say that antiquity was in the habit of ascribing supernatural birth to its great personages and

---

46 Attested by the Verona Codex of the Old Latin, Irenaeus and Tertullian.

47 *The Date of the Acts and of the Synoptic Gospels* (1911) , p. 148.

48 G. Vos, *The Self-Disclosure of Jesus* (1926) , pp. 210-213. Cf. Zahn, *op. cit.,* p. 136.

49 *Op. cit.,* pp. 123-130.

50 Except on the part of the heretical Ebionites and the Cerinthian Gnostics.

that Christianity has followed the conventional pattern is misleading. Are the so-called virgin births of antiquity the same in kind as that ascribed to Jesus in the Gospels? The words of Louis Matthews Sweet are worth recalling:

> After a careful, laborious, and occasionally wearisome study of the evidence offered and the analogies urged, I am convinced that heathenism knows nothing of virgin births. Supernatural births it has without number, but never from a virgin in the New Testament sense and never without physical generation, except in a few isolated instances of magical births on the part of women who had not the slightest claim to be called virgins. In all recorded instances which I have been able to examine, if the mother was a virgin before conception took place she could not make that claim afterwards.[51]

Even if paganism offered an adequate parallel, which is not to be expected in view of the divergent concept of God,[52] the necessity remains of showing how such a doctrine could have secured favorable rootage in the Jewish-Christian soil whence the New Testament doctrine of the virgin birth sprang. The prejudice against paganism was too strong for such borrowing.[53]

If the idea of a virgin birth for the Messiah lay ready to hand in the theology of Judaism, it is conceivable that the early Christians could have taken it over from this source. But the difficulty is that no evidence can be cited in favor of such a Jewish expectation. Isaiah 7:14 was not given a messianic interpretation among the Jews of our Lord's time,[54] unless the use of *parthenos* (virgin) in the Greek translation of the Old Testament be regarded as proof of such an expectation in some quarters of Judaism. At any rate it cannot be demonstrated that Matthew worked from Scripture to event rather than vice versa. Though there is an undoubted miraculous element in the birth of certain individuals in the Old Testament period, such as Isaac, these cases are

---

51 *Op. cit.*, p. 188.

52 A. M. Fairbairn, *Studies in the Life of Christ*, 14th edition (1907), pp. 39-42, sets forth the dissimilarity between the Christian doctrine of incarnation and that of the Hindus and the Greeks. See also W. L. Knox, *Some Hellenistic Elements in Primitive Christianity* (1944), p. 25.

53 Box, *op. cit.*, pp. 2-3, points out that the Jewish-Christian character of the nativity narratives (and their Palestinian origin) is inimical to pagan derivation.

54 Edersheim, *op. cit.*, II, 710ff., lists the OT passages cited in ancient rabbinic writings as messianic. Isaiah 7:14 is not among them.

clearly not parallel to the virgin birth of Christ. The very notion of a virgin birth was foreign to Jewish thinking, especially at the beginning of the Christian era, when the transcendence of God was more strongly emphasized than through the Old Testament period.[55] It may be thought that this same aversion to involving God in human origins would operate in the minds of the early Christians, who were themselves Jews, so as to preclude any virgin-birth ideas. But it must be remembered that they had immediate experience of Jesus Christ, who claimed to have come from God in a unique sense. This contact undoubtedly prepared them to accept what their background and training would lead them otherwise to reject.

Still another possibility remains, namely, that the virgin birth is a fabrication of Christian origin, intended to magnify the person of Christ. If John the Baptist, the forerunner, was filled with the Holy Spirit from the womb, it was easy to reason that with the greater person, Jesus Christ, the influence of the Holy Spirit began with the conception of life. Then the Isaiah 7:14 passage was used to buttress this belief. However, it may justly be doubted that any such tendency, if it existed at all, could effectively surmount the barrier that the Hebraic opposition to a virgin birth, noted above, would impose. The introduction of such a theory would at the very least be the occasion of controversy within the church; yet of such controversy we have no evidence whatsoever. And if invention is at work here, how strange that it is so reserved, confining itself to a few verses! When early Christianity really undertook to invent, it did not content itself with such limited expression, as the apocryphal gospels attest. The New Testament, however, cannot justly be accused of inventing "facts" on the basis of Old Testament prophecy. The event came first, then the linking with prophetic testimony followed.

Some moderns would brush aside the whole subject of the virgin birth on the ground that such a doctrine is unnecessary for Christian faith. This may well be an admission that the grounds for this article of Christian belief are too strong to be overthrown. When it is pointed out that multitudes of people became adherents of the church in its early days without knowing anything

55 The paradox that must be explained is this: "The belief . . . embodied in our narratives was not a natural product of Judaism, and cannot be explained by any normal evolution of thought within it. Yet the men who first made and held it were Jews" (Fairbairn, *op. cit.*, p. 42).

about such a teaching, a wrong inference is easily made from such an observation, as though ignorance amounted to rejection. Actually, we have no right to assume that on learning of the virgin birth converts held such information to be of slight consequence, any more than that they repudiated it as false.

Brunner treats the virgin birth as an impertinence, since it is an attempt to explain what should be left as a mystery.[56] He proposes that the incarnation be retained as central to Christianity but that the virgin birth be regarded as an attempt of human minds to explain the miracle. Granting that the incarnation is the greater of the two, it is just this factor of greater importance that accounts for the preponderance of its mention in Scripture. There is no solid basis for distinguishing the two as divinely-revelational on the one hand and humanly-interpretative on the other. Brunner cannot see how the origin of Jesus from a sinful human pair would be qualitatively different from the origin of Jesus from a sinful mother. If God is not hindered in achieving his intended purpose through the latter means, why could he not have achieved it through the former? Suffice it to say that the neo-orthodox theologian, with his insistence upon complete freedom of action for God, is in a poor position to raise a question here. Doubtless God could have given us a Savior through the ordinary processes of generation had he chosen so to do, but he did not choose this method. The overshadowing of Mary by the Holy Spirit was clearly intended to safeguard the holiness of her offspring. Despite her own limitations, the babe could be called the holy Son of God (Lk. 1:35).

That Brunner's position is untenable will readily be seen when it is appreciated that the brevity and sublimity of the virgin-birth narrative in the Gospels is what we should expect if it belongs to revelation, but not what we should expect if it is the attempt of human minds to explain the incarnation. It is just the absence of labored explanation, it is just the refusal to delve into the physiological problem involved in the conception, that places this portion of the story on the same high level as the Scripture assertions that in Jesus Christ God has become manifest in the flesh.

Admittedly the virgin birth is a mystery, but so is the gospel to which it forms an introduction. Both need to be received with

56 Emil Brunner, *The Mediator* (1934), p. 322, n. 1.

humility. "The records of the Virgin Birth in Matthew and Luke reveal God's ability to enter into human life and history notwithstanding his absolute transcendence."[57]

THE PURPOSE OF THE INCARNATION

Closely associated with the birth of Jesus are certain indications of the objectives to be gained by his advent. He comes first of all to reveal God. Zacharias calls the one to be born the dayspring from on high, who shall give light to those who sit in darkness (Lk. 1:78-79). Simeon's statement is similar (Lk. 2:32). Here belongs also the name Immanuel (Mt. 1:23). The theme of the Prologue of the Fourth Gospel is the knowledge of God, now made sharp and clear at last through the tabernacling of the Word in flesh (Jn. 1:14, 18).

A second and closely related purpose is the accomplishment of the salvation of men. If incarnation had to take account of the barrier of finiteness, removing it by presenting God in human form, it also had to take account of the barrier of sin by presenting a Savior who could meet man's responsibility in a way acceptable to God. Simeon sees in the babe Jesus God's provision for salvation (Lk. 2:30). His very name betokens his mission (Mt. 1:21). He has been born a Savior (Lk. 2:11).

It is significant that of the three main elements of world preparation for the coming of Christ—the Greek, which provided the cultural milieu and the language; the Roman, which provided the facilitating elements of communication, law, and order; and the Jewish, which provided the religious background—only the latter was a positive preparation. The other two were at best neutral in their contribution, for they simply implemented a gospel when it was ready for dissemination. But the Jewish preparation provided something that dealt directly with the content of the gospel. Jewry had tried the law and had failed under it, proclaiming thereby the necessity for a Savior from sin.

A third purpose of the incarnation is dominion. "And he will reign over the house of Jacob for ever; and of his kingdom there will be no end" (Lk. 1:33). He was born a king (Mt. 2:2). Such pronouncements of royal sovereignty serve to emphasize the expectation that he will unquestionably succeed in carrying out his redemptive mission. The crown is won by means of the cross.

57 Otto Piper, "The Virgin Birth," *Interpretation*, 18 (1964), 142.

This threefold purpose lay deeply imbedded in the consciousness of our Lord also, and is reflected in his teaching. One can know the Father truly and fully only as the Son reveals him (Mt. 11:27). He knew he had come to minister and to give his life a ransom for many (Mk. 10:45). He foresaw a glorious consummation despite his rejection by his own nation (Mk. 13:26; 14:62). In fact, New Testament teaching as a whole follows the same threefold pattern. Paul taught that Christ is the image of God, so that we know God in Christ (II Cor. 4:4, 6), and that he came to redeem (Gal. 4:4-5), and that to him belongs supremacy over all things (I Cor. 15:24-28). The same three strands make up the texture of the Christology of the opening chapters of Hebrews. God has spoken by a Son who is the express image of his person (Heb. 1:1-3). It is the divine will that Christ should taste death for every man, that through death he should destroy the devil and deliver those who were held in the bondage of fear (Heb. 2:9; 2:14-15). In the present age Jesus is seated on the right hand of the Majesty on high, crowned with glory and honor, awaiting the hour when God will make his enemies the footstool of his feet (Heb. 1:13; 2:9).

When the gospel was first made known through the apostles and others, it had as an initial obligation the explanation of the offense of the cross (I Cor. 1:23); but as the message came into contact with Greek thought the point of tension shifted to the incarnation, and this is reflected especially in the Johannine writings. In the struggle with imperial power, it was natural that the supreme issue should be the kingship of Jesus Christ. But through all time these three aspects of our Lord's mission will retain their relevancy and will challenge the faith of men.[58]

BIBLIOGRAPHY

Lancelot Andrewes. *Seventeen Sermons on the Nativity*. London: Griffith, Farran, Okeden and Welsh, n.d.

C. K. Barrett. *The Holy Spirit and the Gospel Tradition*. New York: Macmillan, 1947. Pp. 5-24.

[58] Into the questions that the incarnation poses for modern thought we cannot enter. A good statement of them will be found in *Conflict in Christology* by J. S. Lawton (1947). See also W. R. Matthews, *The Problem of Christ in the Twentieth Century* (1950).

G. H. Box. *The Virgin Birth of Jesus*. London: Pitman, 1916.

C. A. Briggs. *The Incarnation of the Lord*. New York: Scribners, 1902.

R. J. Cooke. *The Incarnation and Recent Criticism*. New York: Eaton and Mains, 1907.

Douglas Edwards. *The Virgin Birth in History and Faith*. London: Faber and Faber, 1943.

Paul Lobstein. *The Virgin Birth of Christ*. New York: Harper, 1930.

J. Gresham Machen. *The Virgin Birth of Christ*. New York: Harper, 1930.

Paul S. Minear, "The Interpreter and the Birth Narratives," Uppsala: *Symbolae Biblicae Upsalienses*, 1950.

G. Campbell Morgan. *Crises of the Christ*. New York: Revell, 1936. Pp. 64-101.

J. K. Mozley. *The Doctrine of the Incarnation*. London: Bles, 1949.

James Orr. *The Virgin Birth of Christ*. New York: Scribners, 1907.

R. L. Ottley. *The Doctrine of the Incarnation*. London: Methuen, 8th edition, 1946. Pp. 3-35.

Otto A. Piper, "The Virgin Birth," *Interpretation*, 18 (Apr. 1964), 131-148.

W. M. Ramsay. *The Bearing of Recent Discovery on the Trustworthiness of the New Testament*. London: Hodder and Stoughton, 4th edition, 1920. Pp. 238-300.

————. *Was Christ Born at Bethlehem?* London: Hodder and Stoughton, 2nd edition, n.d.

William Childs Robinson, "A Re-study of the Virgin Birth of Christ," EQ, 37 (Oct.-Dec. 1965), 198-211.

A. N. Sherwin-White. *Roman Society and Roman Law in the New Testament*. Oxford: Clarendon, 1963. Pp. 162-171.

G. S. Streatfeild. *The Incarnation*. London: Longmans, Green, 1910.

L. M. Sweet. *The Birth and Infancy of Jesus Christ*. Philadelphia: Westminster, 1906.

Vincent Taylor. *The Historical Evidence for the Virgin Birth*. Oxford: Clarendon, 1920.

T. J. Thorburn. *A Critical Examination of the Evidence for the Doctrine of the Virgin Birth*. London: S.P.C.K., 1908.

B. B. Warfield. *Christology and Criticism*. New York: Oxford, 1929. Pp. 447-458.

CHAPTER III

THE INFANCY AND BOYHOOD

> *A simple-hearted Child was He,*
> *And He was nothing more;*
> *In summer days, like you and me,*
> *He played about the door,*
> *Or gathered, when the father toiled,*
> *The shavings from the floor.*
>
> *And when the sun at break of day*
> *Crept in upon His hair,*
> *I think it must have left a ray*
> *of unseen glory there—*
> *A kiss of love on that little brow*
> *For the thorns that it must wear.*
>
> —Albert Bigelow Paine

THE LORD OF GLORY BEGAN HIS EARTHLY LIFE IN A MANGER IN THE city of David, as Mary with her own hands took the babe and wrapped him in swaddling clothes[1] and laid him on the straw. No attendants stood by, nor host of admirers such as would welcome the arrival of a king's son.[2] "He became poor" (II Cor. 8:9), and this was true from the very beginning.

[1] As described by B. S. Easton, "The oriental swaddling-clothes consist of a square cloth and two or more bandages. The child is laid on the cloth diagonally and the corners are folded over the feet and body and under the head, the bandages then being tied so as to hold the cloth in position," ISBE, V (1930), 2874.

[2] D. A. Hayes, *The Most Beautiful Book Ever Written* (1913), pp. 129-133, contrasts the birth of Jesus with the glitter and pomp that marked the birth of Louis XIV of France.

THE SHEPHERDS

To devout and unsophisticated men, tending their sheep like David long ago, came suddenly on that wonderful night the tidings that a Savior was born in Bethlehem (Lk. 2:8ff.). The revelation was accompanied by a display of glorious light to mark its supernatural character and by choirs of angels to indicate that this momentous birth, fraught with the possibility of great joy for all the people, brought rejoicing in heaven as well. Without any expression of skepticism and without delay, these humble shepherds made their way into the city to behold with modest wonder what God had wrought. Departing from the presence of the child, they became the first witnesses of Christ to the people, telling what they had heard and seen. Their quiet routine, as they returned to it, was irradiated with joy and praise to God.

THE CIRCUMCISION AND NAMING OF THE CHILD

These two acts took place on the eighth day and designated Jesus as a son of Israel (Lk. 2:21; cf. Phil. 3:5). Beyond this obvious fact lay the deeper significance that identification with those he came to redeem, as expressed in circumcision, was a necessary condition of effecting their salvation. The naming of the child was the carrying out of the explicit direction given both to Mary and to Joseph (Lk. 1:31; Mt. 1:21). In this name *Jesus* was contained the prophecy that he would be the Savior. Through the years it was a reminder to the one who bore it that he was under obligation to fulfill the implication of that name.

THE REDEMPTION OF THE FIRSTBORN AND THE PURIFICATION OF THE MOTHER

Approximately a month later, two other legal requirements were met by a visit to the temple. According to the Mosaic code, the firstborn of man and beast belonged to the priest as his portion; but in the case of men, to relieve from the necessity of priestly service, redemption was prescribed, consisting of the payment of five shekels (Num. 18:15-16). The mother's purification terminated a period of forty-one days (Lev. 12:1-4) and was marked by the presentation of a burnt offering and a sin offering. Ordinarily a lamb was offered for the former and a bird for the latter; but if means were not sufficient, it was allowable to offer two turtle-doves or two young pigeons (Lev. 12:8). Mary's offering is a commentary on the poverty of the holy family (Lk. 2:24). The visit to the temple was above all for the purpose of presenting the child to the Lord (Lk. 2:22). Like Samuel, Jesus was a special gift of God befitting acknowledgment in his house.

SIMEON AND ANNA

During the presentation in the temple, these two saints came forward to behold the child and give thanks to God for him (Lk. 2:25-38). In a day when formalism and commercialism had cast their blight upon the holy precincts, these two represented the finer side of Israel's piety. Simeon recognized in the babe Jesus the salvation of God for his people Israel and for the Gentiles, and he saw by the Spirit that the child would be the touchstone of destiny for men. His sufferings would stab the heart of Mary also. This meeting in the temple was a high occasion for Simeon; he was ready thereafter to depart this life in peace. But for Anna, probably more advanced in years, the glimpsing of the infant Jesus was such a stimulation that she busied herself to speak of him "to all who were looking for the redemption of Jerusalem."

THE VISIT OF THE MAGI

When the wise men from the east appeared in Judea, the holy family was still in residence at Bethlehem, dwelling now in a house in the city (Mt. 2:11). It is impossible to say how much time had passed since the birth, but the edict of Herod about the slaying of the children two years old and under suggests quite an interval.

The uneasiness of Jerusalem at the coming of these men is understandable. One born king of the Jews could readily stir the old fanatical enthusiasm for independence. Herod was committed to resisting any such thing, and behind him stood the power of Rome. Jerusalem had already experienced its full measure of turmoil and bloodshed since the days of the Maccabees. It was not anxious for more. The dominance of Herod may also explain, at least in part, the indifference of the scribes. They knew where the Christ was to be born, but they made no move to investigate, leaving that to the visitors from the east. If they had any genuine concern over the fulfillment of the prophetic word, it would not be healthy to indicate that fact in a public way. They were under the thumb of Herod. Even so, the zeal of the pilgrims from the east and their bold inquiry stand in reproachful contrast to the numb apathy of Israel and its leaders.

The long trek of the Magi was now ended, and they proceeded at once to the realization of their announced objective—to worship him who was born as Israel's king. Mary was there with the child, but they worshiped him alone (Mt. 2:11). They understood enough of the nature of worship not to confound it with the offering of their gifts, which they presented as a separate act.

THE FLIGHT TO EGYPT

When the Magi did not return to him, the infuriated Herod, who had anticipated precise information about Jesus which would enable him to locate the child and do away with him, proceeded to deal with the situation in a characteristic way which revealed his own peculiar brand of savagery. He decreed the death of the male infants of Bethlehem and environs. Though Herod was an Idumean rather than a Jew, his act seems prophetic of what was to follow in the career of Jesus. Bethlehem is not far from Jerusalem, nor the cradle from the cross. Herod's act only throws into sharper relief the love for children that Jesus manifested during his ministry.[3]

Warned of God concerning Herod's intentions, Joseph took his family down to Egypt. As it had been a refuge in days gone by for the people of God (Gen. 12:10; 46:3-4; Jer. 42:14), so now it was destined to offer asylum to the Lord's anointed. Scripture is content to state that the family remained in the country until the death of Herod, when Joseph was again informed by a dream that it was safe to return to the land of Israel. But the apocryphal gospels embellish the simple narrative by accounts of the adoration of wild beasts along the route of travel, the supernatural shortening of the journey, the falling down of the idols when the holy family entered a temple to find lodging, and other fancies.[4]

The canonical record tells us nothing about the life in Egypt or how the exiles were sustained. Doubtless the gifts of the Magi were looked upon as a providential help toward their maintenance. Matthew is concerned, however, to point out that the summons to leave Egypt was in fulfillment of the prophecy of

3 B. B. Warfield, art. "Children," HDCG, I, 302b.
4 See especially the Gospel of Pseudo-Matthew, chs. 18–24.

Hosea 11:1, "Out of Egypt have I called my son." Once again the attention of the reader is drawn to the purposeful identification of the Redeemer with the nation he came to save.[5] It is possible to see here also an intentional correspondence with Moses, the great deliverer and lawgiver.[6] One of the major contributions of Matthew's Gospel is the placing of the teaching of Christ against the background of the Mosaic legislation.

THE RETURN TO NAZARETH

From Matthew's account it is plain that Joseph was intent upon settling in Judea after the return from Egypt (Mt. 2:22). He evidently felt that Jesus the Messiah ought to be reared in or near his birthplace, the city of David.[7] But persuaded otherwise by divine guidance, he turned aside and proceeded to Nazareth in Galilee. It is a peculiarity of Matthew's Gospel that he says nothing about Nazareth as the original home of Joseph and Mary. That he was ignorant of the tradition as stated in Luke is improbable. Perhaps the kingly emphasis in Matthew, so clearly shown in chapters one and two, dictated the exclusion of any mention of Nazareth (belonging to Galilee of the Gentiles) at this point. From the standpoint of historical fact, the important thing is that both Matthew and Luke agree in fixing upon Nazareth as the place of Jesus' residence prior to his public ministry. It would be inept to argue, on the other hand, that Jesus must have been born in Galilee because he was known in mature life as Jesus of Nazareth. The general public would not be likely to know anything about the earliest years and so would naturally think of him as originating in Nazareth (Jn. 1:46; 7:52).

In connection with the settling at Nazareth, Matthew states that this was in fulfillment of prophecy to the effect that Jesus should be called a Nazarene (Mt. 2:23). The conception of fulfillment entertained by New Testament writers was a rather fluid thing. In this case Matthew is basing his statement upon the fact that Nazareth and Nazarene appeared to have a verbal con-

5 C. H. Dodd, *According to the Scriptures* (1952), p. 103.
6 R. V. G. Tasker, *The Old Testament in the New Testament* (1947), p. 43.
7 Some have thought that Joseph planned not to return to Nazareth because of gossip concerning Mary. Cf. David Smith, *Our Lord's Earthly Life* (n.d.), p. 16. Another opinion puts Joseph's original home at Bethlehem. See Box, *The Virgin Birth of Jesus* (1916), p. 56, n. 2, also p. 57.

nection with *netser* (branch), which occurs in Isaiah 11:1, a definitely messianic passage. Since other prophets also spoke of Messiah in terms of the Branch, although a different Hebrew word was used (Jer. 23:5; Zech. 3:8; 6:12), the Evangelist could legitimately say that this prediction was spoken through the *prophets.* Nazarene has nothing to do with Nazirite.

One often hears the comment that Nazareth had an unsavory reputation in the time of Christ, and that this is reflected in Nathanael's pessimistic query, "Can any good thing come out of Nazareth?" (Jn. 1:46). For this opinion there appears to be no real foundation. The basis of Nathanael's thinking was probably rather this, that if Galilee as a whole could not produce the Messiah (Jn. 7:52), how much less such an insignificant part of it as Nazareth.

Various negative assertions have been made about Nazareth to the effect that the place had no existence or that Jesus never lived there. Its omission from ancient Jewish literature, including the Old Testament, is far from being conclusive evidence that there was no such place.[8] If the evidence of the Gospels be accepted, and there is no valid reason for rejecting it, Nazareth was the home of Jesus until he adopted Capernaum as his own city (Mt. 4:13; 9:1). This latter site was better suited to his need for a central headquarters during his public ministry than the more secluded Nazareth, which resented him anyway.

This hamlet[9] of Nazareth in northern Palestine was a miniature of the whole country in the sense that its situation afforded ready contact with the outside world, yet considerable separation from it, the very features Israel historically had enjoyed. Their land lay at the crossroads of the world but was detached by its peculiar topography, which confined the flow of travel largely to the lowlands, passing by the plateau where the life of the nation centered.

From the hill back of Nazareth, Jesus as a boy must often have scanned the horizon in all directions. Travelers attest the magnificence of the view from this spot. The panorama would include the Mediterranean Sea to the west, Mount Carmel and the plain of Sharon south of it, the broad valley of Esdraelon, with Mount

[8] G. F. Moore, in F. J. Foakes-Jackson and K. Lake, *The Beginnings of Christianity,* I (1942), 429.

[9] Matthew and Luke call it a city, perhaps out of regard for its importance in the gospel story.

Tabor on the north, the hill of Moreh and Mount Gilboa on the south, and Samaria beyond—all of these in an almost perfect line north and south. To the east, beyond the depression made by the Sea of Galilee and the Jordan, rose the hills that marked the beginning of the Bashan-Gilead country. To the north lay the somewhat broken terrain of Galilee, rising to plateau proportions in the distance, with glistening Mt. Hermon to the northeast capping the scene.

No patriotic son of Israel could allow his eye to sweep these vistas without being reminded of the stirring events of history that would forever be associated with them: Elijah's triumph over the prophets of Baal, the victory of Deborah and Barak, the crushing of the Midianites by Gideon and his band, the lamented death of Saul and Jonathan—these and other episodes would easily rise out of the past and in fancy be reenacted. Yes, Nazareth was secluded, but just beyond its sheltering quiet lay the world of affairs. Its immediate gift to Jesus was an opportunity to live a life of simplicity. More remotely, it provided a door of entrance to the busier and more complex life in which he would minister.

Nazareth depended for its livelihood upon the tillage of its grain-fields and the cultivation of its vineyards and groves, which ranged up and down the neighboring hills. Though his labor kept him in the village, Jesus loved the out-of-doors, and must often have tramped through the countryside enjoying its sights and sounds. Years later, when he chose to slip away from human companionship to commune with the Father, he was remaining true to the influence of the environment of the early days.

Judging from his parables Jesus must have cultivated early in life the habit of observing what went on around him. He saw that not all the sower's seed fell on good ground. He knew that a good tree was needed to insure good fruit. He had many times stuffed dried grass into his mother's stove to heat it for baking, grass that only a short time before had been growing in the field. Perchance he had watched Mary light a lamp and look carefully for the coin that had slipped from her hand and rolled out of view. Whether indoors or out he was alert to all that was going on. This panorama of early days furnished him with many a true-to-life illustration as he stood before the multitude and taught.

A place the size of Nazareth would hardly need more than one

person or family for most of its trades. It is not surprising that
Jesus should be known in the community as "the carpenter" (Mk.
6:3). There was no other following the death of Joseph.[10]

THE FAMILY OF JESUS

Joseph does not appear in the narrative following the infancy
period except by name (to indicate Jesus' family relationship),
so it is safe to assume that he died before the opening of the
public ministry. Doubtless this placed heavier responsibility
upon our Lord in providing for the needs of the others. The
Gospels mention four brothers of Christ. His sisters are unnum-
bered and unnamed.[11] The precise relation between Jesus and
his brothers has been a matter of keen debate in the history of
the church. Three men, living about the same time,[12] espoused
views that are still associated with their names. Epiphanius contended that the brethren of the Lord were children of Joseph by
a former marriage, the term brethren being used in the same
accommodated sense as is the word *father* when applied to
Joseph's relation to Jesus. Helvidius maintained that the brethren
were blood brothers of Jesus, born to Joseph and Mary subse-
quent to his birth. In opposition to Helvidius, Jerome (Hierony-
mus, hence the name Hieronymian for his view) insisted that
the brethren were kinsmen, specifically first cousins, being sons
of Mary's sister, namely, that Mary who was the wife of Clopas
(Jn. 19:25).

The last position is too tenuous to merit serious consideration.
It involves supposing that two sisters bore the name Mary; that
brother can be used for cousin (not in NT usage otherwise), and
that James the Lord's brother (Gal. 1:19) is identical with James
the son of Alphaeus among the apostles. Epiphanius' view was
popular from the beginning because it fitted the ascetic mood of
the early church, which delighted in emphasizing the perpetual
virginity of Mary. Yet many moderns have endorsed it strictly on
scriptural grounds, especially the unwillingness of Jesus to commit Mary to the care of his "brethren," despite the fact that they

10 A. T. Olmstead, *Jesus in the Light of History* (1942), p. 6.
11 Matt. 13:55-56. The word *all* suggests that there were at least three
sisters.
12 Late fourth and early fifth century.

were destined to believe on him in a matter of days.[13] Great weight is laid, too, on Luke 1:26-38 as teaching the perpetual virginity.[14] Yet it is doubtful that Mary's words, "How can this be, since I have no husband?" are intended to express a settled purpose to maintain a celibate state in the future. They seem clearly to refer to her perplexity in the present situation only. The most natural position, in the light of the impression made by the statements of the Gospels, is the Helvidian.[15] In spite of some slight indication that early in the ministry the brethren may have been rather neutral in their attitude toward Jesus (Jn. 2:12), as time went on they became offended in him and refused to believe in his messianic status (Jn. 7:5).

EDUCATION

Taken in the larger sense, the entire earthly life of the Lord constituted his education, particularly in the area of temptation and affliction, since he learned obedience by the things he suffered.[16] But we are thinking here of the more limited sphere of child training.

The Palestine of Jesus' day represented a commingling of cultures and languages. When the Jews returned from the captivity, the Persian empire of which they were a part used Aramaic as its official language. That this tongue had already become familiar to the Jews is seen from the fact that when Ezra and his associates read the law to the people, it was necessary to give the sense of it in a language the people understood (Neh. 8:8). This can only have been Aramaic. That Hebrew continued to be used for the writing of the last books of the Old Testament is not surprising, since it was only natural that there should be a conscious effort to maintain the language of the fathers for this holy use. Hebrew continued to be used, in fact, for the public reading of the Scriptures, which were then rendered into Aramaic for the benefit of the hearers. Among the scribal class, the duty to maintain a knowledge of Hebrew was fully recognized; but the evidence is clear that points to the use of Aramaic in popular

---

13 J. B. Lightfoot, *Galatians* (1896), p. 272.
14 C. Harris, HDCG, I, 235ᵇ, 236ᵃ.
15 See J. B. Mayor, HDB, I, 320-326.
16 W. M. Ramsay, *The Education of Christ* (1911), pp. 132-133.

speech.[17] This evidence includes certain utterances of Jesus that are retained in the Gospels in their Aramaic form, place names, and personal names.[18] In the early church at Jerusalem, those who are called Hebrews in distinction from the Hellenists were Aramaic-speaking Jews who had become Christians (Acts 6:1). It has long been recognized that Jesus' discourses were spoken in Aramaic.

Modern research is making it increasingly apparent that there were writings in Aramaic in the time of our Lord, some of which would be of interest to him and would enrich his education. Apparently, written Targums (paraphrases of Scripture in Aramaic) were in existence by that time.[19] Olmstead lists several works in Aramaic to which Jesus could have had access.[20] Among modern discoveries in Palestine has been the finding of fragments of the Aramaic text of *The Testaments of the Twelve Patriarchs*, previously known only in various translations from the Aramaic.[21]

Did our Lord know Hebrew in addition to Aramaic? An affirmative answer is indicated by the fact that he was able to stand up in the synagogue and read the Scriptures.[22] The acquisition of the knowledge of Hebrew, so closely related to Aramaic, would not be at all impossible for him, even though he did not attend a rabbinical school. His intense interest in the Scriptures would provide the necessary motivation. Finding a teacher would be a secondary problem.[23]

[17] It is now generally conceded that the approach used by Dalman in seeking to reconstruct the Aramaic of the first century was wrong. He sought to connect it with the Aramaic of the official Targums of Onkelos and Jonathan. But these are written in a literary Aramaic which was artificial. Kahle has shown by the study of certain fragments found in the Cairo Genizah that the Palestinian Targum was written in the spoken Aramaic and affords a better basis of comparison with the Aramaic at the beginning of the Christian era than do the aforementioned Targums.

[18] For a full statement see G. Dalman, *Jesus-Jeshua* (1911), pp. 11-14.

[19] P. E. Kahle, *The Cairo Genizah* (1947), pp. 123-124.

[20] *Jesus in the Light of History*, pp. 16-20.

[21] C. Burchard, *Bibliographie zu den Handschriften vom Toten Meer* (1965), p. 334.

[22] Dalman, *op. cit.*, p. 37.

[23] The term "Hebrew" as used in the New Testament means generally, if not universally, Aramaic. In most instances it serves to differentiate the language in question from others of a non-Semitic character, and for this purpose the historic, sacred term is preferred to Aramaic, the technically correct designation. However, this view has been challenged by J. M. Grintz, "Hebrew as the Spoken and Written Language in the Last Days of the Second Temple," JBL, 79 (1960), 32-47.

Another language almost certainly entered into Jesus' background, for ever since the conquests of Alexander the Great, Greek influence was strong through most of the Near East. First under Egyptian (Ptolemaic), then under Syrian influence, Palestine was subjected to a process of hellenization. Because the Syrians, Antiochus Epiphanes in particular, sought to impose the Greek language, culture, and religion upon the Jews, their political revolt against their Syrian overlords naturally included a revolt against hellenization, including the language. Yet the revolt against the language could not be universal or permanent. Galilee, by reason of its position alone, was exposed to Greek influences which were inescapable. It was flanked on the eastern side by the Decapolis, a string of Greek cities that challenged Semitic isolationism. Apparently our Lord had some contact with this area, which is most easily explained if he had some knowledge of Greek (Mk. 7:31). Presumably he would need this language also for any ministry in the territory of Tyre and Sidon.[24] Dalman is no doubt correct in assuming that Jesus spoke to Pilate without an interpreter, and that the medium of communication was Greek.[25] As a boy in Nazareth, Jesus is likely to have made trips from time to time to Sepphoris, only three miles away, where Greek influence was predominant.[26]

Of formal education, the chances are that Jesus had little. Although popularly known as a religious teacher or rabbi, his reputation was not due to technical training (Jn. 7:15). Almost certainly he attended the synagogue school as a child and unquestionably received instruction in the Scriptures at home, in accordance with the ancient requirement (Deut. 6:7). The local synagogue services had their place also in shaping his formative years. Then at the age of twelve, if not before, he began those periodic pilgrimages to Jerusalem to attend the feasts of the Lord, which brought him into contact with the hub of Judaism at Jerusalem. Fortunately Luke has included an account of one especially significant visit (Lk. 2:41ff.).

On this occasion the boy Jesus caused astonishment in two directions, to his parents for his deliberate tarrying in the temple after their departure for home, and to the doctors of the law for his understanding of spiritual matters. Jesus met the complaint of Joseph and Mary by expressing his own astonishment that they

24 Mk. 7:24. Note that Jesus *talked* with a woman of this area (vv. 26-29).
25 *Op. cit.*, p. 6.
26 Olmstead, *op. cit.*, p. 24.

did not realize the necessity of his being in the house of his Father.[27] Whether or not the reader is intended to catch here a tension between Mary's "thy father" and his own "my Father," it is remarkable that the first recorded utterance of Jesus should reflect such a clear-cut consciousness of divine sonship.

As to the amazement of the Jewish teachers, there is no suggestion that this was due to omniscience on Jesus' part such as is attributed to him in the apocryphal Gospel of Thomas.[28] Nor is there any of that impertinence which mars the apocryphal account. If such had been displayed by Jesus, the doctors of the law would not have tolerated his presence. Rather, he began by listening to their teaching, then proceeded to ask questions. This led to further interchange in which the teachers put questions to him. They were amazed at the quality both of his questions and of his answers. He fulfilled the ideal of the pupil just as he fulfilled the ideal for every other phase of normal life.

It is not unreasonable to suppose that in the course of those few days the savants in the temple introduced Jesus to the traditions of the elders, which by this period had grown to considerable proportions. Certainly by the time of his public ministry our Lord had become proficient in this area as well as in the Scriptures and could discuss such matters with the Pharisees from time to time.

Those days in Jerusalem gave to the lad from Nazareth a much clearer picture than he had before of what Roman occupation meant for his nation, since at festival time the governor and his cohorts were much in evidence as a warning against revolutionary violence. Before many years had passed Jesus would be under the necessity of deciding what his own attitude should be, whether to be sympathetic to the Zealots in their passionate advocacy of active resistance to Rome with a view to regaining independence, or to resist the temptation to prostitute his mission to political ends. That he came to a clear-cut decision to avoid entanglement is apparent throughout his ministry and comes to expression in the incident of the tribute money (Mt. 22:15-22).

---

27 Lk. 2:49. As to whether we should render "my Father's house" or "my Father's business," both are possible, but the former is preferable. As Plummer justly remarks, "The words indicate His surprise that His parents did not know *where* to find Him. His Father's business could have been done elsewhere" (Com. on Luke, ICC, *in loco*). See also Matthew Black, *An Aramaic Approach to the Gospels and Acts*, 2nd edition (1954), p. 3.

28 Chs. 6, 7, 19.

The story of the incident in the temple is preceded and followed by statements dealing with Jesus' boyhood development
(Lk. 2:40, 52). Both of them emphasize his possession of wisdom,
the very thing that impressed those who heard him speak as a
man, even the people of his own district (Mk. 6:2). Wisdom is a
more comprehensive thing than knowledge, though it presupposes knowledge. In wisdom Jesus of Nazareth stands unrivaled.
A comparison of the two verses in Luke shows considerable similarity, but whereas verse 40 pictures natural growth, verse 52
stresses personal determination to advance.[29] Then, too, in the
former passage, wisdom follows physical development; in the
latter passage, it precedes. As time went on, the boy Jesus learned
to put a higher evaluation on wisdom than upon attention to the
body.

Many readers of the New Testament have expressed regret
that so little is given there about the boyhood of Jesus.[30] This
very fact, however, makes the little we possess the more precious.
But whereas the early church, as represented by the writers of
the apocryphal gospels, sought to fill the gap by making Jesus
a wonder worker even in those tender years, we now see that
the reason for the silence of Scripture is simply that there was
nothing extraordinary to record. So far as miracles are concerned,
the canonical Gospels imply that these began only with the public
ministry (Mk. 6:1-3; Jn. 2:11).

The conduct of Jesus in the home as a boy and as a youth is
gathered up in the one word obedience (Lk. 2:51). What he was
in relation to the Father in heaven throughout his ministry he
was in relation to those whom God had placed over him in
authority, and the lesser was preparation for the greater (Phil.
2:8). This subjection to parents raises the question of their understanding of the true nature of their son. Throughout his narrative of the infancy and boyhood, Luke persistently emphasizes
the wonder of the parents, especially Mary, over the things said
of the child Jesus or the things he did. Does this mean they
grasped the full significance of his deity? If they had, it would

29 Paul uses the same verb *prokoptō* to state his advance in Judaism (Gal.
1:14).
30 Robert Aron, *Jesus of Nazareth* (1962), p. 12, observes that the pattern
set by Scripture in telling of Moses' career is followed here. After the account
of his birth there is a gap until he comes to manhood. Details of private life
could be sacrificed to make room for a man's contribution to the world in the
fulfillment of the purpose of God.

have rendered a normal relationship in the home impossible. Let Edersheim speak on this point:

> Christ could not, in any true sense, have been subject to His parents, if they had fully understood that He was Divine; nor could He, in that case, have been watched, as He "grew in wisdom and in favor with God and men." Such knowledge would have broken the bond of His humanity to ours, by severing that which bound Him as a child to His mother. . . . We can thus, in some measure, understand why the mystery of His Divinity had to be kept while He was on earth. Had it been otherwise, the thought of His Divinity would have proved so all-absorbing, as to render impossible that of His Humanity, with all its lessons.[31]

It is Jesus' likeness to us, then, that shines through these narratives of the early years. But the peculiar circumstances of the time and place of his entrance into our humanity demanded a companion emphasis which is summarized in Paul's word, "made under the law." So it is that the presentation of the babe in the temple is said to be after the custom of the law (Lk. 2:27; cf. Lk. 2:39). Likewise, the one incident chosen from the boyhood for special notice is that momentous occasion when the lad of twelve prepares to become a son of the law, assuming formal responsibility to live before God in the light of his holy commandments. His very first test under this discipline was that ready subjection to parents which is called for in the fifth commandment. We ought not to assume that such subjection was easy, when preference for his Father's house was so marked. Nor was it easy in the ensuing years, which he must spend under the authority of parents who were hardly his superiors intellectually, who were fallible, and would choose for him what he would not always choose for himself. But in all this we see the shaping of the Man who preferred the Father's will above his own.

BIBLIOGRAPHY

Robert Aron. *Jesus of Nazareth.* London: Hamish Hamilton, 1962.
William Barclay. *The Mind of Jesus.* New York: Harper, 1960. Pp. 3-15.
Eric F. F. Bishop. *Jesus of Palestine.* London: Lutterworth, 1955.

[31] *The Life and Times of Jesus the Messiah,* I, 192.

G. Dalman. *Sacred Sites and Ways.* London: S.P.C.K., 1935. Pp. 57-78.

Henri Daniel-Rops. *Jesus and His Times.* New York: Dutton, 1954.

George Farmer, "Boyhood of Jesus," HDCG. New York: Scribners, 1924. Vol. I, pp. 224-230.

G. Campbell Morgan. *The Crises of the Christ.* New York: Revell, 1936. Pp. 123-136.

A. T. Olmstead. *Jesus in the Light of History.* New York: Scribners, 1942. Pp. 1-27.

John Oxenham. *The Hidden Years.* New York: Longmans, Green, 1927.

W. M. Ramsay. *The Education of Christ.* London: Hodder and Stoughton, 1911.

David Smith. *The Days of His Flesh.* New York: Doran, n.d. Pp. 14-24.

Maisie Spens. *Concerning Himself.* London: Hodder and Stoughton, 1937. Pp. 3-13.

Ethelbert Stauffer. *Jesus and His Story.* New York: Knopf, 1960. Pp. 43-62.

L. M. Sweet. *The Birth and Infancy of Jesus Christ.* Philadelphia: Westminster, 1906. Pp. 19-54.

CHAPTER IV

THE BAPTISM

> *"I have baptized you with water: but he will baptize you with the Holy Spirit."*
>
> —John the Baptist

IN THE PROVIDENCE OF GOD, THE EMERGENCE OF JESUS INTO PUBLIC life came in conjunction with the ministry of John the Baptist. After the centuries of dearth when no prophetic voice was heard to challenge or comfort the nation, the effect of John's proclamation was electric. "The end time has come, because God speaks through his prophets again."[1] All Jerusalem and Judea and the territory around the Jordan turned out a stream of people eager to catch a glimpse of this desert-reared figure and hear the man to whom the word of the Lord had come. In Mark's language, this was the beginning of the gospel of Jesus Christ (Mk. 1:1). The same consciousness is reflected in the preaching of the early church (Acts 10:37; 13:24-25). In choosing a replacement for Judas the apostles felt the necessity of having someone who had followed Jesus from the early days of his contact with John (Acts 1:21-22).

Josephus mentions John in a passage that seems to be entirely independent of the Gospels, though in substantial agreement with them.[2] The allusion to John is somewhat incidental, being introduced in order to explain a military reverse that Herod suffered in a conflict with Aretas, the Nabatean king whose daughter had been Herod's wife until he rejected her in favor

[1] O. Cullmann, *The Christology of the New Testament* (1959), p. 15.
[2] *Antiquities* xviii.5.2.

of Herodias. The popular reaction to this defeat, according to Josephus, was the belief that it constituted a divine punishment upon Herod for putting John to death. Josephus says nothing about the imprisonment of John for his rebuke about the marriage, nor does he recount the festivities that led to John's death. Rather, he assigns the murder to Herod's fear that a revolt might gather force around the person of John, giving him no little trouble in his domain. The Jewish historian speaks of John's preaching of righteousness and of the baptism to which he summoned the people. Herod's fear of John's political potential may not unfairly be taken as an attestation of the Baptist's preaching about the imminence of the kingdom.

Discovery of the Dead Sea Scrolls has attached new importance to the question of John's possible relation to the Essene movement or something akin to it. The previously known *Zadokite Fragments* reveal the existence of a reform movement in Judaism in the first century B.C. with affinities to the Essenes as they are described by Josephus, Pliny, and Philo. Of the newly discovered materials, the *Manual of Discipline* is especially instructive as to the tenets and practices of the Qumran sect. Since John spent his sheltered years in the Judean desert, the possibility of contact with this group must be admitted. His asceticism may be explained in this way. But his practice of baptism can hardly be so explained, for the Essenes were noted for their repeated lustrations, which were ceremonial in character, whereas John's baptism was once-for-all and was related definitely to sin and righteousness. The fact that it was not repeated underscores its eschatological character. It was a preparation for the denouement of the messianic era.[3]

The stern warnings of judgment upon sin that characterized John's preaching were accompanied by the command to repent and to manifest works in keeping with a true repentance. Various groups who came to him sought instruction as to the type of conduct expected of them (Lk. 3:10-14), and John replied in terms appropriate to their special situations. This looks like a species of catechetical instruction, and it may well have served as a sort of model for the early church, although in the latter case information about the person and work of Jesus naturally formed the groundwork for the teaching on ethical and moral matters.

3 A. Feuillet, "Le baptême de Jésus," RB, 71 (1964), 337.

John's baptism is probably to be linked to proselyte baptism, the rite whereby Gentiles were formally received into Judaism, accompanied as it was by circumcision and the assumption of the burden of the law.[4] But the new element in John's baptism was its application to those who had been born and reared in Judaism. The prophet would not allow his hearers to take refuge in the fact that they were Abraham's children (Lk. 3:8). No wonder he met opposition from some of the people, especially the religious leaders.[5] They were not prepared to be treated like sinners of the Gentiles.

A note of special urgency in John's preaching was the announcement that the kingdom of heaven was at hand. This particular emphasis is found only in Matthew (3:2), but it is closely connected, no doubt, with John's prophetic announcement of one to come who was mightier than he (apparently because he would not baptize with water but with the Holy Spirit). In all the Gospels this anticipation of the coming of another is coupled with a statement of John's own unworthiness to be even his menial servant. But the disconcerting thing, as G. S. Duncan has observed, is that John nowhere identifies this figure, as we might have expected him to do, with the Messiah.[6] Was John indifferent to the person and office of the coming one by reason of his engrossment in his work? We have no warrant for concluding this. Are we to seek an explanation in the circumstance that the Old Testament had made prophetic announcements that were capable of being interpreted in terms of more than one person? This situation is reflected in John 1:19-24. A deputation from the Pharisees asked John to identify himself, starting off with Messiah, then passing to Elijah, and concluding with the prophet (predicted in Deuteronomy 18). The very positiveness of John's rejoinders about himself suggests that he had a reasonably well-defined conception of the identity of the one whose way he was preparing. Strangely enough, even after the baptism of Jesus and a considerable period of ministry, John continues to speak in the same fashion, sending representatives to inquire of Jesus if he is the one who was to come (Mt. 11:3).

---

[4] I. Abrahams, *Studies in Pharisaism and the Gospels,* First Series (1917), ch. 4. H. H. Rowley, "Jewish Proselyte Baptism," *Hebrew Union College Annual,* 1940, pp. 313-334. However, dependence on Qumran baptism is suggested by J. A. T. Robinson, *Twelve New Testament Studies* (1962), pp. 17-18.

[5] T. W. Manson, *The Servant-Messiah* (1953), pp. 44-45.

[6] *Jesus, Son of Man* (1949), p. 83.

The reluctance of the forerunner to use the term Messiah of Jesus is probably best explained by our Lord's own avoidance of the title. It was too easily misunderstood, too easily associated with merely temporal and political hopes, to be safely appropriated and promiscuously used in reference to his own mission. It is suggestive that when Andrew, a disciple of John, rushed to find his brother Simon and share with him his discovery about Jesus of Nazareth, he did not shrink from announcing that he had found the Messiah. It would be arbitrary to base this confidence merely on Andrew's interview with Jesus apart from any conditioning through his period of association with John the Baptist. What John could not openly proclaim he could nevertheless divulge to an intimate follower like Andrew.

According to the Fourth Gospel, John's testimony to Jesus was twofold: as Son of God and Lamb of God (Jn. 1:29, 34). The former title gives no particular difficulty, since it fits in with the acknowledgment of Jesus by the Father on the occasion of the baptism as reported in the Synoptic Gospels. The phraseology of John 1:34 suggests that the Baptist's habit of speaking thus of him dated from the baptism scene. But the title Lamb of God is hard to cope with. It seems to run counter to the conception of Jesus' mission that the forerunner held as reflected in the Synoptics. And to look at it from another point of view, why would the Baptist send a message of doubt to Jesus from prison if he really entertained the conviction that he would go on to die as the Lamb of God? At least two things can be said that go far to relieve the difficulty. The pronouncement about Jesus as the Lamb of God was a prophetic utterance, and prophets did not always understand their own predictions. Especially was this true in relation to the sufferings of the Christ (I Pet. 1:10-11). Until the actual event, almost no one understood the death of the Lord even when its necessity was clearly stated to those closest to him. It was a subject dark with mystery, to be avoided if at all possible. Secondly, John's self-identification as the voice of one crying in the wilderness suggests that he leaned heavily upon the prophecy of Isaiah for the understanding of his mission. One would not have to read far beyond chapter forty in order to find the portrayal of the Suffering Servant, who is likened to a lamb in his death, a death that avails for the sheep who have gone astray (Isa. 53:6-7).

If John had certain things to say about Jesus, it is true also that Jesus had a testimony to bear concerning John as a courageous soul, thoroughly self-disciplined, a fearless prophet and more than a prophet in view of his office as forerunner. In summary, of those born of women, none is greater than John (Lk. 7:24-28). Yet this generous acclaim is followed at once by the observation that the one who is least in the kingdom of God is greater than he (Lk. 7:28). This saying is probably to be understood as pointing to the fact that John the Baptist marked the conclusion of an era, since the prophets and the law prophesied until John (Mt. 11:13). Jesus could not absorb this great man into the fellowship of the Twelve, even though he was glad to take those who had been his followers.

Some modern writers have concluded that Jesus did not want John, that although these two started out with similar ideas and purposes, a rift grew up between them. Goguel[7] posited a period of collaboration when John and Jesus saw eye to eye, when both proclaimed judgment and doom which could be avoided only by repentance. But a change in their relations came when Jesus began to preach the gospel, the good news. This change is connected with a supposed shift in Jesus' conception of the nature of God. When he came to understand God as completely transcendent, absolutely righteous, he sensed the futility of all human attempts to become acceptable to God by repentance and baptism. So Jesus gave up the effort to bring about a national repentance on the part of the old Israel. Goguel found evidence of dispute between Jesus and John in John 3:25–4:3.

However one is to explain the fact of a continuing movement centering around the Baptist (evidence of it is found in Acts 19 in a community as far away from Palestine as Ephesus), it does not appear that Goguel's thesis can be sustained. When John was buried, his disciples came and reported his death to Jesus (Mt. 14:12). They would hardly have done this in person if they had become embittered toward him by their leader. If it be argued that this is deliberate invention in order to fit into the pattern the Evangelists have created of John's subordination to Jesus, then it is hard to account for such a passage as Luke 11:1, where the disciples of our Lord ask him to instruct them in the art of prayer as John had done for his disciples. John's priority is admitted here, and the disciples appeal to his example without any evidence of restraint or lack of appreciation. If it be insisted

[7] Maurice Goguel, *Jean-Baptiste* (1928), pp. 235-274; *The Life of Jesus* (1949), pp. 264-279.

that the action of John's disciples in reporting the death of their leader to Jesus is found only in Matthew, and that Mark knows nothing of it, this omission is counterbalanced by the circumstance that Mark contains a notice to the effect that even after John's death Jesus sent his own disciples out to preach a message of *repentance* (Mk. 6:12-14). Carl Kraeling has pointed out how damaging Mark 11:30 is to Goguel's hypothesis. "To adopt Goguel's interpretation of the break between the two men would be to imply that Jesus must have regretted ever having been baptized by John. This would reduce to a mere farce Jesus' action in posing the question, 'John's baptism, was it from heaven or from men?' "[8] Here Jesus speaks approvingly of John's baptism at a late period in his ministry, long after the supposed rift with John. One may say also that the very readiness of the disciples at Ephesus who had been adherents of John's message and baptism to accept Christian baptism is not congenial to the idea of enmity between John's disciples and the followers of Jesus. Goguel's thesis fares no better when the testimony of Josephus is consulted. Nothing stated there supports the notion of rivalry,[9] and Josephus' account is clearly independent of the Gospels.[10]

Jesus' baptism at the hands of John needs no defense as to its historicity, for his followers would not have invented something that seemed not only to make him in a sense inferior to John but also to raise serious question as to his sinlessness. The event is related in all the Synoptics, and in all three accounts it is stated that following the baptism three phenomena occurred: the opening of the heavens, the descent of the Spirit upon Jesus, and his approval by the divine voice.

Luke has two distinctives, declaring that Jesus was baptized after all the people had been baptized and that our Lord was engaged in prayer immediately after the rite was administered to him (Lk. 3:21). Both notices may suggest that Jesus' baptism took place when few were present, perhaps at the close of the day. More important is the hint provided here that Jesus' baptism was climactic, for it was that which alone could give meaning to the baptism that the people had received.

It is in Matthew's account, however, that we have the only semblance of an attempt to set forth the meaning of the event.

8 *John the Baptist* (1951), pp. 149-150.
9 H. St. J. Thackeray, *Josephus: the Man and the Historian* (1929), p. 131.
10 I. Abrahams, *op. cit.*, pp. 31-33.

Matthew introduces a conversation in which John evidences his reluctance to baptize Jesus, feeling that their positions should be reversed (which raises the interesting question as to whether John himself was ever baptized). But when Jesus insists that the baptism be carried through "to fulfil all righteousness," John's reluctance is overcome. Matthew's account differs from the others also in his report of the divine commendation of the Son, which is put in the third person rather than the second—"this is my beloved Son." The change may have been dictated by Matthew's concern to make it clear that the baptism of Jesus was appropriately witnessed, which was a requirement of Jewish proselyte baptism. This accords with the implication of Jesus' words in Matthew 3:15 that his baptism had more than a personal significance. It had a bearing on his relation to the nation.

Various attempts have been made to state the significance of this event in Jesus' life. David Strauss felt that it pointed to his consciousness of sin, and he has been followed in this by some more recent writers. But against it is the total impact of the Christian tradition, which affirms his sinlessness unequivocally, whereas it just as unequivocally affirms the sinfulness of all others. Against it also is the shrinking of the Baptist from the performance of the rite upon our Lord. The same prophetic penetration that enabled John to discern the hypocrisy of the Pharisees who came to his baptism enabled him to see in Jesus one who did not need his baptism.

It is scarcely more satisfactory to affirm that Jesus sought baptism because of a consciousness on his part of a possibility that he might sin. Bowman's comment on this position is just: "One thing is certain about that [John's] baptism, namely, that it was a baptism of repentance from *sin*, and not from any hypothetical 'liability to sin.' "[11] Perhaps this thought about Jesus fearing a liability to sin is derived from the passage in the Gospel according to the Hebrews, a lost work known today only through allusions in several of the Church Fathers. The text runs: "Behold, the mother of the Lord and His brethren said to Him: 'John the Baptist baptizeth for remission of sins; let us go and be baptized by him.' But He said to them: 'Wherein have I sinned that I should go and be baptized by him? Except perchance this very thing that I have said is ignorance.' " Dunkerley is disposed to credit the tradition as genuine and as possibly recalled by Jesus'

---

[11] John W. Bowman, *The Intention of Jesus* (1943), p. 21.

brethren during the days of waiting before Pentecost.[12] But there are evidences of idealization here. Jesus is called the Lord prior to his ministry. His awareness of a qualitative difference from others seems to be something read back into this early period, whereas our canonical records lead us to think that Jesus gave no particular evidence of being distinctive, as attested by the offense created in Nazareth at the fame that came to him after he left their midst.

The surest approach to the problem is made by appealing to the explanation attributed to our Lord himself in Matthew's account: "Let it be so now; for thus it is fitting for us to fulfil all righteousness." Josephus also associates John's baptism with righteousness. "For John was a pious man, and he was bidding the Jews who practiced virtue and exercised righteousness toward each other and piety toward God, to come together for baptism. For thus, it seemed to him, would baptismal ablution be acceptable, if it were used not to beg off from sins committed, but for the purification of the body, when the soul had previously been cleansed by righteous conduct" (*Antiquities* 18, 5, 2, Thackeray's translation) . In other words, John's baptism was not a convenient means of getting rid of sins previously committed but a symbolic act attesting the attainment of righteousness by one's good deeds. This conception may be explained by Josephus' Pharisaic connections. But the view of righteousness entertained by the Pharisees was quite different from that of John and Jesus. Josephus' account does not contain the word "repentance," which is so prominent in the Synoptists' report of John's activity. So we get little help from this quarter.

What did Jesus mean by his words to the Baptist? His first concern was to deal with John's unwillingness to baptize him. The words "Let it be so now" recognize the essential soundness in John's reticence. Baptism is not needed by Jesus for his own sake, but for *now* (the present occasion) it has a relevance that cannot be denied. John must cooperate with him (it is fitting for *us*) in seeing to it that all righteousness is fulfilled. The exact expression *all righteousness* is not found again in the Gospels. In fact, outside of Matthew, the Gospels contain only three occurrences of the word, and in Matthew the only other occurrence outside the Sermon on the Mount is Jesus' statement about John, that he came "in the way of righteousness" (Mt. 21:32) .

12 Roderic Dunkerley, *The Unwritten Gospel* (1925) , pp. 39-40.

The Sermon on the Mount contains five references. Schrenk maintains that Matthew always uses the word in the sense of doing right in the sight of God, and he concludes therefore that the baptism of Jesus was to fulfill all duty to God, not every ordinance, which would have been expressed by *dikaiōma* instead of *dikaiosunē*.[13] This corrects the interpretation of Montefiore, who makes the fulfilling of all righteousness to consist in satisfying all divine ordinances.[14] It might indeed be replied that the point of the *all* is to include externals along with moral obligation of the law. But as the theme of righteousness is developed in the Sermon on the Mount, the emphasis is intensive rather than extensive. One must have a righteousness that exceeds that of the scribes and Pharisees, and this is immediately explained as going far deeper than formal obedience to the letter of the law (Mt. 5:20-24).

√ By his statement to John about fulfilling all righteousness, Jesus seems to mean that for the purpose of accomplishing his mediatorial work it is necessary for him to be baptized. This must be understood as a deliberate identification of himself with the nation, and so is in line with his birth, circumcision, presentation, and assumption of the yoke of the law. Since John's baptism was bound up with the forgiveness of sins (Mk. 1:4), and no personal sin is involved in Jesus' case, the conclusion is fairly obvious that the baptism was the first public step taken in the direction of bearing the sins of the people. It may be significant for the understanding of Matthew 3:15 to recall that the servant who was destined to bear the iniquities of the people is called righteous (Isa. 53:11). That Jesus' statement stops short of a forthright declaration of purpose and is rather couched in general, almost enigmatical terms is a token of historical accuracy. Invention would hardly be careful to observe such restraint.

Later developments in the gospel story reveal that our Lord's conception of the baptism moved along this vicarious line. His experience at the Jordan meant more to him than a consecration to his ministry. "I have a baptism to be baptized with; and how I am constrained (or hemmed in) until it is accomplished!" (Lk. 12:50). He was anticipating the baptism of blood that came to him at the cross. Again, in dealing with the sons of Zebedee, he linked his baptism of the future with the cup he must drink, and then applied both of them to these two disciples (Mk.

[13] TDNT, II, 198.
[14] C. G. Montefiore, *The Synoptic Gospels*, 2nd edition (1927), II, 16.

10:38-39). They would share his suffering. Clearly baptism is associated with death. Jesus seems to have been the first one to state a connection between these two items, and in stating it he revealed his understanding of his own experience of baptism. The teaching of the early church followed this same pattern, depicting Jesus as coming both by water (baptism by John) and blood (the death of the cross) (I Jn. 5:6), and also coupling baptism and death in the case of the believer as the ground of his sanctification (Rom. 6:3). If John had perceived the depth of meaning in Jesus' submission to baptism he would not have faltered in his faith later on. But in the nature of the case Jesus could not unfold to the forerunner all that was in his own heart with reference to what this experience meant to him. Once again the restraint of the narrative is noteworthy. For Jesus the baptism was not so much the event that launched him upon his ministry, although it was that; even more it was a consecration to the death that awaited him.

No treatment of the baptism can ignore the accompanying phenomena. These are named in the same order in all the accounts. First is the opening of the heavens. Mark uses a term meaning "to rend," and the only other time he uses it is in connection with the rending of the veil of the temple at the death of Christ (Mk. 15:38). The two may be easily related, for the Son not only has access to God but also makes it possible for others to have it by his saving work. Pious souls in Israel no doubt often took up the plaintive cry, "Oh that thou wouldest rend the heavens, that thou wouldest come down" (Isa. 64:1). This was the moment of providential intervention, but not to vindicate Israel by apocalyptic judgments. A closer parallel in the Old Testament is Ezekiel 1:1-3. The heavens become opened to the prophet so that he has visions of God; the word of the Lord comes to him and the hand of the Lord is laid upon him. Heaven is concerned and heaven is acting.

Revelation is usually by act before it is by word. This is the order here. Jesus sees the Spirit in the likeness of a dove descending upon him out of the opened heavens. In rabbinic teaching the dove is often an emblem for Israel, but also occasionally for the Spirit.[15] Abrahams feels certain that Genesis 1:2 has influenced the account of the Synoptists.[16] The new creation is breaking, a new order is dawning. He who will baptize with the Spirit

15 SBK, I, 123-125.
16 Op. cit., p. 50.

first receives the Spirit. The man Jesus as he steps across the threshold of his ministry is more mature than the lad of twelve whom we glimpse momentarily in Luke's Gospel, but the records do not place the explanation for the achievements of his mission in his greater maturity or ripened wisdom. More is needed anyway than wisdom. His ministry is one of power, and this is associated with the enduement he receives at the baptism. Incidentally, as the book of Acts opens we find the same factors: prayer, the coming down of the Spirit, and the resultant power for the opening of the ministry of the church.[17]

Most important of all the manifestations which marked the baptismal experience was the heavenly voice. As God speaks at the initial creation expressing his satisfaction, so he now speaks his good pleasure in the Son. But Son in what sense? Vos thinks the sonship in question goes beyond messianic position. "Jesus is in a peculiar sense, and antecedently to his calling, the Son of God; secondly, the divine good pleasure has come to rest upon Him for the Messianic appointment."[18] The statement attributed to the heavenly voice is a quotation derived from two Old Testament passages (Ps. 2:7; Isa. 42:1).[19] The setting for both statements strongly emphasizes office, that of kingly (messianic) office in Psalm 2 and that of the servant in Isaiah 42. Ontological sonship, while not clearly present, is suggested in the epithet "Beloved," which, as Plooij points out, is found in the Targum of Psalm 2:7 and also in Matthew 12:18, where a free rendering of Isaiah 42:1 is given. Vincent Taylor states of Mark's account: "The Evangelist's idea is . . . that Jesus is by nature the Son of God, and that the Voice at the Baptism declares Him to be such."[20] The same writer remarks on the New Testament usage of the title in question as follows: "Sometimes the meaning is Messianic, but for the most part, and even in the words of the Divine Voice at the Baptism, it is Messianic with a plus."[21]

The Western text of Luke 3:22 reads somewhat differently, having nothing from Isaiah 42:1, simply giving the full text of Psalm 2:7 as it appears in the Septuagint: "Thou art my Son,

---

[17] G. W. H. Lampe, *The Seal of the Spirit* (1951), p. 44.

[18] G. Vos, *The Self-Disclosure of Jesus* (1926), p. 187.

[19] Zimmerli and Jeremias, *The Servant of God* (1957), p. 81, favor the notion that Isaiah 42:1 is the sole quotation involved, but this is far from certain.

[20] *The Gospel According to St. Mark* (1952), p. 121.

[21] *The Names of Jesus* (1953), p. 70.

this day have I begotten thee." But it is quite clear that this variant is due to "testimony" influence. This verse was often cited in the early church as a christological proof-text, and so appears in Hebrews 1:5 and 5:5, and also in Acts 13:33. The Western text of Luke 3:22 simply accommodates its reading to the commonly used wording of the passage from Psalm 2.[22]

So we should try to explain the heavenly message from its two-fold background in the Old Testament. Judging from the Second Psalm, the sonship is closely connected with heirship, for the very next verse mentions the nations as the divinely appointed inheritance of the Son. This becomes the issue in the third phase of Jesus' temptation. In the parable of the wicked husbandmen sonship and heirship are closely conjoined. The son and heir will die, not because the divine appointment has been withdrawn, but because of the wickedness of those to whom he is sent (Mt. 21:38).

The second portion of the message at the baptism is drawn, as we have seen, from the servant section of Isaiah. From the context in Isaiah 42, it appears that the prophetic office of the Servant is immediately in view here. One notices the reference to the placing of the Spirit upon the servant—"I have put my Spirit upon him"—in the next line of Isaiah 42:1 (cf. Isa. 61:1), which makes the use of this Scripture exceedingly appropriate for an occasion in which the Spirit comes upon our Lord. The heavens had opened when the birth at Bethlehem was announced, and a word had been spoken about men of (God's) good pleasure. Now a similar word comes to point out the Man of God's good pleasure *par excellence*. It is possible, as Campbell Morgan holds, that the commendation is intended to cover the thirty years in which the Son has lived a life of quiet obedience hidden away in the obscurity of Nazareth.[23] The aorist tense here, however, does not necessitate a backward look, for it can readily express a momentary action or decision, and is best rendered as having the force of a present tense, not only here but also in Luke 12:32.[24]

When the two statements attributed to the divine voice are considered in the light of their Old Testament contexts, they are seen to combine with an affirmation of messianic dignity (Ps. 2:7) not only an indication of a prophetic ministry but also a hint of that suffering as the Servant that looms large in Isaiah 53,

22 See D. Plooij in *Amicitiae Corolla* (1933), ed. H. G. Wood, pp. 245-246.
23 *The Crises of the Christ* (1936), pp. 120-122.
24 Cf. C. F. D. Moule, *An Idiom-Book of New Testament Greek* (1953), p. 11.

where the servant motif reaches a climax. Certainly this accords with Jesus' own consciousness of his unique sonship, and with his awareness that death as the Servant lay at the very heart of his mission (Mk. 10:45). Strikingly enough, the one who participated with him at the baptism in the Jordan, speaking with that event in view, not only calls him the Son of God (Jn. 1:34) but also the Lamb who takes away the sin of the world (Jn. 1:29).

That this is a correct reading of the baptism event is confirmed by Jesus' transfiguration, where once again the heavenly voice is heard declaring with evident approval the standing of Jesus as the Son, and doing so in a setting where his death at Jerusalem is involved (Lk. 9:31, 35).

The complex of ideas clustering around the words from heaven is not foreign to other parts of the New Testament. A close parallel is found in Philippians 2:5-11, where "the form of God" connotes sonship in the highest sense, to be followed in turn by "the form of a servant" obedient unto death, and concluding with attained heirship.

What this divine commendation meant to the Son on the occasion of the baptism we can only dimly surmise. At the very least it must have been a word of comfort to which he reverted many times in later days, when men denied to him any special relationship to God and took deep offense at his claim of possessing a kingdom as God's chosen heir. By putting him to death in disbelief of his sonship they unwittingly provided the ground on which he was exalted to his heirship.

The early church came to appreciate the baptism as the occasion when God anointed Jesus of Nazareth with the Holy Spirit and with power (Acts 10:38). By speaking of Jesus as God's Servant, Peter in his preaching reflected an understanding of the event that may well have been communicated to the disciples by our Lord himself (Acts 3:13, 26). This understanding passed into the possession of the Christian community and became a part of its christological vocabulary (Acts 4:27, 30).

BIBLIOGRAPHY

William Barclay. *The Mind of Jesus.* New York: Harper, 1960. Pp. 16-30.
C. K. Barrett. *The Holy Spirit and the Gospel Tradition.* New York: Macmillan, 1947. Pp. 25-45.

John W. Bowman. *The Intention of Jesus*. Philadelphia: Westminster, 1943. Pp. 11-40.

W. H. Brownlee, "John the Baptist in the New Light of Ancient Scrolls," *The Scrolls and the New Testament*, ed. K. Stendahl. New York: Harper, 1957. Pp. 33-53.

O. Cullmann. *Baptism in the New Testament*. London: SCM, 1950. Pp. 9-22.

—————. *The Christology of the New Testament*. Philadelphia: Westminster, 1959. Pp. 23-50, 66-69.

A. Feuillet, "Le baptême de Jésus," RB, 71 (July 1964) , 321-352.

W. F. Flemington. *The New Testament Doctrine of Baptism*. London: S.P.C.K., 1953. Pp. 13-33.

A. E. Garvie. *Studies in the Inner Life of Jesus*. New York: Armstrong, n.d. Pp. 116-127.

Maurice Goguel. *Jean-Baptiste*. Paris: Payot, 1928.

—————. *The Life of Jesus*. New York: Macmillan, 1949. Pp. 264-279.

J. K. Howard, "The Baptism of Jesus and Its Present Significance," EQ, 39 (July-Sept. 1967) , 131-138.

Carl H. Kraeling. *John the Baptist*. New York: Scribners, 1951.

T. W. Manson. *The Servant-Messiah*. Cambridge, Eng.: Cambridge University Press, 1953. Pp. 36-49.

G. Campbell Morgan. *The Crises of the Christ*. New York: Revell, 1936. Pp. 107-148.

D. Plooij, "The Baptism of Jesus," *Amicitiae Corolla*, ed. H. G. Wood. London: University of London Press, 1933. Pp. 239-252.

J. A. T. Robinson, "The Baptism of John and the Qumran Community," *Twelve New Testament Studies*. Naperville, Ill.: Allenson, 1962. Pp. 11-27.

CHAPTER V

THE TEMPTATION

". . . made like his brethren in every respect . . ."

". . . because he himself has suffered and been tempted, he is able to help those who are tempted."

—Hebrews 2:17-18

AT THE BAPTISM JESUS EMERGED FROM OBSCURITY INTO PUBLIC LIFE, and there received an induction into his task and the equipment for its fulfilling. The next step, however, was not into the arena of national affairs, but rather a sudden return to privacy and solitude more complete than that of Nazareth, yet far more disturbed. His home became the wilderness, his companions the wild beasts.

There is no lack of integration, however, with the preceding stages. Echoes of the baptism are discernible in the prominence given to the title Son of God and in the leadership assigned to the Holy Spirit. It is because the baptism and the temptation are so intimately related that they are placed next to each other in the narrative.

The inspiration of the divine approval given through the heavenly voice must surely have remained with the Son, stimulating to such fidelity that the good pleasure of God would continue, and with even deeper satisfaction. By implication the narrative carries us back also to the days of Nazareth, where the foundations of Scripture knowledge were laid in reading, meditation, and prayer. It was out of these treasures stored up in the soul that Jesus was able to draw the truths that by their pertinency and authority repulsed the suggestions of the evil one.

Modern thought has difficulty with the realism of the biblical portrayal of a malevolent spirit world. The tendency is to rule it out as antiquated by increased knowledge of nature and of human psychology, coupled with the observation that such a dualism is unworthy of a faith that posits the sovereignty of God. Then it is fashionable to account for this element in Scripture by assigning it to Persian influence. But the attempt to make Persian dualism the scapegoat has run far ahead of the evidence and must be viewed with suspicion. Both Jesus and the early Christians in general take this aspect of evil seriously. It is woven into the very texture of the biblical revelation. If the devil be reduced to a symbol of the evil tendencies lurking in human nature, then the inclusion of the temptation narrative in the Gospels becomes far more inexplicable than the presence of the baptism account. Jesus' sinlessness is even more drastically imperiled.

No explanation is forthcoming from the Gospel accounts of the temptation as to the necessity for this encounter. But the Gospel history unfolds it with sufficient clarity. Satan's kingdom is not confined to evil spirits and to the upper reaches of the atmosphere. It has invaded the souls and bodies of men. This same sphere of human life is the territory where the kingdom of God should operate. Hence the collision is inevitable. If Jesus would spoil the house (by delivering from demonic power), he must first bind the strong man (Satan) who stands in control (Mk. 3:26-27). The temptation, then, has immediate relevancy to the ministry of healing which was to occupy our Lord so largely in days to come.

That it has wider implications cannot be doubted. A glance at Luke 3:38 in conjunction with 4:3 suggests a far-reaching connection. Adam is God's son. So is Jesus of Nazareth. The story of the failure of Adam under Satanic pressure stands in the background. Now the Second Man comes on the scene. Redemption history revolves around him. If he fails as the first man failed, all hope for the race is gone.[1]

We turn to the vexed problem of the proper relation of the temptation to the sinlessness of Jesus. To insist that he could not have sinned takes the incident out of line with the primeval probation. By reducing the temptation to a demonstration of sinlessness the nerve of connection is cut with believers also,

---

[1] The issue is obedience to God (Rom. 5:19; Phil. 2:8; Heb. 5:8).

for then it would be logically impossible for New Testament writers to appeal to Jesus' temptation as a ground of confidence for the believer's overcoming of temptation by his sympathetic help (Heb. 2:18; 4:14-16). The inclusion of the words "Lead us not into temptation" in the Lord's Prayer eloquently testifies to the rigor of this experience for Jesus himself. This is not to deny at all the difference between temptation and testing. What was from Satan's standpoint a diabolical attempt to ensnare and ruin was from God's standpoint a probation similar to that which he appointed for the first man. But if we affirm the inability of the man Jesus to sin, we are affirming a qualitative difference between the humanity of the first Adam and that of the Last Adam.

No satisfactory explanation has been given for the extreme brevity of Mark's account.[2] In it we have the bare essentials: that the temptation immediately followed the baptism, that the Spirit took the initiative in leading the Son, that the scene was the desert, and that the temptation at the hands of the devil continued over a period of forty days. His mention of the fact that Jesus was with the wild beasts is peculiar to his narrative. Since this feature stands in combination with the locale of the wilderness, it may be intended to convey a judgmental emphasis—man's failure due to sin and disobedience, as in certain Old Testament passages where the divine judgment turns an area into a place devoid of habitation except for wild animals (e.g., Isa. 13:19-22).[3]

Since Jesus is alone in this experience, he is the natural source of information concerning what happened. The alternative is to suppose, as Birger Gerhardsson does, that "the Temptation narrative is an early Christian midrash, based on a text from the Old Testament, as this was interpreted in the late Jewish period."[4] William Manson is prepared to grant that the tradition

[2] Roman Catholic scholars, in line with their theory of the priority of Matthew's Gospel, tend to make Mark's account a summary of Matthew. If this were the true state of affairs, it would represent a situation quite in contrast with what we usually find, namely, that Mark's narratives are longer than Matthew's and therefore not a digest of them. One Catholic scholar, however, has suggested that Matthew and Luke drew on a source that had filled out Mark's brief statement "with a dramatic synopsis of the type of temptations Jesus actually faced during his life" (R. E. Brown in CBQ, 23 [1961], 155).

[3] The word "desert" or "wilderness" as used in the New Testament does not require us to think of a sandy waste but of a spot somewhat removed from ordinary habitation (Mk. 1:35).

[4] "The Testing of God's Son," *Coniectanea Biblica*, NT Series 2:1 (1966), p. 17.

incorporates symbolical features, but contends that "there is no reason why it should not go back to an actual conflict in the life of Jesus."[5]

In passing it is well to observe what all three accounts emphasize, that instead of being cornered by the evil one, Jesus was led out to meet him. The initiative was on the side of the divine and not of the diabolical. It was in the divine purpose that Jesus was thus tempted. From this may be gathered the imperative necessity of the encounter from God's standpoint, and the equally important fact that the genius of the Christian movement, which it received as a legacy from its victorious Master, is to press the fight against its spiritual foe rather than be put on the defensive. Here the close connection with the baptism needs again to be borne in mind. As A. E. J. Rawlinson remarks, "The newly baptized Christian must be ready, like his Lord, to face immediately the onset of the Tempter."[6] The sequence of baptism-temptation in the life of Jesus must have proved highly suggestive in terms of catechetical instruction.

The representative character of Christ's participation in the temptation links it, as we have seen, with all humanity. But there are features that link it representatively with the covenant nation Israel in a special way. First of all, one cannot fail to be impressed with the fact that the title "Son of God," which is so prominent here, as well as in the baptism, is used in the Old Testament of Israel in the form "my son" (Ex. 4:22-23). The importance of this is greatly increased in the light of Matthew's application of Hosea 11:1 to the child Jesus (Mt. 2:15). Added to everything else is the fact that Deuteronomy 8:5, which belongs to the context of the passages attributed to Jesus as quotations in the temptation, includes the word "son"—"Know then in your heart that, as a man disciplines his son, the Lord your God disciplines you" (Deut. 8:5). We get help from Paul also, who pictures Israel as "baptized" in the Red Sea experience and then tested in the wilderness (I Cor. 10:1-13). So we are invited to see that Jesus, now baptized, must also go on to submit to severe testing as the true Israelite. Where the nation failed, he stood fast in quiet dependence upon God.

Less important, but nevertheless serving as pointers in the same direction, are the elements of locale (the desert setting

[5] *The Gospel of Luke* (Moffatt Com., n.d.), p. 36.
[6] *The Gospel According to St. Mark* (Westminster Com., 7th edition, 1949), p. 12.

serving to recall the wilderness wanderings of Israel), the hunger, and the duration of the testing (the forty days recalling the forty years). Gerhardsson notes also that "The presence of the Spirit at the time of the desert wandering is a popular motif in the targums and midrashes"[7] (as well as being in the Old Testament text).

That our Lord was conscious of this intimate connection between his situation and that of Israel appears to be sealed by the fact that all three of the citations he used in the temptation are from Deuteronomy. One of the distinctive features of this book is the way in which the combination of human failure and divine faithfulness over the period of the wilderness wanderings becomes the leverage for injunctions to future obedience. Deuteronomy is drawn upon as the Psalms and the prophecy of Isaiah figured in the baptism narrative. It so happens that these three books are the very ones that were most popular with the Qumran sect, judging from the Dead Sea Scrolls. Dwelling in the wilderness, they sought to be a purified remnant of the nation that would be at once a rebuke to the rest of Israel and a suitable preparation for the nation's glorious future. "The Essenes were called basically to repeat the experience of their forefathers who had lived forty years in the desert, while overcoming the trials through which that generation had failed to come successfully."[8]

If there is a close bond between the testing of Israel in the wilderness and the testing to which the Son was subjected, then if the purpose of the former testing can be ascertained, it will likely throw light on the objective of the latter testing. G. H. P. Thompson writes, "Deuteronomy 8:2 gives a theological interpretation of the wilderness wanderings: they had the purpose of testing and proving Israel to see whether the people of God would be loyal to their Redeemer."[9] He goes on to observe that whereas Israel's testing was done by God himself, the probing and proving of Jesus is done through the instrumentality of Satan, as was the case with Job.

Inasmuch as two of the three approaches of the tempter to Jesus are prefaced by the remark, "If you are the Son of God . . . ," the understanding of this title should be of distinct help toward

[7] Op. cit., p. 38.

[8] J. T. Milik, Ten Years of Discovery in the Wilderness of Judaea (1959), p. 115.

[9] "Called—Proved—Obedient: A Study in the Baptism and Temptation Narratives of Matthew and Luke," JTS, n.s., 11:1 (April 1960), 2.

a correct interpretation of the whole situation. Does the use of the title mean that the temptation impinges on the deity of the Son? Hardly, in view of the nontemptability of God (Jas. 1:13). But the use of the title at the baptism indicates a certain uniqueness of relationship to God as well as approval by God and endowment with the Holy Spirit. It will be Satan's effort to persuade to such action as will be contrary to complete dependence on him, by asserting a measure of independence based on self-interest. It must be remembered that Jesus was committed to living man's life and sharing his lot, despite his supernatural origin. If he fails in principle now, he cannot succeed in practice later. Submission to the sovereign will of God, no matter how difficult it may prove, is the only right course for him as well as for any man.

It is probably necessary to hold that in the third phase of the temptation the messianic status of the Son becomes involved, but this is not obvious in the first two. This double reference in the word Son is not arbitrary, for "in late Jewish times both the idea of Israel as God's son and that of the Anointed One as God's son existed side by side in the sacred texts."[10] Two ideas of Messiahship were prominent in the Judaism of Jesus' time. One view proclaimed a detached, transcendent figure who would answer to apocalyptic expectations, whereas the other had in mind an earthly figure of Davidic descent whose reign would fulfill the political aspirations of an oppressed and restless nation. Neither view paid any special attention to moral and spiritual qualifications keyed to a divine standard. The idea of a Messiah whose kingly office would rest upon a perfect manhood, which could vindicate itself in a probation such as Jesus endured, seems to have been foreign to the Judaism of the period.

THE FIRST PHASE

In his initial approach the evil one bade Jesus turn stones into bread. A wilderness landscape in Palestine is filled with them, and the use of the plural not only accords with this fact but suggests a gratifying sight to a hungry man. The famine would be replaced by great abundance. A state of hunger is presupposed by this solicitation, and this condition is confirmed by the statements of Matthew and Luke. Now it should be evident that the satisfaction of hunger is not sinful, for eating was a part of man's

10 Gerhardsson, *op. cit.*, pp. 22-23.

life before the fall. Incidentally, it does not seem to be accidental that the opening phase of the temptation should come in the same realm as the first man's probation (Gen. 3:3).

Insight into the true nature of this suggestion on the part of Satan is best gleaned from a consideration of Jesus' reply, "Man shall not live by bread alone, but by every word that proceeds from the mouth of God." The Lord does not minimize the importance of bread ("man shall not live by bread alone") in the interest of magnifying the sustenance of the inner man by feeding upon the word of God (Scripture), as though to affirm that he had been feeding upon the word and had found it so satisfying that he did not need ordinary bread. Nor does this reply mean that just as man needs bread for the body, so he needs the word of God for his soul. To be sure, this is often assumed to be the meaning; but if that were the sense we would expect an *also* following *but*.

It is more profitable to note with Vos that the statement about the word of God is somewhat peculiar, in that what is stressed is not the word as bestowed by God and possessed by man, but on the word as spoken, and spoken in solemn, oracular fashion.[11] It denotes a sovereign purpose in relation to a specific objective. A rough parallel is found in Isaiah 55:11, "so shall my word be that goes forth from my mouth; it shall not return to me empty, but it shall accomplish that which I purpose, and prosper in the thing for which I sent it." The thought moves in the realm of supernatural interposition. So we understand Jesus to mean that although he has a bodily need which bread would supply, yet, since no bread was given to him when he went aside into the wilderness and no direction was given to him about meeting his need, it would be wrong for him to use any special power such as his status as Son, together with the Holy Spirit, might provide in order to produce bread apart from divine direction. Rather, he must wait upon divine provision. In Deuteronomy 8:3 it is stated that God humbled Israel and allowed the people to hunger before feeding them with the manna from heaven. This seems to warrant the thought that "every word that proceeds from the mouth of God" refers primarily to the divine response to the need that arose because of the hunger. Can the Son refuse to be afflicted by God in like manner as the nation Israel in the days of its youth? God gave bread then and he will not fail to meet

11 G. Vos, *Biblical Theology* (1948), p. 360.

the need now. If an earthly father will not give a stone to a son who asks bread (Mt. 7:9), surely the heavenly Father will provide for his sons, *this one* no less than others. Jesus refuses to imitate Israel in its murmuring; he is content to look to the Father in the full assurance of faith.

The importance of Jesus' stand appears in the Johannine account of the feeding of the five thousand. On that occasion the people interpreted the miracle as a token that the expected bread of the messianic age might now be provided for them, and so they were ready to acclaim Jesus as king. Their materialistic view of the kingdom carried over to their understanding of the bread. Jesus, on the other hand, having resisted the Satanic suggestion regarding the turning of stones into bread, rejected also the materialistic notions of the Jews.[12]

In coming days Jesus was to make stringent demands upon his followers in terms of discipleship. Fundamental among those demands would be the insistence upon self-denial. The right to make such a requirement and the vigor of its statement come right out of the temptation experience. Jesus established a pattern that must be reproduced in those who seek to come after him. If our Lord had yielded to this temptation by providing himself with bread through means at his command, discipleship would have been out of the question for those who must earn their daily bread by the sweat of their brow. Jesus could not say, "Learn of me," apart from giving a worthy demonstration of selflessness, one that would have meaning to his followers.

THE SECOND PHASE

The setting for the second round of the struggle with Satan is the pinnacle of the temple. Does this necessitate the supposition that Jesus was actually transported to this high point in person? Not necessarily, any more than the mention of a high mountain in the next incident could be expected to give a panorama of all the kingdoms of the world. The sphere of conflict need only be mental. On the other hand, if the crux here is the gaining of a following, physical presence at the temple would be virtually demanded. Since Satan's suggestion that Jesus cast himself down from the temple does not have the same obvious relation to some need as the turning of stones into bread, we are left to our own

12 Bertil Gärtner, *John 6 and the Jewish Passover* (1959), pp. 21-22.

inquiries. Suppose we follow for a moment the line of thought that what is in view is the urge to create a spectacle that will simply overpower the nation and win its allegiance at one stroke. One of the last prophecies of the Old Testament stated that the Lord would come suddenly to his temple (Mal. 3:1). The Jews might readily regard this prediction as fulfilled before their eyes. But of course such an action on Jesus' part would amount to a call to discipleship based on sight rather than on faith, with no personal contact as the basis for adherence and without self-testimony from the Lord himself or any revelation of his mercy and compassion through beneficent works. It could be said that in line with his rejection of this enticement by the evil one was his refusal during the ministry to work a miracle for the sake of creating a spectacle that would dazzle the fancy of men.

However, since nothing whatever is said in the narrative about the presence of men in connection with the temple, and since the quotation from Psalm 91:11-12 properly relates to preservation from danger in the ordinary course of life, it is safer to interpret the situation along different lines. There must be some significance in the fact that this particular temptation had the temple as its locale. Psalm 91 begins thus: "He who dwells in the shelter of the Most High, who abides in the shadow of the Almighty, will say to the Lord, 'My refuge and my fortress; my God, in whom I trust.'" Though God was available anywhere to his people, the sense of his presence was naturally greatest in the spot where he had caused his name to dwell. We are told that this second phase of testing occurred on the pinnacle (lit., "little wing") of the temple. Psalm 91 has a rather evident point of contact. "He will cover you with his pinions, and under his wings you will find refuge" (v. 4). We are informed that the rabbis associated this psalm not only with the temple but with the wilderness wanderings.[13] Satan is seeking to sell Jesus on the idea that here in the temple area the pledge of God to keep his own takes on a heightened challenge. Will the Son dare to step out on faith and claim this protection, or will he show himself a weakling?

Matching the statement from Scripture with one of his own, Jesus declares that to follow the suggestion of Satan would be to tempt God. The quotation is from Deuteronomy 6:16, where it stands as a warning from Moses to Israel not to put God to

13 Gerhardsson, op. cit., p. 58.

the test as the nation had done at Massah. This was the occasion where water was brought from the rock in the wilderness in answer to the murmuring and complaining of Israel (Ex. 17:1-7). The people were putting the Lord to the test by doubting his presence and provision. "Is the Lord among us or not?" Although Israel is said to have tempted God ten times during the forty years of wandering, the one incident that is reported in detail is the one referred to by Moses. Massah is not so much a place as a term given to commemorate an experience. In Deuteronomy 6:16 the Hebrew word carries the definite article, and this is reflected in the Septuagint rendering, which has simply "the testing." Echoes of the same event are found in Psalms 78:18 and 95:8-9. The allusion in Psalm 106:14 is more general, but evidently takes in Massah. It is not impossible that Jesus, with this latter passage also in mind, shrank from having such a barren result as Israel gained, getting their request but along with it experiencing leanness of soul.

To cast himself down from the temple would mean a demand laid upon God to rescue him, a demand no other servant of God could rightfully make, a demand that was not really consonant anyway with the passage quoted by Satan. The psalm breathes the atmosphere of trust, but to put God to the test is proof that one is not really trusting him. God would become in reality a servant, obliged to give aid no matter how foolhardy the venture undertaken by his own. An act that Satan sought to make alluring by picturing it as an exercise of trust in God's power of deliverance was perceived by Jesus to be essentially a new Massah, a demand for dramatic, momentary intervention in place of patient waiting upon God for the revelation of his will. The New Testament stigmatizes such conduct as unbelief (Heb. 3:7-12, 19).

The Third Phase

The scene changes to a high mountain. Matthew and Luke both state that the kingdoms of the world were exhibited before our Lord, Luke adding, "in a moment of time." The emphasis here may well be not on the time naturally required but on the time purposely taken—a rapid, sweeping glance at the magnificence of worldly empire (the glory is emphasized in both accounts). Satan would dazzle Christ by the prospect of beauty, wealth, and power that would be his, then would hope to sweep him off his feet by means of a sudden proposal to transfer them—at a price.

Mention of the glory of the kingdoms of the world shows that an outward kingdom is proposed to Jesus. That is all Satan could offer. He could not offer a kingdom of which the essence was righteousness and joy and peace in the Holy Spirit. He could offer only a kingdom of outward splendor and inward corruption. It was part of the purpose of the incarnation that Jesus would prove his right to the kingdom in the external sense by proving his ability to found a kingdom of God in a spiritual sense, so that when the time came to establish that kingdom in its outward aspect it would be purified of just those base elements which permit Satan to exercise his sway.

Luke's account is notable for the prominence of personal pronouns, as the evil one advances his suggestion that what is his can become our Lord's, all at the cost of bowing the knee in worship. There is no mention of God at all. He is merely hinted at in the acknowledgment that the authority "has been delivered to me." This deliberate exclusion of God makes the reply of Jesus all the more crushing, for his reply gives prominence to the Almighty. "You shall worship the Lord your God, and him only shall you serve."

In this final episode Satan is unmasked. Gone is any suggestion that he is working for the best interests of the Son of God. No citation from Scripture is offered. Satan reveals the inmost secret of his being. Much as he enjoys the distinction of being the prince of this world, a distinction only sin has enabled him to achieve, he covets something else infinitely more. He would be like the Most High. He would receive to himself what is most characteristically and exclusively the prerogative of God, namely, worship. A true angel abhors the very thought of being worshiped (Rev. 22:8-9), but this fallen angel fiercely, cravenly covets it.

That such an offer was extended to Jesus is a testimony to his greatness. The stakes are high. When Satan made Judas his victim, his bait was a mere thirty pieces of silver. Indeed, Satan could not well offer a lesser inducement to our Lord, for the nations were the promised inheritance of the Messiah and the uttermost parts of the earth were his anticipated possession (Ps. 2:8). In Psalm 2 this passage follows immediately the divine recognition of the sonship of the Messiah, the focal point of the temptation. "Ask of me," says God, but Satan brazenly usurps the place of the Almighty.

Jesus' reply, taken from Deuteronomy 6:13, belongs to a chapter that enshrines Israel's great confession of the one God, who calls for love with all the heart and soul and strength. In the same chapter there is a solemn warning against idolatry. As a devout Son of Israel Jesus repudiates with instant indignation a course of action that would strike at the very foundations of the faith of the fathers as well as his own relation to God. The situation called for the repetition of a great pronouncement out of the past, "You shall worship the Lord your God." But there is more to Jesus' quotation. The fact that he includes the words, "and him only shall you serve," shows that he is taking seriously the role of the Servant of Yahweh. As we have seen, this office has prominence at the baptism, and it is not forgotten now in the hour of severe testing. He will be obedient even unto death. Then he will be in position to receive from the hands of God the reward of his faithfulness—the name above every name, the kingdoms of this world, together with power and everlasting glory. And with all this will come worship, as the Lamb is honored equally with the Father in the grateful praise of the myriad host of the redeemed.

By his rejection of Satan's last attempt, Jesus indicated his own understanding of the messianic role into which he had been inducted and his determination to repudiate any counterfeit. "By refusing to do what the Messiah is expected to do, *he rejects in fact the traditional messianism.* He declares that the idea of a Messiah with worldly power and glory is of the evil one, a satanic temptation."[14]

The arsenal from which our Lord has drawn the weapons of his spiritual warfare is Deuteronomy 6–8. At the head of this section stands the central command: "Hear, O Israel: The Lord our God is one Lord; and you shall love the Lord your God with all your heart, and with all your soul, and with all your might" (Deut. 6:4-5). The rabbis interpreted the word *might* in the sense of resources, wealth, or property.[15] So when Jesus talked about the threat of mammon (Mt. 6:24) he was speaking existentially, against the background of his final testing at the hands of the evil one. "The Son of God is here tempted to forget his God for the sake of the riches of this world and to fall into idolatry (worship of Satan)."[16]

14 R. Leivestad, *Christ the Conqueror* (1954), p. 54.
15 Gerhardsson, *op. cit.*, p. 78.
16 *Ibid.*, p. 66.

In leaving Jesus after his third failure, Satan did not abandon his attacks, which now take other forms. Having tested the power of the word of God when turned against him, he bends his efforts toward snatching away the word when it has been sown in human hearts (Mk. 4:15). The early church found that it needed this sword of the Spirit in contending against the devil (Eph. 6:17). What is especially noteworthy in the succeeding days of the ministry is Satan's attempt to embarrass and thwart Jesus by tempting him through other agencies. The people came to him after the feeding of the five thousand, bent on making him their king. How could he resist them, the very people upon whom he had compassion, the multitude to whom he could furnish the right kind of guidance and leadership? But our Lord recognized behind this plea, however innocent it might appear, the sinister portent of Satanic suggestion. From an entirely different motivation, certain people pleaded with him to come down from the cross and thus demonstrate that he was the Son of God—the title that is central in the baptism and the temptation (Mt. 27:40-43).

Satan was successful in penetrating the circle of Jesus' apostles, making their leader his unwitting dupe and instrument. At Peter's suggestion that he should dismiss all thought about the necessity of facing a cross, Jesus brusquely censured him as Satan and turned his back on him (Mt. 16:23). This has special relevance because Peter had just acknowledged Jesus as Son of God, that title which reverberates through the accounts of the baptism and the temptation. The continuing impact of Satan is attested by the word Jesus addressed to his disciples just before the ordeal of Gethsemane, "You are those who have continued with me in my trials" (Lk. 22:28). But the ineffectiveness of the evil one is confirmed in Jesus' remark about Satan falling from heaven like lightning (Lk. 10:18). The disciples were able successfully to invade the kingdom of darkness and bring deliverance to many through the power of God shared with them by the Master. The fruits of the victory in the wilderness were already apparent, though the full harvest awaited the consummation of the age.

BIBLIOGRAPHY

A. M. Fairbairn. *Studies in the Life of Christ.* London: Hodder and Stoughton, 1907. Pp. 80-98.

Austin Farrer. *The Triple Victory*. London: Faith, 1965.

Alfred E. Garvie. *Studies in the Inner Life of Jesus*. New York: Armstrong, n.d. Pp. 128-142.

Birger Gerhardsson, "The Testing of God's Son," *Coniectanea Biblica*, NT Series 2:1. Lund: Gleerup, 1966.

W. H. Hutchings. *The Mystery of the Temptation*. London: Rivingtons, 1875.

Henry A. Kelly, "The Devil in the Desert," CBQ, 26:2 (April 1964), 190-220.

H. J. C. Knight. *The Temptation of Our Lord*. London: Longmans, Green, 1907.

Ragnar Leivestad. *Christ the Conqueror*. London: S.P.C.K., 1954. Pp. 1-80.

G. Campbell Morgan. *The Crises of the Christ*. New York: Revell, 1936. Pp. 149-210.

Maisie Spens. *Concerning Himself*. London: Hodder and Stoughton, 1937. Pp. 14-39.

Helmut Thielicke. *Between God and Satan*. Edinburgh: Oliver and Boyd, 1958.

G. H. P. Thompson, "Called—Proved—Obedient: A Study in the Baptism and Temptation Narratives," JTS, n.s., 11:1 (April 1960), 1-12.

Carl Ullmann. *The Sinlessness of Jesus*. Edinburgh: T. & T. Clark, 1882. Pp. 123-144.

CHAPTER VI

JESUS AS TEACHER

"No man ever spoke like this man!"
—John 7:46

THE SYNOPTISTS MAKE IT CLEAR THAT THE LORD'S PUBLIC MINISTRY began by preaching (Mt. 4:12-17; Mk. 1:14-15; Lk. 4:14-15). Luke uses the word teach instead of preach, which creates a problem to which we will return presently. At any rate, Jesus presented himself to the nation first by proclamation of the spoken word. Burkitt claims that as a result of the temptation Jesus' course of action was no clearer than before, and that the call came from without, from the course of events, specifically John's arrest by Herod.[1] It would be better to say that the temptation gave guidance on the negative side, determining that Jesus would not pursue a type of ministry that would be self-seeking and characterized by independence of action in reference to the Father. The positive guidance belongs more particularly to the baptism. These two events together provided the elements of personal dedication and divine direction. The Spirit, who came upon the Son at the baptism and led him into the desert for the temptation, now rested upon him mightily for the discharging of his commission (Lk. 4:14, 18).

Nothing was more natural than that Jesus should come before the people as a teacher. The office of teacher had a long and honorable history in Israel, especially from the time of the giving of the law. In its wider sense, *Torah* means "instruction."

---

[1] F. C. Burkitt, *Christian Beginnings* (1924), p. 24.

Moses was called to teach the law that he introduced (Deut. 4:14; cf. Ex. 24:12). In this work the sons of Levi were associated (Lev. 10:11; Deut. 33:10), for the people were many and so were the ramifications of the law. This public instruction rested on the foundation of parental tutelage in the home (Deut. 4:10; 6:7). Even a king could teach, judging from Solomon's proficiency in proverbs; but it was a somewhat detached and academic thing with him, and unfortunately lacked the seal of consistent example. King Jehoshaphat commissioned certain princes to teach (II Chron. 17:7). The word "teach" rarely occurs in connection with the ministry of the prophets. This strange omission is probably due to two considerations: the prophet was appealed to more for occasional guidance than for constant instruction, and his work of prophesying, whether related to the present or the future, was more in the nature of preaching than teaching. Finally, the Lord God himself is represented as the supreme Teacher, working through all these constituted channels (Isa. 48:17; Jer. 32:33).

Some difficulty attaches to the attempt to distinguish preaching and teaching in the ministry of Jesus. The terms seem to be intermingled. Unquestionably the training of the Twelve involved instruction, and deserves to be called teaching; but what about the addresses to the multitudes? Perhaps the best we can do is to say that in proclaiming the kingdom of God, with its demand for a decision involving repentance and faith, Jesus was preaching (Mt. 4:17). But insofar as his message to the people was in the nature of instruction based on the Old Testament Scriptures and directed to the covenant nation, it could properly be called teaching. We will make no further attempt to differentiate as we examine the spoken word of Jesus addressed to the people as a whole. The instruction of the Twelve will come before us later.

That Jesus was popularly recognized as a teacher is evident from the titles given to him. Among these is *rabbi*, meaning "my great one," the pronominal suffix originally reflecting individual veneration but in time becoming otiose.[2] It was a natural title for Jesus to have, especially in view of the fact that he gathered disciples around him. For the same reason it was applied to John the Baptist. More frequent is the word *didaskalos*, meaning "teacher," but often translated "Master" in recognition of the

[2] *Jewish Encyclopaedia* (1901), art. "Rabbi."

peculiarly authoritative character of Jesus. Luke alone makes use of a term that strictly means "Master" (*epistatēs*), in addition to his use of the word "teacher" (Lk. 5:5, etc.)

CHARACTERISTICS OF THE TEACHING

What impressed his hearers and astonished them was the *authority* with which Jesus spoke (Mk. 1:22; Mt. 7:29; Lk. 4:32). As Swete has observed, this testimony of his auditors is the more remarkable because of his comparative youth at the time and because it was accorded him at the very outset of his teaching ministry.[3] As to its nature, ". . . The authority which held the audience spellbound was not the magic of a great reputation, but the irresistible force of a Divine message, delivered under the sense of a Divine mission."[4] The contrast the multitude felt between Jesus as a teacher and the scribes was not altogether that he founded his message on the Scriptures and they upon the traditional teaching of the elders. Jesus himself acknowledged that the scribes could be legitimate exponents of the Mosaic law and as such were worthy of being followed (Mt. 23:2-3). Of course, when scribal teaching in effect set aside the word of God, he was ready to object strenuously. This authority which others recognized in our Lord does not seem to have resided primarily in a superior knowledge of the Scriptures or in a dominance of personality. It was rather a God-given quality linked with his messianic office and the fullness of the Spirit resting upon him. It explains the powerful effect of both his words and deeds.

Modern Jewish scholars tend to regard this distinction between Jesus and the scribes as not altogether in his favor. If he expected the nation to rally to him, he should have stood in the tradition of its acknowledged teachers, men who built upon the opinions and deliverances of their predecessors. His very independence was bound to cast suspicion upon him. More than that, in his teaching Jesus disregarded the national and cultural aspects of Judaism, generalizing the law in terms of human life rather than Jewish.[5] The point that is left untouched in this criticism is the vital one. Why should this one rabbi out of the great mass of Israel's teachers take such an independent course? The more

3 H. B. Swete, *Studies in the Teaching of Our Lord* (1903), pp. 17-18.
4 *Ibid.*, pp. 18-19.
5 Cf. J. Klausner, *Jesus of Nazareth* (1925), pp. 369-376.

the difference is emphasized, the more mysterious the figure of Jesus becomes and the more impossible to explain on naturalistic grounds.

If Jesus' authority as a teacher connoted a certain independence of tradition, it did not involve independence of God. "My teaching is not mine, but his who sent me" (Jn. 7:16). "I do nothing on my own authority, but speak thus as the Father taught me" (Jn. 8:28).

That the early church recognized his authority in a unique sense is clear. His own word and that of the Old Testament stand on an equality. After all, it was he who enabled the disciples to understand their Scriptures (Lk. 24:27, 45). Wherever the apostle Paul could do so he appealed to the spoken word of Christ in support of his own teaching (I Thess. 4:15; I Cor. 7:10, 25; Acts 20:35).

Experience leads us to realize that the arrogation of authority to oneself apart from a substantial basis for the claim ends in exposure to ridicule. The higher the claim the greater the risk. Though Jesus' authority was challenged on occasion, it was never unmasked as pretension. To the very end of his course his message had the same confident, positive character, free alike from conjecture and from craven dependence upon human opinion. "Verily, verily, I say unto you . . ." is the familiar formula which reminds us that his utterances are clothed with the mantle of majestic certitude and finality.

The note of authority in Jesus' teaching is confirmed as historically genuine by his disclaimer of knowledge as to the time of his return (Mk. 13:32). If the authoritarian emphasis in his teaching as a whole were a "build-up" by apostolic writers in order to enhance the person of Jesus, this admission of ignorance could not have found a place.

Jesus' teaching was also noted for its *wisdom*. This was the reaction of the people in his own community when they listened to his discourse (Mk. 6:2). During his youth he had not appeared among them in the role of a teacher, but had quietly pursued a life of toil. For this reason the townsfolk felt obliged to conclude that the wisdom had been given to him (from God). The citizens of Jerusalem were impressed with his erudition, particularly in the light of his lack of technical rabbinic schooling (Jn. 7:15). Even the scribes and Pharisees in the capital were willing to address him as teacher (the equivalent of rabbi), and thereby acknowledged that he was no mean opponent in disputa-

tion, even if they were not willing to abide by his conclusions
(Mk. 12:14, 32). Yet it was not knowledge as such that per-
meated his utterances. Wisdom implies a saturation with goodness which knowledge does not necessarily imply. Jesus emphasized the good life and grounded it on the nature and will of
God.

The teaching of our Lord could well be called *radical*.[6] In this
connection two things must be somewhat distinguished. The
extravagant use of language that Jesus permitted himself was
a device to stimulate interest and impress the point being made.
Such, for example, is the comment about the man with a plank
in his eye trying to remove a speck from the eye of another, and
the observation that the Pharisees were prone to strain out a
gnat and swallow a camel (Mt. 7:3; 23:24). This is largely a
formal aspect of his teaching. But the term radical has special
bearing on the content. If one has faith, he can bid a mountain
to be removed and be cast into the sea (Mt. 17:20). Here form
and content are both of an extreme nature; they cannot be successfully dissociated. Then there are sayings in which the radical-
ism is purely one of content, for no figure of speech is present.
One must renounce all that he has to be a disciple (Lk. 14:33).
One must be perfect as the heavenly Father is perfect (Mt. 5:48).

In this respect Jesus stood apart from the trend of contemporary Judaism, which became crystallized in the maxim, "We
should not impose a restriction upon the community unless the
majority of the community will be able to stand it."[7] Jesus made
no attempt to adjust his ethical demands to the limitations of
human nature. The loftiness of the standard was not allowed to
soften the edge of requirement. Certainly the teaching was not
given to create amusement in the frivolous or despair in the
earnest. It was given that one might build his life upon it (Mt.
7:24-27; Lk. 6:46ff.).

This radical element has sometimes been denominated im-
practical, and has been explained and defended on the ground
that the teaching was not intended to be permanent. It was
rather an "interim ethic," according to Albert Schweitzer, until
the kingdom of God should come. Followers of Jesus could be
expected to live abnormally, maintaining an extravagantly
sacrificial type of conduct, for it would not be required very

6 Cf. E. C. Colwell, *An Approach to the Teaching of Jesus* (1947), pp. 11-34.
7 J. Klausner, *From Jesus to Paul* (1944), p. 488.

long. But nothing in the teaching itself calls for this interpretation. As T. W. Manson has written,

> If the object of the teaching is to give direction rather than directions, to point to the goal of all good living rather than to legislate for particular cases, then the important thing is not whether the goal is near or far away, but whether the direction is correct. If the object of Jesus was so to guide His followers that their lives should fit into the great purpose of God, the question whether that purpose would be realized in ten years or ten thousand became a minor consideration. Now we must maintain that this was precisely the object of Jesus.[8]

An outstanding quality of the sayings of Jesus is their *simplicity*. Technical terms such as require a detailed knowledge of Judaistic background are almost nonexistent, and theological expressions are held to a minimum. One suspects that the multitudes flocked to hear him because they could understand him. It would be interesting to know whether the children who were present when the Lord fed the five thousand were there because their parents compelled them to go along or because of their own eagerness to hear the Master. Similarly, one would like to know whether the children who sang hosannas to Jesus as the Son of David in the temple did so in imitation of their elders or out of a passionate persuasion that he was their champion also, one whose speech was intelligible to them.

A certain peril lurks behind this simplicity. It is the danger that the reader of the Gospels may assume, without realizing it, that the truths Jesus enunciated are as easy of comprehension (and execution) as the linguistic medium that conveys them to the ear.[9] His words are simple, yet no words could be more profound. Stripped of all needless accessories, they transmit the truth in all its boldness and severity such as only an unheeding familiarity can obscure.

Closely allied to simplicity in Jesus' teaching is the element of *concreteness*. The speculative and the theoretical have no place. Again and again spiritual truths are brought into touch with human thought and life by the power of illustration. Though Jesus was keenly conscious of the gulf separating the heavenly from the earthly, he also understood the feasibility of unveiling

---

8 Major, Manson, and Wright, *The Mission and Message of Jesus* (1938), p. 329.

9 W. A. Curtis, *Jesus Christ the Teacher* (1943), p. 105.

the heavenly by means of some earthly counterpart. The Father's love is unforgettably etched in the story of the prodigal son, even as the duty of love to neighbor is strikingly memorialized in the story of the good Samaritan. Examples of this concreteness are legion.

The teaching was also *occasional*. Jesus did not come to a situation with a prepared message in the formal sense. He had no use for notes, for the instruction was spontaneous. This makes its cogency and abiding worth all the more amazing. Of course certain great themes, such as the nature and purpose of God, his own mission in the world, and the destiny of men, were so central to his thinking that they came readily to expression; but they took shape in accordance with the immediate need.

To assert that the words of Jesus possess *originality* is to invite contradiction. At least the point has been vigorously debated in recent years and the tendency of modern scholarship is to deny any clear-cut uniqueness. This is based on research into extrabiblical literature of the Jews as well as upon a careful comparison of his utterances with the Old Testament. Many students of Scripture would say that the Golden Rule is the ‘ crown of our Lord's ethical teaching. Originality in a sense belongs to this saying, but only in the way it is formulated. Tobit 4:15 has it in the negative form, "And what thou thyself hatest, do to no man." When Hillel was asked by a prospective proselyte to Judaism to teach him the entire law while he stood on one foot, he made reply, "What is hateful to you, do not to your fellow: this is the whole Torah, and the rest is commentary."[10] It should be noted that both Hillel and Jesus refer the truth involved in their statements to·the Old Testament. So the sentiment may have been quite generally current in New Testament times. Israel Abrahams contends that Hillel's form is the more basic, upholding as it does "the claim of each to be free from his fellow-man's injury."[11] It may be replied that Jesus' form is the loftier, moving in the realm of love as well as justice, and demanding divine grace for its realization.

Gerald Friedlander represents the extreme of depreciation among Jewish writers. "The Jews of the days of Jesus had nothing to learn from his message."[12] He attempts to show that the so-called inwardness of Jesus' teaching, the probing of mo-

10 *Shabbath* 31a.
11 *Studies in Pharisaism and the Gospels,* First Series (1917), p. 24.
12 *The Jewish Sources of the Sermon on the Mount* (1911), p. 4.

tive as well as act, is really not new but is anticipated in the Old Testament.[13] In connection with Jesus' warning against hatred as a violation of the command not to kill, he cites Leviticus 19:17-18. What he does not mention is that the two things are brought together by Jesus, which the Old Testament does not do. Again, he observes that the words "You shall not covet your neighbor's wife" answer to Jesus' warning about looking on a woman with lustful desire, but fails to note that this specification from the tenth commandment falls somewhat short of the range of Jesus' declaration.

Montefiore has shown considerable appreciation of Jesus' teaching. Along with his demonstration that most of what Jesus taught can be duplicated in rabbinic writings, he has introduced two factors that are in danger of being overlooked. One is the observation that the parallels in Jewish literature were written (and spoken) after Jesus' time, for the most part.[14] The other is the recognition that verbal comparison is not the end of the story. A spirit, an atmosphere, pervades the teaching of Jesus that is not found elsewhere.[15] Jesus seems to have understood the inwardness of character better than the rabbis.[16] He affirmed the blessedness of the humble, even though unlearned, in a way that was unprecedented among the Jewish teachers.[17]

Practically all writers, Jewish and Christian alike, grant a difference between Jesus' teaching and the rabbinic in that his words are free of the wearisome casuistry that clutters the Talmud. The explanation on the Jewish side is that the leaders of Judaism were driven to this because of their ideal—the meticulous application of the law to all life, down to details.[18] The fact remains that Jesus insisted on the vital and essential in a way that is seldom approached among the rabbis. Chesterton notes the absence of platitudes and truisms.[19]

Perhaps the word "originality" is somewhat unfortunate in such a discussion as this. If by it we mean absolute newness, then there is very little that can be attributed to Jesus on this basis. But if originality is the proper word to use for the reasser-

13 *Ibid.*, pp. 42-43.
14 C. G. Montefiore, *Some Elements of the Religious Teaching of Jesus* (1910) , p. 10.
15 *Ibid.*, p. 85.
16 *Rabbinical Literature and Gospel Teachings* (1930) , p. 21.
17 *Ibid.*, p. 8.
18 J. Klausner, *Jesus of Nazareth* (1925) , pp. 372-373.
19 G. K. Chesterton, *The Everlasting Man* (1925) , pp. 220-221.

tion of old truths that were in danger of being forgotten, and for moving against the stream of contemporary thought, and for presenting the truth with a sustained quality of excellence, an inimitable artistry of expression, a penetrating inwardness, and a glow of moral intensity, then the stamp of his own genius must be admitted to rest upon the spoken word of Jesus of Nazareth.

Forms of the Teaching

For popular instruction, Jesus relied on the *parable* as the medium of communication. It was a common enough method among the rabbis, but was brought to its highest level of excellence by the master Teacher. Etymologically, the word "parable" should denote a comparison or similitude (the putting of one thing alongside another) ; and this is usually the case, observations about nature or human life constituting the foil for a spiritual lesson related more or less closely to the natural counterpart. But the word is used also where the notion of comparison is absent, as in Luke 4:23, where it has the sense of proverb. This is due to the fact that in the Septuagint *parabolē* is regularly employed to render the Hebrew *mashal*, which means "proverb" (literally it denotes a ruling expression, a decisive word, a master statement). So in the New Testament *parabolē* may be used of what is generally recognized as a wise saying or it may be used of a comparison newly introduced to impart spiritual information and insight.

T. W. Manson has observed that in the Old Testament the parable (*mashal*) is often used for warning as well as for an example (see Ezek. 17), and further, that "a parable may be perfectly intelligible in itself while its application is hidden from the hearers."[20] These considerations prepare us somewhat for a strange phenomenon in the Gospels, that the method of parabolic instruction, which should theoretically make the truth simple and luminous, actually operates to veil the truth from some minds. In fact, Jesus seems to say in Mark 4:12 that the parabolic medium is deliberately employed in order that people may hear and not understand, lest they turn and forgiveness be granted to them. It seems incredible that the Lord would hide truth that could bring forgiveness. This stands in opposition to the whole spirit of his mission.

[20] T. W. Manson, *The Teaching of Jesus* (1939), pp. 63-65.

The situation would be somewhat relieved if the expression of purpose in Mark (*hina*) could be made equivalent to Matthew's *hoti*, meaning "because" (Mt. 13:13). While there is a slight basis in usage for this possibility, it is very slight indeed, and probably does not help here. As A. T. Robertson notes, "If Matthew changed *hina* to *hoti* to avoid purpose, that would argue against the causal use of *hina*,"[21] at least in this instance. The real difficulty is that in both Matthew and Mark the text goes on to incorporate Isaiah 6:10, "lest they . . . turn for me to heal (Mark—"forgive") them." The element of divine purpose seems to be present no matter what is done with the grammatical problem of the conjunction.

Manson and Jeremias have approached the problem through the Aramaic.[22] Jeremias would translate the *mēpote* from the Septuagint of Isaiah 6:10 as "unless," on the ground that its Aramaic equivalent *dilᵉma* may be so rendered. In other words, the sense of the passage then is that the auditors are designed to hear and yet not understand *unless* they turn and thus find God's forgiveness. This greatly simplifies the situation and offers the best explanation, provided the Semitism be allowed.

The words we have been considering are found in connection with the Parable of the Sower. One writer has made the interesting suggestion, based on the fact that the verbs in Mark 4:2 are in the imperfect tense, that it was our Lord's habit to present this particular parable when he spoke to a new company of people.[23] The parable itself has to do with the response made by various groups to the disseminated word, so it is a fitting introduction to anything further that Jesus might teach at any given time.

Christ's teaching owes something of its effectiveness to his use of *metaphor*. John the Baptist's rugged independence is neatly capsuled in the question, "What did you go out into the wilderness to behold? A reed shaken by the wind?" The saying fits both the character of John and the locale. A tottering fence would have conveyed the idea fairly well, but it belongs to civilization rather than to the desert. By bidding his followers beware of the leaven of the Pharisees and Sadducees, Jesus gave a lively picture of the inflating and corrupting influences found in these circles.

21 "The Causal Use of *hina*," *Studies in Early Christianity* (1928), ed. S. J. Case, pp. 51-57.
22 T. W. Manson, *op. cit.*, pp. 75-80; J. Jeremias, *The Parables of Jesus* (1954), pp. 11-16.
23 A. H. Curtis, *The Vision and Mission of Jesus* (1954), p. 210.

Although the Twelve were themselves Orientals, it appears that they frequently missed his allusions by tending to take what he said too literally. Only by degrees did they learn to expect the enigmatical from his lips and frame their own understanding of it accordingly (Jn. 16:29).

Much of our Lord's teaching found in individual sayings is couched in the form of the *proverb*. This is sometimes a saying in common use, like the observation on tomorrow's weather based on the color of the evening sky (Mt. 16:1-4). Others are apparently original with Jesus, or at least known parallels are lacking. "Where your treasure is, there will your heart be also" is an example.

Hyperbole is evident in connection with the mote and beam, and with the saying about the camel and the eye of the needle.

Epigram has its place too. At least this is a convenient term to use for those sayings of Jesus which are not merely aphoristic but present challenge or command. The world has not ceased to admire the masterly summation of obligation contained in the saying, "Render therefore to Caesar the things that are Caesar's, and to God the things that are God's."

Paradox is a frequent ingredient in these terse utterances. The saying employed more often than any other, it seems, occurring no less than four times with characteristic variations befitting each separate occasion, is this: "He who finds his life will lose it: and he who loses his life for my sake will find it."

Jesus' skill in debate is attested by his use of the *dilemma*. Questioned as to the source of the authority under which he carried on his work, he parried the question by posing another in its place. "Was the baptism of John from heaven or from men?" Matthew 22:15-46 leaves with the reader the distinct impression that the Master was equal to any situation that involved him in disputation.

Finally, we note that Jesus found the *a fortiori* argument useful. "If you then, who are evil, know how to give good gifts to your children, how much more will your Father who is in heaven give good things to those who ask him!"

In addition to these recognized categories of rhetoric, our Lord displayed appreciation of the value of *repetition*. The Beatitudes owe their effectiveness in part to the piling up of one "blessed" upon another. Repetition makes possible the achievement of a climax. For example, anger toward a brother puts one in danger of the (local court of) judgment; the use of *raca* invites action by the council (Sanhedrin), whereas to call him a fool puts one in danger of hell fire.

Jesus was adept also in the handling of *contrast*. One recalls the pointed application of the Sermon on the Mount made by the story of the two houses, one built on rock, the other on sand. Then there is the story of the two sons whose father requested them to work in his vineyard. Their word and their deed stand out in sharp opposition.

It is widely recognized today that there is a poetic structure discernible in many of our Lord's sayings. The subject has been explored by C. F. Burney.[24] This poetic form served as a mnemonic aid and incidentally attests the accuracy of the reported sayings in their written form. One can hardly miss the cadence in such lines as these:

> Ask, and it will be given you;
> Seek, and you will find;
> Knock, and it will be opened to you.

It is well to recognize that one may possess a captivating style and yet have nothing worthy to communicate. In the case of Jesus, admiration for his style does not overshadow appreciation of the content. Form and substance are in satisfying equipoise.

THE IMPORTANCE OF THE TEACHING

Despite the admiration and gratitude Christians have for the words of Jesus, it should be realized that we possess no statement from his lips to indicate that teaching was the prime object of his mission. We look in vain for such a saying as this: "The Son of man has come to teach." Those who magnify out of proportion the importance of the prophetic character of Jesus' ministry can escape only with great difficulty from the logical consequences of their emphasis. Other prophets spoke too, speaking for God and about him. We are led thus perilously close to the old liberalism of Harnack, who made out that Jesus' gospel pertained to God, not to himself.[25]

If it be granted that Christ came to redeem the lost, the question that needs determination here is the relation between his teaching and the work of salvation that climaxed his career on

---

24 *The Poetry of Our Lord* (1925).
25 Cf. J. K. Mozley, *The Doctrine of the Incarnation* (1949), pp. 31-32.

earth. W. A. Curtis contends that he taught in order to save and that he actually did save by his teaching.[26] It is true that we have the saying attributed to Jesus, "The words that I have spoken to you are spirit and life" (Jn. 6:63). Instances are on record of Jesus' granting forgiveness by his word to the sinner. But these declarations find their efficacy in the fact that the speaker was destined to die for the sins of men. He was gathering the fruits of his redemptive victory in advance. His own testimony is that his life, apart from the cross, would be as fruitless as a grain of wheat that does not fall into the ground and die (Jn. 12:24). It must be admitted, even so, as Curtis points out, that without the teaching we would be left in the dark as to the meaning of the cross from the standpoint of the Suffering Servant himself.[27]

That the teaching of Jesus was intended to have abiding significance for the church is suggested by his own prediction that among the functions of the Spirit in the days following his return to the Father would be the recalling to the remembrance of the disciples of the things he had spoken to them (Jn. 14:26). While this statement has special bearing on the instruction given to the Twelve, there does not appear to be any good reason for excluding from its scope the things they heard in his public ministry. In themselves his words have the quality of pure truth, and so will endure (Mt. 24:35).

Apparently Christ was fully aware that he occupied a supreme and unique position as teacher in relation to his followers. He warned them against allowing themselves to be called rabbi, on the ground that one was their teacher and they were brethren (Mt. 23:8). The whole New Testament supports this very situation. In the Gospels we find enshrined the golden sayings of one great teacher and one only. The future leaders of the church are learners (that is the meaning of disciple). Only when he is gone do they become teachers, and in that capacity they consciously stand in his light (note the *verba Christi* in James and I Peter, for example). In the Judaism that formerly nurtured them, on the other hand, the individual teacher is relatively unimportant. The rabbis stand on much the same plane with one another. What is regarded as important is the broad outline of a sustained tradition to which they all subscribe.

The words of this preeminent teacher are not simply wise sayings calculated to strengthen and better one's life. They are words

26 *Op. cit.*, p. 12.
27 *Ibid.*

filled with destiny. To ignore them means ruin (Mt. 7:26-27). These very words will judge such people in the last day (Jn. 12:48). To be ashamed of Christ's words is tantamount to being ashamed of him, and this shame will reap a terrible harvest in the last day (Mk. 8:38). The men of Nineveh will rise up at the judgment and condemn the men of Jesus' generation, for they repented at Jonah's word, and lo, a greater than Jonah is here (Mt. 12:41).

The message of Jesus has its imperative in the fact that he was more than a mouthpiece for the will of God. He himself was in the process of carrying out that will, obedient even unto death. He stood in the tideway of the movement of God in human history at its most crucial point, and he summons all who would be obedient to the truth to stand with him.

BIBLIOGRAPHY

Israel Abrahams. *Studies in Pharisaism and the Gospels.* Cambridge, Eng.: Cambridge University Press, First Series 1917, Second Series 1924.

C. F. Burney. *The Poetry of Our Lord.* Oxford: Clarendon, 1925.

E. C. Colwell. *An Approach to the Teaching of Jesus.* New York: Abingdon, 1947.

W. A. Curtis. *Jesus Christ the Teacher.* London: Oxford, 1943.

D. Daube. *The New Testament and Rabbinic Judaism.* London: Athlane, 1956. Pp. 205-223.

C. H. Dodd. *Gospel and Law.* Cambridge, Eng.: Cambridge University Press, 1951.

—————,"Jesus as Teacher and Prophet," *Mysterium Christi*, ed. Bell and Deissmann. London: Longmans, Green, 1930.

Gerald Friedlander. *The Jewish Sources of the Sermon on the Mount.* London: Routledge, 1911.

A. E. Garvie. *Studies in the Inner Life of Jesus.* New York: Armstrong, n.d. Pp. 197-219.

A. C. Headlam. *The Life and Teaching of Jesus Christ.* London: Oxford, 1923. Pp. 209-266.

H. H. Horne. *Jesus the Master Teacher.* Grand Rapids: Kregel, 1964.

T. W. Manson. *The Teaching of Jesus.* Cambridge, Eng.: Cambridge University Press, 1931.

William Manson. *Jesus the Messiah.* Philadelphia: Westminster, 1946. Pp. 79-133.

C. G. Montefiore. *Some Elements of the Religious Teaching of Jesus.* London: Macmillan, 1910.

————. *The Synoptic Gospels.* 2 vols. London: Macmillan, 1927.

————. *Rabbinic Literature and Gospel Teachings.* London: Macmillan, 1930.

H. H. Sharman. *Jesus as Teacher.* New York: Harper, 1935.

H. B. Swete. *Studies in the Teaching of Our Lord.* London: Hodder and Stoughton, 1903.

G. Vos. *Biblical Theology.* Grand Rapids: Eerdmans, 1948. Pp. 375-383.

H. H. Wendt. *The Teaching of Jesus.* 2 vols. New York: Scribners, 1892.

A. Lukyn Williams. *The Hebrew-Christian Messiah.* London: S.P.C.K., 1916.

CHAPTER VII

THE MIRACLES

> *"There is an indissoluble connexion of proclamation, miracle, and faith. The Gospel miracle cannot be isolated from this service. None of the miracles takes place in a vacuum. None of them takes place, or is recounted, or claims significance, in and for itself. Their significance is only as actualizations of His Word, as calls to repentance and faith."*
>
> —Karl Barth

THE IMPACT OF JESUS CHRIST WAS MADE NOT ONLY THROUGH HIS words, but equally by means of his works of power. These are the two streams by which his person refreshed the world during the days of his flesh (Acts 1:1). Nicodemus was willing to concede a connection between the two. The miracles entitled Jesus to be respected and heard as a teacher sent from God (Jn. 3:2). If his contemporaries were impressed by his teaching because it had authority, the same was true of his deeds of mercy, many of which meant an invasion of the realm of Satanic power. In Mark's account of the first activity of Jesus in Capernaum, these two aspects are drawn together sharply, for the people in the synagogue expressed astonishment first at the teaching, then at the ability to heal a demon-possessed man (Mk. 1:22, 27). It was a new teaching—with authority. Far from being theoretical, it was a whole program of life revealing its relevancy to human need in practical demonstration.

Modern man, however, is apt to have quite a different reaction to the record of the miracles in the Gospels. He welcomes the religious teaching but is embarrassed by the presence of the miracle-stories. He may even applaud the various attempts that have been made to get rid of this element in the narratives by rationalistic devices. The search for the historical Jesus, he is convinced, must take account of the fact that the first century was unscientific and prone to attribute to supernatural causes things we can now satisfactorily explain on a natural basis. What cannot be so explained may justifiably be ignored as unreliable. Those who reject or explain away the miracles of Jesus seldom realize that logically they are endorsing an atheistic, pessimistic view of history. They exclude the guarantee, and therefore the hope, of the triumph of righteousness.

But it is antecedently improbable that miracles would be imported into the record without having basis in fact. Wace has put the matter well:

> It is difficult to conceive that any writers, at all within the range of contemporary evidence, would presume to state as the most open and public feature of our Lord's ministry a characteristic by which in reality it was never marked, and which would have been inconsistent, not merely with the evidence of particular witnesses, but with the total impression subsisting in the Jewish nation respecting our Lord's work.[1]

Recent historical criticism has found itself obliged to abandon the arbitrary tactics that the old liberalism employed in its attempt to rescue the kernel by abandoning the husk. Liberalism has found itself in something of a dilemma. On the one hand it has gloried in the magnifying of the worth of Jesus as a great and good man, and on the other has shied away from the supernatural. To sense the resulting embarrassment we have only to ask ourselves how greatly reduced a Christ we would have, in terms of love and good will toward men, if the miracles were removed. How central the miracles are, after all, to the best ingredients even in a liberally constructed Christ!

This dilemma has been overcome in part by the increased recognition of the power of the mind in dealing with bodily ailments, so that a portion of Christ's miracles may be safely admitted, it is felt, even though others must still be treated with skepticism. D. S. Cairns speaks to this point:

> Modernism has here partially followed the lead of science, and is now willing to accept many, if not all, of the healing miracles of Jesus. But again, it patiently accepts the limits which

---

[1] Henry Wace, *Some Central Points of Our Lord's Ministry* (1890) , p. 185.

our present-day experience still sets. We have no real analogies to the walking on the waters and to the control of the storm, and we have certainly none to our Lord's resurrection, and so applying the standards of our everyday experience and making them the limits of the credible, these narratives are treated precisely as those of the healing miracles were treated seventy years ago.[2]

That this observation is true may be seen in a fairly recent work which, while it admits the possibility of the miraculous in the realm of nature (such as stilling the storm), expresses doubt that Jesus actually did work miracles in this realm.[3]

Modern man likes to think of primitive man, with his animistic beliefs, as governed by superstition from which he himself has been delivered by increased acquaintance with the actual character of the universe and its laws. But is there not a danger that scientism, with its exaltation of natural law alone, may become merely a refined animism? Cairns should be heard again: "If the system of physical nature can be deflected by the mind of man, is it really coherent thinking to say that it is unscientific to believe that its course cannot be influenced by the Mind and Will of God?"[4]

It is not convincing anyway to say that man in the first century of our era was a gullible creature who expected a generous portion of the miraculous with any religion proffered to him. The fact is that the old mythologies were dead. Philosophy had driven them from the field. Granted, the lower forms of religion still flourished in many quarters; magic and the occult are not exactly dead even today, despite all our enlightenment. Though Christianity appealed more to the lower classes at the beginning than to others, it had to accredit itself increasingly to educated minds. To such minds the miraculous may have been a stumbling block to faith rather than a help, but the credentials of the gospel were strong enough to win them over.

To avoid misunderstanding, it is necessary to define the sense in which one uses the term "miracle." The definition of John D. Davis will serve the purpose well. "Miracles are events in the external world, wrought by the immediate power of God and intended as a sign or attestation."[5] When thus defined, miracles

2 *The Faith That Rebels* (1928), p. 40.
3 Vincent Taylor, *The Life and Ministry of Jesus* (1954), p. 100.
4 *Op. cit.*, p. 40.
5 *A Dictionary of the Bible*, 3rd edition (1923).

may be the more readily distinguished from special providences that are wrought through secondary means and are not necessarily for the purpose of attesting any message or messenger of the Lord.

The popular notion that the Bible abounds with miracles, so that they are present on practically every page, is refuted by a simple reading of the Scriptures. As Sir Robert Anderson showed in his volume, *The Silence of God*, miracles generally have occurred in periods, the major ones being the creation, the exodus, the age of Elijah and Elisha, the time of Daniel, and the days of Christ and the apostles. That we should be living in a period of the silence of God (so far as miracle is concerned) should not trouble us unduly, seeing there have been other times when this was true. The need in the first Christian century for accrediting the gospel by special signs does not exist today, when Christianity is well known and widely diffused and its message incorporated in a Book available to readers in hundreds of languages.

CLASSIFICATION

According to Acts 2:22, Peter in his Pentecost sermon used three categories in setting forth the wonderful works of the Lord Jesus. The first word, "miracle" (*dynamis*), means a mighty work. The same word is used of the gospel in Romans 1:16. The second word, "wonder" (*teras*), means a marvel, something that makes its appeal to the senses. The third, "sign" (*sēmeion*), points to a spiritual truth of which the miracle is the outward expression. Jesus used all three terms, although the second refers to his own works only by implication (Lk. 10:13; Jn. 4:48; 6:26; cf. Heb. 2:4). Of these three terms, the third is the most important in relation to Jesus' mission. In its aspect as a sign, a miracle was a kind of acted parable, whose value lay in its correspondence with the spiritual lesson it was intended to convey. While all three terms could be applied to one event, they represent the varied aspects under which a miracle could be apprehended and appreciated.

Passing beyond the use of terms, we should try to classify the mighty works according to the sphere in which they were wrought. Westcott divided them according to their respective reference to nature, man, or the spirit-world.[6] An equally good arrangement differentiates those performed in the realm of nature (such as the

---

[6] B, F. Westcott, *Characteristics of the Gospel Miracles* (1859), p. 8.

stilling of the storm), of super-nature (the expulsion of demons),
and of the derangement of nature (sickness, disease, and death).
C. S. Lewis divides them into miracles of the old creation and of
the new, putting in the former category events "in which we see
the Divine Man focussing for us what the God of Nature has
already done on a larger scale," and in the latter the transfiguration, the resurrection, and the ascension.[7] Walking on the water
belongs to the second group also.

CHARACTERISTICS

The miracles of Jesus are set in a framework of the *truly historical*. They are represented as having really happened. This
must be emphasized in order to gain a proper perspective for
comparison with wonders reported in other contexts. McGinley
has made a study of miracle-stories from rabbinic and Hellenic
sources and has noted in the Gospel accounts "a completely
different historical and spiritual tone."[8] In these other sources
one finds the operation of the superstitious, curiosity-loving elements of the human mind playing an important role. The stories
are in the nature of wonder-tales, which are designed to excite
the imagination. A partial exception is the record of cures effected
by medical treatment in connection with cult-centers of the god
Asklepios.

Our Lord's miracles should be recognized as *eschatological*, for
in him the powers of the age to come (Heb. 6:5) were at work.
"The miracles of help and healing that He performed were the
fulfillment of the promise of salvation . . . signs of the dawn of
that final revelation of salvation which was to call Israel to
repentance."[9] So they do not stand as isolated phenomena but are
part and parcel of the inbreaking of the kingdom of God through
the person and mission of Jesus.[10]

The mighty deeds of our Lord may be said to be *reasonable*, not
in the sense that reason can explain them in their entirety, but
in the sense that they are not inherently improbable or fantastic.
Whatever difficulties they may present to a mind predisposed to
unbelief, they are not impossible when the theistic position in its

[7] *Miracles* (1948), pp. 169-170.
[8] L. J. McGinley, *Form-Criticism of the Synoptic Healing Narratives* (1944),
p. 153.
[9] L. Goppelt, *Jesus, Paul and Judaism* (1964), p. 54.
[10] Cf. W. Grundmann, TDNT, II, 302.

full implications is cordially received. This quality of reasonable-
ness takes on added significance when the sober and restrained
narratives of our canonical records are set over against the fanciful accounts contained in the apocryphal gospels.

His works were *useful* also, calculated to meet pressing human
needs, such as the relieving of hunger, the cleansing of leprosy,
the restoration of bodily powers atrophied through crippling ill-
ness, and many other conditions. One good reason for refusing to
perform a miracle in the presence of Herod and his men was the
inappropriateness of the situation, since it presented no genuine
human need.

Jesus' signs and wonders were *wrought in a variety of spheres.*
Had they been of one sort only, confined to a single type or even
to a few spheres of operation, suspicion concerning their authenticity could well arise. Jesus delivered from sickness (Mk.
1:29-31), from disease (Mk. 1:41-42), from demon possession
(Mk. 5:1-19), and from death (Mk. 5:35-43).

Being *performed openly*, in the view of many spectators, without paraphernalia or accomplice, they were so completely devoid
of dishonesty or artifice that not only the multitudes but even
the leaders of the Jews, who opposed him in many respects, were
obliged to acknowledge the reality of his good deeds among the
people (Jn. 11:47). They felt driven to give the lame explanation that his exorcisms were accomplished because he was
possessed by the prince of demons (Mk. 3:22).

Jesus' healings were *completed instantly* in nearly every case.
Where there was deviation from this norm, doubtless we are to
posit an educative design (Mk. 8:22-26).

A feature of his works of mercy that is easily overlooked is their
gratuitous character. No fee of any kind was levied. This was
possible because of the entire absence of apparatus or supplies or
equipment of any kind. More important, it was entirely in accord
with the whole movement of God that centered in Christ, a movement of good will and grace. In contrast, a payment was expected by visitors to the shrines of the Hellenic healing cults.[11]

Jesus' miracles are marked by *freedom from retaliation*. No
case is on record of the use of his power to inflict punishment on
individuals who opposed or displeased him, although pressure
was put upon him by his disciples on at least one occasion to do

---

11 McGinley, *op. cit.*, p. 126.

this very thing (Lk. 9:52-56). McGinley notes that in this respect Jesus stands apart from both Hellenic and rabbinic healers.[12]

PURPOSE

This was not the same in every case. Examination of the data seems to warrant the following observations. Although it would probably be wrong to contend that Jesus deliberately chose to perform miracles in order to gain a hearing for his message (John the Baptist performed no miracle, yet had a vast audience for his preaching), the use of miracle actually had the effect of bringing together throngs of people who were then favorably disposed to listen to the spoken word. It is well to note, for example, that a great multitude were in position to hear the Sermon on the Mount because they had brought their sick from far and near and he had healed them (Mt. 4:24-25).

The miracles were intended to accredit the person and mission of Jesus (Lk. 4:16-21). They were expected of the Messiah (Jn. 7:31). This concept meets us in the apostolic preaching (Acts 2:22), which simply reflects Jesus' own thought in the matter. His expulsion of demons betokened the coming of the kingdom of God upon the people (Lk. 11:20). The success of his disciples in expelling demons testified to the breaking of the hold of Satan. This was his victory, since they ministered in his name (Lk. 10:18). In his eyes the mighty works rendered his rejection by the nation inexcusable (Jn. 15:22-24). It must be remembered, however, that our Lord did not use every occasion of the display of his miraculous power as an opportunity to press his messianic claim. This means either that he was too preoccupied with the meeting of the needs of the multitudes to press upon them the personal, messianic significance of the signs, or else that he realized that deeds speak more loudly than words. The constant assertion of a messianic claim in conjunction with the miracles could eventually pall upon his hearers and be discounted accordingly.

Cairns complains that the traditional explanation of the miracles has so exclusively stressed the evidential aspect that it has lost sight of other features. He thinks that "the idea . . . that they are primarily evidential portents, seals attached to the Divine

---

12 *Ibid.,* p. 146, n. 5.

message to authenticate it, is mistaken, and . . . they are instead part of the message itself."[13] Yet it remains true that many writers who have expressed the traditional viewpoint have also seen the other element that Cairns emphasizes. Westcott wrote, "They [miracles] are essentially a part of the revelation, and not merely a proof of it."[14] Warfield expressed himself similarly. "Miracles are not merely credentials of revelation, but vehicles of revelation as well."[15] Others have taken the same tack.[16] If the miracles were designed simply to authenticate the claim of Jesus to be sent of God, the execution of a few signs here and there would have been sufficient.

It is clear from apostolic testimony that Jesus' works as well as his words belong to his message. If the thrust of the preaching was contained in the challenge, "Repent and believe . . . ," the same may be said of the miracles. Jesus lamented the fact that the cities of Galilee, among which his mightiest works had been done, failed to repent (Mt. 11:20). As for faith, many statements connect this with the purpose of the signs, John 20:30-31 serving as a convenient summary.

Further, the miracles were revelations of the sympathy and compassion of Christ. It is repeatedly declared in the Gospels that the sight of human need strongly moved our Lord and led him to act without delay in relieving the distress (Mt. 14:14; Lk. 7:15). Since he had the power to heal at a distance (Lk. 7:1-10; Jn. 4:46-54), the question arises why he did not exercise this power more freely and so restore even more people than he was able to reach in person. Presumably it was because the compassion of Jesus, however successfully it could bridge the miles, could not communicate itself to suffering humanity so as to bring appreciation on the part of the beneficiary. The Savior's compassion led him to touch many who were avoided by society because of the gruesome or communicable nature of their diseases. This was not necessary in order to effect their recovery, but it symbolized the impartation of himself and his love to them. His mighty works would have fallen short of their objective if they acquainted people with his power but not his person. That Jesus' healing activity was somewhat selective is not surprising. A universal riddance of sickness

---

13 *Op. cit.*, p. 47.

14 *Op. cit.*, pp. 3-4.

15 B. B. Warfield, *Revelation and Inspiration* (1927), p. 47.

16 Otto Borchert, *The Original Jesus* (1933), p. 405; E. Y. Mullins, *Why Is Christianity True?* (1905), p. 182.

and disease could only be regarded as bizarre. Not all should be relieved of these limitations, for many have need of the discipline of suffering.

Although Jesus healed in his own right, so to speak, not calling upon God in prayer in order to gain the needed power from on high,[17] it was doubtless his intention that the miracles should serve as a revelation of the divine nature and purpose. Men could well reason that with such an unlimited display of power as they saw before their eyes, the same infinity might attach to the divine love for them, that very love which they traced in the Master's manner, in his personal concern for them, and which they saw irradiated from his countenance. They could also learn the great truth of the wideness of God's mercy, which knows no favorites and is no respecter of persons. There was no bypassing even of the untouchables, whether physically or morally leprous. The word commonly employed of our Lord's gracious acts is *heal*, but now and again the word is *save* (to make sound or whole), pointing to a connection between the restoration of afflicted bodies and the saving of the soul. The Lord came to redeem the whole man. Not infrequently the healing of the body was closely linked to a pronouncement of forgiveness of sins, as in the case of the paralytic who was brought by his four friends (Mk. 2:1-12). The Savior bore men's sicknesses and infirmities in the days of public ministry, and their sins he bore at its close.

THE RESPONSE

Since faith is the indispensable condition for individual participation in the salvation wrought by the Lord Jesus, it is not to be wondered at that faith should be required on the part of those who would participate in the benefits of his healing ministry. But the nature of this faith must be defined in accordance with New Testament standards.

[17] Luke 5:17 poses a problem, for the statement that the power of the Lord (God) was present for him (Jesus) to heal seems to suggest that there were times when this power was not present, but was for some reason denied to Jesus (cf. R. Otto, *The Kingdom of God and the Son of Man* [1943], p. 342). But this is not a necessary conclusion from the passage, and may be an entirely wrong inference from it. The setting is the presence of a considerable number of Pharisees and doctors of the law. The immediate sequel is the story of the paralytic whose sins Jesus pronounced forgiven before healing him of his affliction. It was especially important on this occasion that there be a demonstration of power, for Jesus was under close scrutiny.

It should be abundantly clear that the stress upon *faith* in the healing miracles bears small relation to modern psychological examples of faith-healing. The modern use of the word 'faith' in the psychological sense has little in common with the faith of which the Gospel-writers are speaking; that is, a saving, personal, believing relationship with Christ.[18]

Faith is everywhere laid down as the requirement for the renewal of the soul, but it is not so universally stated in connection with the reception of bodily healing. Perhaps this difference is intended to point to the greater importance of the redemption from sin. Or it may be that the Evangelists, having marked the presence of faith in connection with our Lord's miracles of healing on many occasions, simply do not deem it necessary to stress the point in every instance.[19]

What are we to make of Mark's observation that the attitude of Jesus' townsfolk was such that he could do no mighty work there apart from laying his hands upon a few sick people and healing them? Mark concludes with the word that Jesus marveled on account of their unbelief (Mk. 6:5-6). The explanation may be simply that only the few who were healed had faith, but possibly Jesus limited himself purposely, refusing to do more because the reception was not cordial. The Lord would no more force a miracle upon a human being than save his spirit contrary to his desire.

Jesus' consciousness of the close integration of miracles with his whole redemptive mission is seen not only in the basic requirement of faith but in the solemn way in which he dealt with those who slandered him by attributing his mighty works to demonic agency (Mt. 12:24-32). They were guilty of unpardonable sin, for it was sin against the Holy Spirit, the one by whose power he was performing his mighty acts, the one who comes with sealing blessing upon every life that admits the Savior and his redemption. It was resistance against God himself, and an attempt to thwart the coming of his kingdom.

On the other hand, there seems to be some disparagement of miracle on the part of the sacred writers, and even of our Lord himself, which demands an explanation. Insofar as his mighty works were acts of mercy they conveyed their own blessing and were no doubt appreciated in greater or lesser degree by those

18 Alan Richardson, *The Miracle-Stories of the Gospels* (1941), p. 63.
19 Cairns, *op. cit.*, p. 72.

who were personally benefited. But of his works as signs pointing to himself and his mission there seems to have been a limitation in value. This is not astonishing in view of the past. Israel saw God's works of power for forty years in the wilderness, yet a whole generation was unable to enter the land of promise and perished because of unbelief.

Several passages in the Gospels seem to reflect the partial ineffectiveness of miracles as signs. The early Judean ministry of our Lord produced a generous following for him, based on the signs that he did. Indeed, the text says that they believed. But the disconcerting thing is that Jesus did not commit himself to them, knowing what was in man (Jn. 2:23-25). At several points in the Fourth Gospel it is noted that men believed, yet some fault is found with this belief. It is fairly evident, then, that there is a type of faith based on the display of miraculous power that is unsatisfactory from the biblical viewpoint. Based merely on observation and mental assent, it does not root itself in heart conviction and lacks devotion to the person of Christ.

Even more depressing is the reaction to miracle in John 12:37-43. In spite of so many miracles, the people as a whole did not believe on him. This is traced to a blindness and hardness of heart, which prevented real faith. The situation seems to be relieved somewhat when John goes on to state that nevertheless many even of the rulers believed on him, a condition that did not exist at an earlier point in the ministry (Jn. 7:48). The interpretation of what follows is not without a degree of uncertainty. These same rulers (members of the Sanhedrin), out of fear of the Pharisees, did not confess their faith lest they face excommunication. John's comment on this is that they loved the praise of men more than the praise of God. Are we to see here a class of secret disciples who are regarded as genuine but are censured for their lack of boldness, or are we to understand the writer as saying that even this apparent exception to the general rule is not truly an exception, for the sort of faith manifested here does not rise to the level of the divine requirement? Westcott may well be right in taking the sterner view of the situation:

> The ground of practical unbelief was moral and not intellectual. Some who remained among the adversaries of Christ were satisfied of the truth of His claims. But the conviction

found no expression in life. Such ineffective intellectual faith (so to speak) is really the climax of unbelief.[20]

One of the greatest of Christ's miracles, reported in all four Gospels, is the feeding of the five thousand. Its importance lies not merely in the magnitude of the event but in the detailed explanation of the sign our Lord gave in the discourse that followed, reported in John 6. Yet we are led to suppose that the final result was desertion by many who had thought themselves his disciples, so that only the Twelve remained gathered about him. Had the sign accomplished anything toward inducing true faith?

To these instances another should be added, one in which Jesus himself seems pessimistic about the value of signs. Certain of the scribes and Pharisees came to him with the request that he show them a sign (Mt. 12:38). His reply was that a wicked and adulterous generation seeks for a sign, but no sign will be given except that of Jonah the prophet. This reply does not condemn signs as such, least of all his own; but it sets forth his refusal to lend his sanction to the working of a sign "on demand" that would make a spectacular impression. These same men had presumably seen some of his signs. If not, they had heard of them from reliable sources. Had one of them been in physical need, without doubt Jesus would have moved to meet that need; but he refused to perform a work to satisfy curiosity. His work was to repair the damage wrought by sin and disease to the human frame, but he did not create new or strange things.

It would be daring to claim that the signs were valueless because the effect was so often negative in producing genuine faith. On the same basis one could assert that the preaching of the gospel is valueless. Rather, the apparent disparagement of signs in the sacred record must be laid to the recognition of the power of sin to harden a heart so that even the clearest and fullest tokens of the divine operation are spurned.

Alan Richardson has set forth the position that Jesus' "signs" were only readable by those who possessed the gift of faith, and must be thought of as strictly parallel to the function of parable in the realm of the spoken word. There was a veiling of the truth from the minds of the unbelieving in both cases.[21] In this connection it is of interest to note that John speaks of the

20 *The Gospel According to St. John* (1896), *in loco.*
21 *Op. cit.,* pp. 48-49, 57.

signs of Jesus as wrought in the presence of the disciples (Jn. 20:30). He records certain of them that his readers may believe (present tense of continuing action) that Jesus is the Christ, the Son of God, and that in so believing they may have (present tense again) life in his name. Yet if this position be pressed too far, it means logically that the signs were wrought for the benefit of believers who had already been convinced by other means, such as preaching or contact with the person of Christ. Very few miracles were performed with only disciples present. The impression persists for the reader of the Gospels that the miracles were designed to induce faith and not simply to stimulate or confirm it. Accompanied as they were by revelation in word, they were elevated above the low level of mere wonders of a thaumaturgic sort.

Unquestionably there were many who were constrained to put their faith in the Lord because of his miracles. Seeing his power in these outward acts, they were led on to confidence in his claims and to love for his person. It must have been reassuring to his immediate followers to witness the continuing demonstrations of his power, especially since the Master seemed to be following a course perplexing to them in the absence of any move toward the setting up of a kingdom of worldly sovereignty.[22] In the signs he manifested his glory. But the greater the opportunity of contact with Jesus himself, the more subordinate becomes the role of miracle. "Believe me that I am in the Father and the Father in me; or else believe me for the sake of the works themselves" (Jn. 14:11). Faith based on the signs is valid, but for those who know him at close range, his self-revelation is sufficient.

The early church, which preserved the traditions about Jesus and then published the Gospel records with their frequent mention of miracle, was bound to feel the pertinency of this element of the tradition to its own situation, since the signs and wonders were still occurring, as the book of Acts and the Epistles testify. Jesus' followers could cherish the recollection of his words to the effect that the works that he had done they would do also, and even greater works than these (Jn. 14:12). What, then, becomes of the claim of Christ that he had done among his nation works that no other man did (Jn. 15:24)? Does this claim of uniqueness apply only with reference to the past? Perhaps it is

22 Borchert, *op. cit.*, pp. 129-130.

safest to conclude that there was a uniqueness that remains un-challenged, inasmuch as the powers of the coming age had their source in him. The miracles he wrought were a part of his work of ushering in the kingdom of God (John the forerunner did no miracle). Operating on authority delegated from him, the apostles were indeed able to do greater works in the sense that more people were affected, a larger number brought into the kingdom of God, and a permanent society established, made up of redeemed men and women, Gentiles as well as Jews. But this, after all, is inconceivable apart from him who continued to work through his own.

BIBLIOGRAPHY

Sir Robert Anderson. *The Silence of God.* London: Pickering and Inglis, n.d.

Karl Barth. *Church Dogmatics,* IV/2. Edinburgh: T. & T. Clark, 1958.

A. B. Bruce. *The Miraculous Element in the Gospels.* London: Hodder and Stoughton, 1886.

D. S. Cairns. *The Faith That Rebels.* London: SCM, 1928.

F. Godet. *Lectures in Defence of the Christian Faith.* Edinburgh: T. & T. Clark, 1881. Pp. 117-161.

C. E. Jefferson. *Things Fundamental.* New York: Crowell, 1903. Pp. 193-221.

James Kallas. *The Significance of the Synoptic Miracles.* Greenwich, Conn.: Seabury, 1961.

C. S. Lewis. *Miracles.* New York: Macmillan, 1948.

L. J. McGinley. *Form-Criticism of the Synoptic Healing Narratives.* Woodstock, Md.: Woodstock College Press, 1944.

J. B. Mozley. *Eight Lectures on Miracles.* London: Rivingtons, 2nd edition, 1867.

Alan Richardson. *The Miracle-Stories of the Gospels.* London: SCM, 1941.

W. M. Smith. *The Supernaturalness of Christ.* Boston: Wilde, 1944. Pp. 109-162.

H. van der Loos. *The Miracles of Jesus.* Supplements to *Novum Testamentum,* Vol. IX. Leiden: Brill, 1965.

B. F. Westcott. *Characteristics of the Gospel Miracles.* Cambridge, Eng.: Macmillan, 1859.

CHAPTER VIII

CONFLICT WITH THE PHARISEES

> *"The ultimate reason for the friction between Jesus and the authorities . . . is not to be sought in a divergence of views on matters of doctrine. The background of the struggle is the claim to unique authority underlying the words and actions of Jesus Christ."*
>
> —Jakob Jocz

NOT ALL THE PEOPLE HEARD THE MASTER GLADLY. OPPOSITION centered in the Pharisees, although later on other groups also were arrayed against him. Because the Pharisees looked on themselves as the godly core of the nation, in the words of Josephus "a body of Jews with the reputation of excelling the rest of their nation in the observance of religion, and as exact exponents of the laws,"[1] they zealously accepted the function of watchdogs ready to investigate any spiritual leader who came on the horizon (Jn. 1:24). For this reason they made contact with Jesus early and maintained it more or less throughout his public life. One is in better position to understand the nature of the conflict if he examines the background of this movement in Israel.

HISTORY OF THE PHARISEES

The name first makes its appearance in Josephus' account of the reign of the Hasmonean ruler, John Hyrcanus[2] (135-105 B.C.); but it is evident that the sect had been in existence for some time before this. Whatever the precise time of its emer-

[1] *The Jewish War* i.110.
[2] *Antiquities* xiii.288-298.

gence, its roots must be sought in conditions following the Babylonian Captivity, when a renewed zeal for the law that was quite the reverse of the laxity that had prevailed prior to that catastrophe began to shape the Restoration along purist lines. In this reformation Ezra had a leading part. Since he was a priest, it was not unexpected that he should instruct the people in the law, for this was a traditional function of the priesthood. But he was also a scribe, a term that carries with it a higher connotation than a mere copyist of the Scriptures. He was skilled in the knowledge of what the law required. In later times the scribes were teachers renowned for their understanding of the Torah and also custodians and expounders of the ever increasing oral traditions that accumulated in the process of applying the law to the daily lives of the people. Their task was to "make a hedge" about the commandments so that people would know exactly what was required of them in order to avoid transgression.

Under the guidance of the scribes a body of people emerged who were committed to faithful adherence to the law, determined to preserve the traditions of Israel at any cost. In the second century B.C., during the period of Syrian oppression, they were known as *Chasidim* or "pious ones." This was a time of ferment, which shaped the course of Judaism for years to come. The Chasidim were quite ready to give their support to the Maccabees during the struggle against Syria, in order to insure the continuance of their way of life, but could not countenance the political ambitions of their leaders during the days of independence that followed. It seems that some of the Chasidim made their protest by a complete withdrawal from society, hoping in secluded communities to cultivate to better advantage the religious life. These became known as Essenes. But the Pharisees, the most influential descendants of the Chasidim, remained as a strong leavening influence among the people, set off from the Sadducees, who constituted the priestly aristocracy.

It is probably incorrect to see in the name Pharisee ("separated") a proof of their tendency to cleavage from fellow Jews such as the Sadducees. More likely the name signifies their determination to maintain moral and ceremonial purity. Under the circumstances it is quite credible that others gave them the title as a nickname.[3]

According to Josephus more than six thousand of them re-

---

[3] A. Finkel, *The Pharisees and the Teacher of Nazareth* (1964), p. 48.

fused to take the oath of allegiance to Caesar and Herod.[4] Whether this was their entire membership cannot be ascertained, but in all probability the Pharisees represented only a small fraction of the population. The impression that all Jews belonged to some party—whether Pharisee, Sadducee, Essene or Zealot— is quite mistaken. Most of the people had no such affiliation. We may be sure that the Pharisees exercised an influence far greater than their numerical strength might suggest. Although a wide gulf separated them from the *Am ha-aretz* (people of the land), who did not live in accordance with the Levitical code (Jn. 7:49), they nevertheless enjoyed the esteem of the vast majority of the Jews. It is a phenomenon common to human experience that people will look up to ministers or priests or so-called holy men, despite discernible blemishes in their lives, feeling that such men are at least far beyond their own pedestrian level of attainment. That the Pharisees sought to increase their numbers in the land by proselyting, but with little success, is the apparent meaning of Jesus' words in Matthew 23:15. Not many cared to make the sacrifices that a rigid adherence to Pharisaic principles demanded. ·

The Pharisees were organized into brotherhoods, binding themselves with an oath to observe faithfully the ordinances of the Levitical code. For the most part they were laymen, but some priests were included (Acts 6:7; 15:5). Although they did not stand aloof from the temple, where the Sadducaic priestly families were in control, or from the Sanhedrin, where they were able to register their point of view sometimes with considerable effect (Acts 5:34-40; 23:6-10), they made the synagogue their stronghold. Here they could exert a formative influence on the life of the common people through instruction and encouragement to participate in the services.

Finkelstein has advanced the theory that in contrast to the Sadducees, who were the landed gentry or patricians of that time, the Pharisees were middle-class folk, mostly artisans, dwelling in the cities, sharing the plebeian animosity toward the wealthy aristocracy.[5] Though he writes with great persuasiveness, one suspects that he has cast the two groups into molds that are too rigid. And when he goes on to suggest that economic position had a determining effect on doctrine (e.g., eschatological hope having appeal to the have-nots whereas it was of little con-

[4] *Antiquities* xvii.42.
[5] Louis Finkelstein, *The Pharisees* (1946).

cern to the well-heeled Sadducees), this amounts to saying that social history is more decisive for doctrinal formulation than revelation.

About the time of Christ two schools of Pharisaic interpretation were coming into being, the one taking its name from Hillel, the other from Shammai. Having come to Palestine from Babylonia, Hillel held to a looser construction of the law than most Palestinians, for the reason that some features of the code were unfitted for life in a foreign land.[6] He was known as a liberal in viewpoint and was noted for his humane outlook and humble character. His disciples often clashed with the Shammaites, who held a stricter view of the application of the law. Eventually the school of Hillel became dominant.

Because the scribes were the legal experts, the Pharisees deferred to them as teachers of the law. They themselves were supremely concerned to practice what the law demanded and even to go beyond the letter of the law to show their zeal for God, as in tithing and fasting. It is not surprising that the presence of scribes along with the Pharisees is noted at several points in the Gospels (Mt. 12:38; 15:1; 23:13, etc.). The expression "scribes of the Pharisees" (Mk. 2:16) suggests that these doctors of the law attached themselves both to Pharisees and Sadducees. They are often mentioned also in conjunction with the chief priests (Mk. 10:33; 11:27, etc.).

With a sense of mission the Pharisees sought to show the way to their compatriots, trying to make the nation holy to the Lord in conformity to the Old Testament ideal. It was because of this that they showed an interest in John the Baptist and in Jesus, and it was because of this that our Lord consented to enter into dialogue with them. He had little in common with the other parties in Judaism.

PHARISAIC OBJECTIONS TO JESUS

A popular observation about the man from Nazareth was that he taught with authority and not as the scribes (Mk. 1:22; Mt. 7:29). This created astonishment. We may be sure that the Pharisees held this against him, because they challenged him on this issue of authority more than once. Here was a man who had received no special training, yet his words had a divine,

---

[6] G. F. Moore, *Judaism*, I (1946), 79.

convicting power about them that was unique.[7] It was galling to see a figure from the backwoods exerting such a powerful influence almost from the very beginning. The resentment of the religious leaders has been likened to that of the medical profession against an unregistered practitioner who seems to be meeting with great success.[8] An attempt has been made to put a somewhat different construction on the passage in Mark. Daube thinks that the meaning of "scribe" in this verse is not that of a scholar or legal expert, but rather an elementary teacher of the Bible such as would be found in almost any village.[9] But it is doubtful that Mark would use the word with a different connotation than it has elsewhere in the Gospels, and that without explanation. Further, Jesus would not have to possess any special qualifications to outstrip such men as these, whereas a comparison with the scribes, the most learned men of the time, indicates the magnitude of the impact made upon the hearers and explains their astonishment.

It was a serious matter in the eyes of the scribes and Pharisees that Jesus claimed the right to forgive sins. This seemed to them outright blasphemy, for this was a prerogative of God alone. By way of answer, the Master indicated that he was acting in terms of delegated authority, that he was forgiving sins on earth (and so was not in competition with the Father in heaven), and that he was making the pronouncement of forgiveness by virtue of his position as Son of man. Apparently his objectors continued to cherish their disapproval.

Another ground of controversy was the activity of Jesus as an exorcist. The Pharisees did not attempt to deny the reality of the cures, but sought to explain them on the basis that Jesus was able to cast out demons because he was in league with Beelzebul, the prince of demons (Mt. 12:24). He lost no time in exposing the folly of this reasoning. It would mean that Satan was arrayed against himself.

Again, Jesus was accused of eating with tax collectors and sinners (Mk. 2:16). With such people the Pharisees refused to associate. It was shocking that a religious teacher would do such a thing. Jesus made no attempt to deny the charge; it was entirely true. But he made it clear that these people were the needy

---

[7] See I. Abrahams, *Studies in Pharisaism and the Gospels*, First Series (1917), pp. 13-17; C. G. Montefiore, *The Synoptic Gospels*, I (1927), 32-33.

[8] R. Travers Herford, *Pharisaism, Its Aim and Its Method* (1912), p. 131.

[9] David Daube, *The New Testament and Rabbinic Judaism* (1956), p. 211.

ones for whom he had come. Evidently the Pharisees counted it more important to remain uncontaminated than to lend a hand to these unfortunates.

Great offense was created by Jesus' disregard of traditional practices such as fasting (Lk. 5:30, 33) and the washing of hands before meals (Mk. 7:1-5). He was not opposed to these things *per se* but refused to magnify such externals as binding.

The feeling against him on the score of these practices was mild compared to the bitter antagonism produced by his attitude toward the law. His denial that he came to destroy it (Mt. 5:17) implies that there were those who were suggesting that his words and actions pointed in exactly that direction. His frequent disregard of the sabbath rest gave his opponents ample ground for the charge that he was a lawbreaker. Many of his healings were done on the sabbath, as though deliberately designed to challenge and infuriate the religious leaders. As T. W. Manson points out, in view of his upbringing such conduct could not be laid to ignorance.[10] While he honored the law as part of the eternal word of God, he insisted that it could be set aside in the interest of the work God had given him to do. If others had broken the sabbath law with good cause, he could do so with greater warrant (Mt. 12:1-8).

If there was anything that competed with the law for the reverent regard of the Jews and held them together as a people, it was the temple, to which the faithful resorted for the national festivals and where sacrifices were offered daily. One of the charges made against Jesus was to the effect that he planned to destroy the temple and boastfully asserted that then he would raise it up again or would substitute for it another not made with hands (Mt. 26:61; Mk. 14:58). The lack of agreement as to the exact statements of Jesus was not allowed to minimize the basic fact that he seemed to have a hostility toward the holy place.[11] The Master did indeed predict the demolition of the temple (Mt. 24:2), but this did not prevent him from regarding it as the house of God (Mk. 11:17). He knew, however, that another house of a spiritual nature was destined to supplant it, the temple of his own body (Jn. 2:21).

The crowning offense was Jesus' claim to a unique relation-

[10] *Judaism and Christianity*, ed. E. I. J. Rosenthal, III (1938), 130.

[11] It is a matter of interest that Stephen and Paul had to face the same charge of alleged disparagement of both the Mosaic law and the temple (Acts 6:13; 25:8).

ship to God (Jn. 5:15-18). Since the Jews were monotheists, this was repugnant to them; and the Pharisees, unlike the disciples, lacked the willingness to sit at his feet and did not have the advantage of intimate contact with him such as enabled his followers to accept this high view of his person. So the gap that had been created by numerous items of friction widened into an impassable gulf.

THE TACTICS OF THE PHARISEES

Almost from the beginning of his ministry Jesus attracted the attention of these men, with the result that he seldom appeared in public without representatives of the Pharisees in the audience. Even in semiprivate situations, when in company with the disciples, he was under their surveillance (Mk. 2:24). The word that is often used to indicate their scrutiny has the force of close observation (Mk. 3:2; Lk. 14:1). The prevailing mood was not that of desire to learn but to establish grounds for criticism.

It is not unexpected, then, that censure should soon be forthcoming (Mk. 2:16; 7:5, etc.). Probably the hope was that if Jesus could be pressed into a corner in the presence of the multitudes this would result in a sharp drop in his popularity and influence.[12]

Another approach was to demand a sign as a token of divine accreditation of his ministry (Mt. 12:38; 16:1; Mk. 8:11; Jn. 6:30). Paul labels this as a national characteristic of the Jews (I Cor. 1:22). Jesus resisted this pressure, regarding the demand for signs as a mark of spiritual decadence (Mt. 16:4; Mk. 8:12).

The use of ensnaring questions was resorted to from time to time (Mk. 10:2), especially toward the close of the ministry, when the Pharisees quizzed Jesus on the touchy matter of paying tribute to Caesar (Mt. 22:15-17). The answer might incriminate him with the Roman authorities, on the one hand, or, on the other, cause him to lose favor with the people. His unexpected reply avoided both dangers.

Banning of a follower from the synagogue is reported on one occasion (Jn. 9:22, 34). This was calculated to make the people afraid to identify themselves with a man whom the authorities

---

12 The warning passed on to Jesus concerning Herod's murderous intentions (Lk. 13:31) seems to have had similar motivation. If Jesus should show fear through flight, it would make a delectable morsel of gossip.

regarded as dangerous. The ban may well have been temporary in its intended duration.

The logical climax of all this maneuvering was the determination that the prophet of Galilee must die (Mk. 3:6; Jn. 11:53). An attempt to take him by force proved abortive (Jn. 7:32, 45-46), but his opponents were willing to bide their time until the propitious season came during the last week in Jerusalem.

Jesus' Reactions to the Pharisees

The notion that the Master had an implacable hostility toward the Pharisees and they toward him is not borne out by the evidence of the Gospels. Luke records three incidents in which he accepted invitations to dine at the house of a Pharisee (Lk. 7:36; 11:37; 14:1). The visit to his quarters by Nicodemus is noted in John 3:1-2. His accusations are regularly addressed to the party rather than to individuals.

Yet the atmosphere of most of the confrontations is undeniably one of tension. Jesus leveled some serious charges at the Pharisees. He accused them of setting aside the commands of Scripture by means of their traditions, as in the case of Corban (Mk. 7:9-13). An undutiful son could withhold support from parents through a vow of dedication of such means to holy purposes (the temple). In so doing he would ironically, it seems, gain the reputation of being devout because of his votive offering.[13]

Accused of blasphemy himself, Jesus turned the tables on the scribes and Pharisees by pronouncing them guilty of blasphemy against the Holy Spirit for daring to assert that he cast out demons by the power of the prince of demons (Mk. 3:22ff.; Mt. 12:24ff.). This was an eternal sin (Mk. 3:29). Lest it be thought that this seemingly harsh verdict proceeded from personal animus toward an adversary, Jesus expressly indicated that a word spoken against the Son of man could be forgiven (Lk. 12:10).

Self-glorification seriously tarnished the image of the Pharisees as Jesus saw it. They loved to be noticed and commended (Mt. 23:5-7). The Master was not erecting a man of straw in his parable of the Pharisee and the tax-gatherer at prayer (Lk. 18:9-14). The figure of the elder brother in the parable of the

13 The accuracy of the representation of the nature of Corban in the Gospel record has been questioned (Montefiore, *The Synoptic Gospels*, I [1927], 148-152). On the other hand, see Vincent Taylor, *The Gospel According to St. Mark* (1952), pp. 341-342.

prodigal son is basically the same (Lk. 15:25-30). He wants recognition and he bitterly resents the loving attention that is being bestowed on his wastrel brother (note in this connection how Luke 15:1-2 forms the background of the entire chapter).

Another charge was casuistry, seen in the distinction made between oaths, some held to be valid but others regarded as not binding because of technicalities (Mt. 23:16-22).

Particularly glaring was the inconsistency between profession and practice. The exterior of the life was kept scrupulously clean, at least to the casual observer, but the inner man was allowed to harbor all sorts of iniquity (Mt. 23:25). Here one should recall our Lord's teaching that the desire to work evil was sinful even though the act might not follow (Mt. 5:28).

Jesus perceived a serious imbalance in the Pharisees in that they were so scrupulous about their tithing, doing more than the law required, yet neglected the weightier matters of the law such as justice and mercy and faith (Mt. 23:23-24).

It is in Matthew 23 that the barrage against the Pharisees is the most sustained and the most intense. No wonder this chapter has become a ground of controversy. Jewish scholars tend to reject many of the charges found here as a distorted picture of Pharisaism. In their judgment, Matthew must have been produced late in the first Christian century or even early in the second, at a time when there was considerable bitterness between the church and Judaism. But there is enough material in Matthew demonstrating the writer's sensitivity to Judaism in the time of Jesus to make dubious this attempt to save the reputation both of Jesus and of the Pharisees at one stroke.

The need of saving Jesus' reputation is alleged by those who find a contradiction between the teaching of our Lord and the violence of the outbursts attributed to him in Matthew 23. There seems to be no manifesting of the love toward enemies of which he spoke (Mt. 5:44).

Other scholars are willing to accept the chapter as historical but are convinced that Jesus would not have delivered such a broadside at the Pharisees as a whole, so they conclude that he must have had in view only certain of their number or else a coterie of them, likely the Shammaites. Finkel[14] has introduced a fairly substantial body of evidence to show that, in the questions of tithing and eating with unwashed hands, the remarks

14 A. Finkel, *op. cit.*, pp. 134-143.

of Jesus fit the Shammaite group rather than the Hillel faction. Further, he is of the opinion that Jesus' charge of shutting the kingdom against men agrees with the fact that the Shammaites denied to the sinner a share in the world to come (Mt. 23:13) and thinks that Matthew 23:31 ("you are sons of those who murdered the prophets") is illuminated by the belligerent attitudes of the Shammaites toward the disciples of Hillel. When one adds the consideration that the period of Jesus' ministry falls in the era of Shammaite supremacy, the view gains in plausibility. Yet it will not explain all the indictments of Jesus. Since it was his practice to consider the Pharisees (and often the scribes attached to them) as a group, the most natural conclusion is that in Matthew 23 he had the Pharisees as a whole in mind, even though some of his charges would be more applicable to a part of them.

How is one to evaluate this chapter, then? Many things have to be brought to bear upon it before anything like a mature judgment is possible. To begin with, this section ought not to be regarded in isolation. John the Baptist's searing criticism of the same group ought not to be forgotten (Mt. 3:7-10). Though the Talmud is not the best guide for conditions in the first century, its jibes at the Pharisees are suggestive of many shortcomings. Of the seven types of Pharisees depicted, some of them closely approximating descriptions in Matthew 23, only one is commended as being genuine in the sense of fulfilling the ideal.[15] It is helpful to reflect that Jesus did not single out the Pharisees for censure. Repeatedly he referred to the nation as a whole as sinful and wicked. On one occasion he uttered woes over certain cities of Galilee for failure to repent in spite of seeing his mighty works (Mt. 11:20-24). Perhaps the "woe" is as much a lament as a judgment pronounced. The same might well apply to Jesus' frequent use of the word in chapter 23. In fact, the lament over Jerusalem at the close reveals the mood of Jesus throughout; and there is no good reason for excluding the Pharisees from those whom he longed to gather to himself, only to be rebuffed.[16] Just

---

[15] Later Judaism could take a more urbane attitude because Pharisaism was no longer in competition with other sects. Pharisaism no longer needed to take itself so seriously or be overly defensive.

[16] If this observation is correct, it goes far to meet the complaint of Montefiore, "Towards his enemies, towards those who did not believe in him, whether individuals, groups, or cities (Matt. xi, 20-24), only denunciation and bitter words!" (*Rabbinic Literature and Gospel Teachings* [1930], p. 104).

as Paul could criticize his countrymen (Rom. 2:17-24) but at
the same time cherish a passionate desire for their salvation
(Rom. 9:1-3; 10:1), so it was with Jesus before him.

Part of the offense created by the chapter lies in Jesus' repeated use of the word *hypocrite.* If it carried anything like the
stigma it conveys today, the Pharisees must have burned with
indignation. With us the word suggests a deliberate intention
to deceive, the word or act being out of line with the motive
of the heart. Sometimes the word has this connotation in the
Gospels, but not always. It may denote the lack of correspondence between the outward and the inward without implying a
deliberate attempt to deceive.

> When Jesus calls the Scribes and Pharisees "hypocrites," He
> does not mean that they were merely "play-acting," "pretend-
> ing," that is, men inwardly aware of their badness but posing
> as good men. The trouble with them was that they sincerely
> thought that they were good men who were championing the
> cause of true religion, while all the time they failed to see that
> their goodness was largely counterfeit as well as lamentably
> deficient, and that what they regarded as the essentials of true
> religion were not its essentials at all. As Jesus pointed out
> they were *"blind* guides" (Matt. xxiii.24), for moral and spiri-
> tual blindness was their chief defect, though all the time they
> fondly supposed that nobody could see so clearly as they did.[17]

Everyone, it seems, is willing to accept at face value the com-
plaints of the Pharisees against Jesus which are found sprinkled
throughout the Gospels. The acceptance of those ought to prepare the reader to accept also the denunciations of Matthew 23.
Jesus is striking back. He cannot be expected to give a calm, balanced statement of the merits and demerits of his opponents.
He is laying bare the faults of his critics.[18] Jesus was not one of
the boorish *Am ha-aretz* who knew not the law. He was called
rabbi. Doubtless he was raised in the Pharisaic tradition (recall
his ability to converse intelligently with doctors of the law at
the age of twelve). All of this background makes his criticisms
of the Pharisees the more telling. He was a critic more or less
from within rather than from the outside. And it should not be
overlooked that the opening of the discourse in Matthew 23 commends his opponents to the extent that they are true interpreters

---

17 L. H. Marshall, *The Challenge of New Testament Ethics* (1947), p. 60.
18 W. K. Lowther Clarke, *New Testament Problems* (1929), p. 55.

of the law (cf. Mk. 12:34). This is no tirade based on ignorance or bias.

The problem facing us is this: if one studies the Pharisees in their historical development apart from their contact with Jesus, one gets a rather consistently favorable impression of them; but when one sees them depicted in Matthew 23, the impression is quite different. This leads to the conclusion that the element of friction between Jesus and the Pharisees, as it is reported in the Gospels, is due to one of two things. Either the Christian documents reflect prejudice against the Pharisees or else the worst features of this group were only really drawn out by their contact with Jesus. That the former alternative is the less likely of the two may be deduced not only from the general trustworthiness of the Gospels but also from the close correspondence between the portrayal of the Pharisees in the New Testament documents and in Josephus.[19]

It is quite understandable that modern Jewish scholars, in their desire to claim Jesus as a leading light in Judaism, should seek to minimize the area of conflict between him and the Pharisees. Quite naturally Matthew 23 dismays them. But the more strenuously the differences are denied, the more difficult it becomes to explain the final chapter in the story, which finds the Pharisees joining in the conspiracy to put out this light. It is part of the greatness of Jesus that he did not spare the lash of criticism, knowing all the while what the ultimate cost to himself would be.

BIBLIOGRAPHY

Israel Abrahams. *Studies in Pharisaism and the Gospels.* Cambridge, Eng.: Cambridge University Press, First Series 1917, Second Series 1924.

W. D. Davies. *Introduction to Pharisaism.* Philadelphia: Fortress, 1967.

Asher Finkel. *The Pharisees and the Teacher of Nazareth.* Leiden: Brill, 1964.

Louis Finkelstein. *The Pharisees.* 2 vols. Philadelphia: Jewish Publication Society of America, 1946.

Leonhard Goppelt. *Jesus, Paul and Judaism.* New York: Nelson, 1964.

R. Travers Herford. *The Pharisees.* London: Allen and Unwin, 1924.

Jakob Jocz. *The Jewish People and Jesus Christ.* London: S.P.C.K., 1949.

[19] Finkel, *op. cit.*, pp. 1-2.

Herbert Loewe, "Pharisaism," *Judaism and Christianity*, ed. W. O. E. Oesterley. London: Sheldon, 1937. Vol. I, pp. 105-190.

T. W. Manson. *The Servant-Messiah*. Cambridge, Eng.: Cambridge University Press, 1953. Pp. 16-35.

G. F. Moore. *Judaism*. 2 vols. Cambridge, Mass.: Harvard University Press, 1946.

A. T. Robertson. *The Pharisees and Jesus*. London: Duckworth, 1920.

A. Lukyn Williams. *The Hebrew-Christian Messiah*. London: S.P.C.K., 1916.

CHAPTER IX

THE CALL AND TRAINING OF THE TWELVE

*"Jesus never wrote on paper; He left no printed book; instead
He wrote his message upon men, and these men were the
apostles."*

—William Barclay

AT THE END OF HIS PUBLIC MINISTRY, JESUS HAD NOTHING TANGIBLE
to leave as a monument of his life work. There was no literature,
nor was there an institution to memorialize him. He had chosen
instead to invest himself in a small group of men. From them
came eventually the literature and the institution of the church.
Looking back from the vantage point of the apostolic age, it is
not difficult to see that the most important work of Christ prior
to his death and resurrection was the selection and training of
the men who would represent him in the world in the coming
days. Significantly, it was to these men that he devoted himself
almost exclusively in the interval between the resurrection and
the ascension, and very largely so in the months prior to his
death.

The strategy of Jesus reveals the value of the principle of
concentration. He came as the gift of God's love to the world;
but in his great prayer, which so faithfully mirrors the practice
of preceding days, he did not pray for the world but for the
men whom the Father had given him (Jn. 17:9). They were
his one great hope of reaching the world.

A striking contrast between Jesus and current Jewish teachers
appears in the way the relationship with disciples was set up.
In the Judaism of the time it was the obligation of the individual

136

to seek out a rabbi to whom he would attach himself for instruction.[1] This may have been the procedure by which John the Baptist gathered his followers. It is favored by the fact that Galileans are noted in his company (Jn. 1), and there is no evidence that John went to Galilee and sought them out. Everything points to the opposite conclusion. These men, out of interest in John and his work, came to him. With Jesus it was different, for he took the initiative in selecting and calling each one of his immediate circle personally (Jn. 6:70). In keeping with this is the singular nature of the tie with which he bound his followers. It was not a philosophical point of view, as with the Greek schools, or the Mosaic law, as in rabbinism. Rather, he bound his disciples to himself.[2]

These disciples were the product of the Lord. They bore his stamp. His summons to them emphasized not their potential fitness for the task but his own creative activity. "Follow me and I will make you become fishers of men" (Mk. 1:17). The same word *make* appears in the account of the appointment of the Twelve, though our English idiom requires some other word to convey the idea (Mk. 3:14, 16). They were not self-made men. We would not have heard of them had not the Master passed their way. "The marvel is not that fishermen of Galilee conquered the world, but that Jesus of Nazareth made them its conquerors. The wonder lies in the making of the men, not in their doings."[3]

THE APPOINTMENT

John's Gospel testifies to a measure of contact between some of these men and Jesus in the very early days of the ministry (Jn. 1:35-51). There is nothing necessarily in conflict with the Synoptic record, since it is wholly natural that Jesus should capitalize on the testimony of John the Baptist to himself by making initial impressions on John's followers that would bear fruit when the definitive call reached them later on. For a time these men returned to their ordinary occupations and were numbered among the ever growing following of the Master. But wisdom dictated that out of this large group of disciples a few should be selected who would share his life and lot, to whom

[1] K. H. Rengstorf, TDNT, IV, 444.
[2] *Ibid.*, p. 447.
[3] A. M. Fairbairn, *Studies in the Life of Christ* (1907), p. 133.

he would seek to impart his vision, and upon whom he would make to rest a measure of his own heavenly authority.

After a night of prayer (Lk. 6:12), indicative of the solemnity of the step about to be taken, he called to himself in a mountainous region those whom he wished, and there set them apart. Our Lord in taking this decisive step consulted not with men but with God. It was a fearful responsibility to launch others upon a vocation the nature of which they could only dimly estimate. Both the glory of it and the cost of it were beyond their ken. But the soundness of the choice is attested by the fact that apart from the special case of Judas no break occurred in the ranks of these men and they proved themselves in the end to be impervious to fear or favor.[4]

If Jesus came to mean everything to his followers, so that they were willing to die for him (Mk. 14:31), it is also true that the Lord became intimately attached to this little company and spoke appreciatively of them (Lk. 22:28; Jn. 17:6). "How much the friendship of His disciples was to Jesus, the whole narrative bears witness. . . . There is an unmistakable note of pathos in His clinging to His disciples, when the natural support of family loyalty is denied Him. They were to Him brother, sister, mother."[5] He called them his friends rather than his servants (Jn. 15:15).[6]

Mark's account discloses a twofold purpose in the ordination (Mk. 3:14). First of all, the Twelve were chosen in order to be *with him*. The simple prepositional phrase suggests such thoughts as association, loyalty, the sharing of the outward circumstances of their common life, and opportunities to learn from him. His own freedom and privacy were on this very account seriously curtailed from this time. He had enlarged his borders, and an enlarged household brings added cares. A second purpose emerges naturally from the first. Jesus had in mind to *send them forth* (the word *apostle* has the same root) with his own authority to do his work, first in a limited way only, then, after his departure from them, as the permanent arrangement for the leadership of the church. In this short statement from Mark's Gospel we have,

4 H. Latham, *Pastor Pastorum* (1910), p. 242.

5 T. B. Kilpatrick in HDCG, I, 290a.

6 This is notably in contrast to the place occupied by the followers of the prophets of the Old Testament; they were servants. See Rengstorf, *op. cit.*, pp. 428-429.

in fact, a miniature of the church—Christ's presence with his people and their responsibility to minister for him.

The number twelve suggests the influence of Hebraic tradition and perhaps warrants the terminology so commonly used today of the church—the new Israel. These chosen few were the nucleus of the new people of God. Their selection and training constitute evidence that the Lord envisioned a church that he would build, contrary to the modern critical assumption that he thought only in terms of a kingdom of power and glory soon to be established. However useful such men might prove in the kingdom, it does not appear that the attention given to them would have been necessary in order to take part in a regime where the personal prestige and authority of the King would be the major factor.

THE PERSONNEL

Concerning most of the apostolic company we have little information. They are scarcely more than names. The same thing is true of the situation in the book of Acts, reminding us that early Christian records were not made to satisfy biographical curiosity. That was left to the postapostolic age. As Schmidt remarks, "It was more important that Jesus had the Twelve with him than that something definite should be known about each of them."[7]

With one exception, the apostles were Galileans. This very fact put a stamp upon them from the beginning. All the prejudice that men of Judea held toward this northern community—due to difference in dialect, difference in occupation, difference in attitude toward pagan life and thought, failure to produce a prophet—meant that these disciples as well as the Master they served were viewed with suspicion. But their greater contacts with Gentiles and presumably greater sympathy toward them helped to fit this company in due time to become witnesses to all men.

Judas, on the other hand, the man of Kerioth, came from Judea. His relation with Jesus probably arose from prior discipleship under John the Baptist. Judea was conservative and exclusive, the center of ecclesiastical control. Its very geography seemed to reflect the spirit of its inhabitants. H. V. Morton says of it, "Judea is

[7] K. L. Schmidt, "The Church," Kittel's *Bible Key Words* (1949), p. 39.

fiercer than anything in Europe—a striped, tigerish country, crouched in the sun, tense with a terrific vitality and sullen and dispassionate with age."[8] From Judea came the traitor.

Our Lord did not choose as his immediate followers farmers who could only with difficulty be weaned away from the soil, or scholars who would be prone to pit their wisdom against his, but men drawn largely from the artisan class, skilled and resourceful, with an eye to practical considerations in whatever they undertook. It should be recalled here that Jesus himself was an artisan, a circumstance that suggests an antecedent affinity with these men. Although they had little formal education, they were by no means lacking in the ability to think and write and speak clearly. The greatness of their Theme brought out the best in them. Had they been more brilliant, we could less readily see through them to the glory of the Lord they served. Their slowness in apprehending the teaching of Christ hardly warrants the assertion that they were "stupid, slow-minded persons."[9] Even Nicodemus, a master teacher in Israel, had some trouble grasping the meaning of Jesus' declarations. Again and again these men, like little children, were left in the lurch by the strange remarks of their leader. But the very literal-mindedness that made them grope for the meaning of his utterances tended to make them faithful reporters of the things they saw and heard. For this the church must ever be grateful. Their very simplicity made them witnesses of the highest caliber.

Let it be said again, these were ordinary men. This very fact enables us to see more clearly what faith in the Lord can do, and so we are encouraged. Had the Twelve been men of extraordinary stature in their intellectual and spiritual development before Jesus called them, we could well question the possibility of a comparable discipleship for ourselves.

Special Features

The group had *leadership*. Although we are not made aware of any organization, and Jesus expressly indicated that to them belonged the equality of brethren (Mt. 23:8), the records give unmistakable prominence to Simon Peter. Named first in all four of the lists of the Twelve, he merited that prominence not on the

8 *In the Steps of the Master* (1934), p. 5.
9 A. B. Bruce, *The Training of the Twelve* (1930), p. 495.

basis of the Lord's prediction in Matthew 16 later read back in such a way as to color the picture of this disciple in the records, but on the basis of his readiness to speak and act before the others did. Perhaps no man ever depended more on trial and error, but scarcely any other could be said to have learned more thereby. To him belonged the leadership in evangelism, for it was his privilege to open the door of faith (Mt. 16:19), first to the Jew on the day of Pentecost, and then to the Gentile in the house of Cornelius. To him belonged also special prominence in the pastoral office, commissioned as he was to strengthen the brethren and to feed the sheep (Lk. 22:32; Jn. 21:15-17).

Some in the circle of apostles were bound by ties of *kinship*. Andrew found a place in this company alongside his brother Peter. James and John made up the other set of brothers. These men seem to have been specially close to the Lord, for on three occasions Peter and the sons of Zebedee were chosen to accompany him (Mk. 5:37; 9:2; 14:33). Andrew is found associated with the other three in their request to Jesus for enlightenment regarding the future (Mk. 13:3). Although Jesus is a divider of men, so that a man's foes are found in his own household, it is not always so. When the ties of faith are added to those of blood, the result is a brotherhood of singular beauty and power.

Friendship also made its contribution to this chosen band. In addition to the intimate relation Peter and John sustained to one another, attested both in the Gospels and in the Acts, we have a broad hint of the same thing for two others, Philip and Nathanael (Jn. 1:45). Although the latter's name does not appear in any list of the Twelve, it is probable that he is to be identified with Bartholomew, whose name follows that of Philip in all the lists found in the Synoptics. These kindred minds found a new sweetness in their friendship as it flowered under the benign influence of the Lord, and a new breadth as they learned to take others to their hearts who, with themselves, had left all to follow him.

More secure than the bond of friendship, which depends upon mutual respect and a certain admiration of human qualities, is that spiritual affinity which men come to share because of their relation to the same Lord. We call it *fellowship*. Both in its obligation, namely, the compulsion to be faithful to the Savior, and in its rewards, the ennobling and glorifying of the human potential through contact with the Master, it surpasses the power of friendship. Whereas friendship may help men to become great, fellowship helps them to become great saints. Two members of the Lord's coterie seemed from their backgrounds to present an almost impossible challenge to the melting and molding process that is essential to oneness in Christ. Matthew the tax-collector had been in the service of Herod Antipas, who was a puppet of the Roman government. Simon the Cananaean (which has nothing to do with Canaanite) was a Zealot, as the term Cananaean denotes, a member of that growing party in Judaism which advocated overthrow of the Roman authority, by violent measures if need be, in order to regain independence. Yet the old prejudices disintegrated under the glow of a common love in the Lord, giving promise of cohesion in the body of Christ down the centuries despite the multiplied diversities and cross-currents among those who would come to him.

Strangely, the apostolic company harbored within itself nevertheless the dark and ugly phenomenon of *traitorship*. Judas did not yield himself to the warmth of the fellowship, though he maintained outward connection with it. Apparently he never came to the place of real faith in the person of Jesus (Jn. 13:10-11), but pinned his hopes on the realization of the messianic kingdom in which Israel would find political salvation and in which he himself would find a place of prominence. Having all the advantages enjoyed by the other disciples, and presumably not behind them in activity when sent out to represent the Master, he remains a warning to all who would substitute outward conformity for inward response to divine grace. Ultimately estrangement from Jesus, coupled with avarice, led him to perpetrate the foul deed that clings to his name like a filthy garment. By yielding to sin he became the dupe of Satan. His remorse could neither eradicate his guilt nor beautify his character.

All efforts to exonerate Judas have failed. The mere fact that he helped to fulfill a divinely ordained event does not suffice to excuse him (Mk. 14:21; cf. Acts 2:23). On the same basis one might as readily argue the innocence of Caiaphas and of the whole Sanhedrin.

Our difficulty is not so much in understanding Judas, enigmatical though he is, but rather in understanding how Jesus, knowing what lurked in the heart of this disciple, could bear with him over the long months when his nefarious purpose was germinating, a purpose that was destined to produce such a bitter harvest.

THE TRAINING

Contact with Jesus brought certain things to this group of men in an incidental way, so as to be almost unconsciously absorbed from him. They must have learned something about the art of meeting people and handling situations as they witnessed their Master threading his way through life with its maze of difficult circumstances occasioned by the public character of his work. Their itinerating activity prepared them for future days when they would go farther afield, in smaller groups or even alone, carrying the gospel message to the ends of the earth.

Having left their various occupations, they were without a means of livelihood. But so was the Master. He had left the carpenter shop behind even as they had left their nets or the counting house. His teaching rebuked them for littleness of faith in the loving care of the heavenly Father (Mt. 6:30). His example taught them to be grateful and content with such things as came to them for their daily provision.

They learned to count on the divine preservation of their lives, so that future dangers would not shake their courage and devitalize their faith. How could they ever forget the lesson of that memorable evening on the lake of Galilee when the sudden squall threatened to engulf their ship and send them to the bottom? They marveled that even wind and wave were subject to his command.

On at least one occasion the Lord thrust these men out to go into the countryside with a ministry modeled closely after his own—healing the sick, casting out demons, proclaiming the glad message of the kingdom of God (Lk. 9:1-6). In coming days they could look back upon this preaching mission and reflect that although the Lord was not with them in person, his power had accompanied them and accomplished great things. Thus were they prepared to labor for him in the long years after he was taken from them.

On the side of more formal training, the disciples profited from the teaching Jesus directed to large groups as well as from that more restricted instruction which he gave them in private. Most certainly the disciples were in the mind of Christ when he pronounced his beatitude upon those who would be persecuted and maligned for his sake (Mt. 5:11). If any were to be thought of as the salt of the earth and the light of the world, this chosen company must have been included.

We read that they came to the Master to request instruction in prayer. John the Baptist had given some help to his own disciples along this line. The particular spur for the request seems to have been furnished, however, by Christ's own example (Lk. 11:1). What ensued was the matchless model prayer with its exaltation of God, its preoccupation with his will, its plea for daily sustenance, its request for the forgiveness of sins committed and for preservation from situations fraught with the danger of further sinning.

More is needed in the shaping of godly men than instruction in righteousness and the introduction to the secrets of prevailing prayer. Sins and infirmities must be exposed and rebuked and corrected. It is significant that the individuals who attained most prominence among the apostles in the early church are singled out for special chastening during the days of his flesh. Concerning Peter, something will be said presently. John the son of Zebedee, whom Christian fancy has somehow pictured as peculiarly free from defect because he was the beloved disciple, appears in quite a different light, at least in the days when he was being molded by the hand of the Savior. This son of thunder had glaring faults, which are no less reprehensible for being so closely linked with his zeal for the Lord he loved. Along with some others who thought that service in Christ's name ought to be limited to the select group to which he belonged, he complained that he had seen someone casting out demons in Jesus' name (Lk. 9:49). But he would like to report now that he had dealt with the situation in summary fashion, telling the offender not to repeat such indiscretion in the future. John was due to receive some of his own medicine. Just because one was not with the apostolic company did not mean he was opposed to them or hostile to their cause. Thus did the Master's lash of rebuke fall upon John's *intolerance*.

Closely connected with this incident in Luke's account is another in which John, together with his brother James, sought reprisal on a certain village of the Samaritans that was unwilling to receive the Lord because he was headed for Jerusalem (Lk. 9:51-56). John proposed that these uncivil folk should be drastically dealt with by calling down fire from heaven in the manner of Elijah the prophet. But the proposal met with no enthusiasm in the Savior, for he rebuked their *vindictiveness* as they moved on together to another village. The same historian has preserved for us the observation that in a later day John with quite a different attitude prayed for Samaritans that they might receive the gift of the Holy Spirit (Acts 8:15).

John was guilty also of unholy *ambition*. The secret desire to have places of distinction and honor on either side of the victorious Son of man could hardly be voiced directly even by spirits as bold as these. But a mother can usually be counted on to do almost anything on behalf of her children, and the wife of Zebedee fell in with their plans (Mt. 20:20-23). The appeal of James and John to Jesus through their mother may have taken into account the fact that she was giving financial support to Jesus and the Twelve (Mt. 27:56). Jesus repudiated any such pressure. When he made answer, he did so publicly before the whole company, for he knew that similar desires lurked in other hearts as well. The wave of indignation toward John and his brother that swept over the disciples was a poor disguise. Their own hearts had been revealed by the Master's rebuke.

The lesson that needed to be inculcated at this point was humility, a willingness to take the lowest place if only it meant an opportunity for service. Jesus could do no more effective thing than to remind his followers that the motivation of his mission was to minister rather than to be served (Mk. 10:45). Not long before, he brought confusion to the faces of his disciples by inquiring about the subject of their conversation as they walked along and disputed one with another, vying among themselves as one after another presented his claim to be the greatest (Mk. 9:33-34). What a miserable occupation for disciples of the lowly Son of man! To shame them into silence and penitence, Jesus set a child in the midst. Matthew's account is the most complete and may have been drawn up from recollection of more than one such incident (Mt. 18:1-6). It is necessary, said Jesus, to become as little children in order to enter the kingdom. In his explanation of this, Bruce combines two elements without being aware, perhaps, of so doing. The unpretentiousness of the child is made the special point of our Lord's teaching, but he goes on to include the possession of a democratic spirit.[10] A child will play with others no matter how different may be the station in life of their parents. Now the question is, do these two things belong together? About the democracy of most children there is little doubt; but there is good ground for questioning their lack of a pretentious spirit, at least in our western culture. They are often more self-assertive

---

10 *Ibid.*, p. 201.

than their elders. For this reason no great number of them can play together without supervision. Warfield finds the point of our Lord's illustration to lie not in the attitude of the child but in his condition. As an infant he enters into life helpless, having nothing. So must it be concerning entrance into the life of the kingdom.[11] The disciples were guilty of thinking of their place in the kingdom in terms of reward, and of taking their place in the kingdom as a matter of course rather than as a matter of grace. Relation to Jesus of Nazareth ought never be viewed as an opportunity for advancement. It is a call to grateful, humble service.

This lesson was so hard to learn that it required still another demonstration, this time in the upper room, where the one who had come from God and was soon to return laid aside his garments, took a towel and a basin of water, and proceeded to wash the disciples' feet, to their great chagrin and shame. When did such lofty dignity ever combine with such lowly labor? More than feet were washed that night. Hearts as well were held in the Master's hands and were cleansed.

It is not difficult to see the necessity for the Savior's insistence that the disciples learn well the lesson of humility. They could enter successfully into the proclamation of his mission to the world and be faithful to that witness only if they themselves possessed the mind of Christ.

Included in their training was instruction about the demands involved in discipleship. Instead of confronting these men at the time of their call with a formidable list of conditions they must meet in order to serve under him, Jesus sought in them a willingness to follow him. With adequate allegiance and dedication, they could be trusted to respond when the full implications of their position were disclosed. Luke gives a convenient summary of the conditions of discipleship (Lk. 14:26, 27, 33). One must "hate" his family, bear his own cross, and renounce all his possessions. These statements were made in the presence of a great multitude and were calculated to impress would-be followers of the Master with the seriousness of such a calling. The situation of Gideon is roughly parallel. Mere numbers mean little. What is needed is a devoted, intelligent following. The severity of the demands of Jesus in the area of discipleship might suggest that he is intent on "using" his followers, tyrannizing them for his own ends; but no evidence for any such motive is forthcoming. Rather,

11 B. B. Warfield, "Children," HDCG, I, 303b.

he seeks to place them in the same servant relationship he himself has assumed, fully committed to the will of the Father.

Peter affirmed that he and the others had left what belonged to them in order to follow their Lord (Lk. 18:28). The expression he used (ta idia) is sufficiently broad to include both family and goods. But what of that third condition of discipleship, the bearing of the cross? The subject was at once unwelcome and obscure. Their leader had left all in the service of God, turning his back on both family and possessions. So they had his example to follow. But the cross was still future. At present it was an idea at best, not yet something confronting them in all the terrifying realism of Calvary. Did it mean martyrdom for them, or was its implication to be sought in death to self no matter what the outward circumstances of life might be?

Obviously some light was needed on this question. Finding a place of detachment and quiet at Caesarea Philippi, our Lord put the matter squarely before the disciples.[12] For him the cross was literal and inescapable. He must go to Jerusalem and suffer many things from the leaders of the Jews, culminating in his death, this to be followed by resurrection on the third day (Mt. 16:21). Matthew's language—"from that time Jesus began to show his disciples"—indicates that the gist of the teaching was repeated on other occasions (cf. Mk. 9:31; 10:33, 45). Since the message of the gospel that would be entrusted to them for proclamation contained at its very center the death and resurrection of the Savior, these facts, despite their present obscurity, must be kept before the minds of those who would be his ambassadors.

Peter's reaction to the announcement was rapid and negative. Flushed with gratification over the Lord's commendation for his statement about his person, this disciple impulsively undertook to dissuade Jesus from entertaining such thoughts about his future. They were unnecessary thoughts anyway. How could the Messiah, the Son of God, come to the place of being killed by his own nation over which he was the divinely appointed sovereign?

Jesus' rejoinder was uncommonly severe. Repudiating Peter's statement by turning his back on him and labeling him "Satan," he pronounced his foremost disciple a hindrance to him. Peter's thoughts and desires were those of men, not of God (Mt. 16:23).

12 Not only this subject but also the teaching on the Fatherhood of God was imparted to the Twelve rather than to the public. See T. W. Manson, *The Teaching of Jesus* (1939), p. 98, and J. Jeremias, *The Central Message of the New Testament* (1965), p. 49.

The best of men can at times be in league with the devil and opposed to God. Having fought and won this battle with Satan when he renounced worldly dominion on Satan's terms, Jesus does not propose to lose it at the insistence of a misguided disciple.

But now the old demand of cross-bearing comes forward again, etched in clearer and sterner lines. The disciple is not above his Master. The cross is for him as well. "If any man would come after me, let him deny himself and take up his cross and follow me" (Mt. 16:24). The Savior is headed for Jerusalem and death. Who will follow him? It was a crisis moment when the whole issue of discipleship had to be reviewed afresh in the light of this new development. Suffering and death? These men had not counted on such a prospect when they left all to follow Jesus of Nazareth. They are stunned, but they do not desert. The next step in their training will show them that the suffering of the Messiah is indeed in the will of God, and it will yield a glory greater than any they have conceived.

NOTE ON THE WORD "DISCIPLE"

Students of the New Testament are apt to be confused concerning the meaning of this word. Does it connote the same thing as believer, or does it point to the element of sacrifice as indispensable to the follower of Christ, so that belief is inadequate unless accompanied by devotion actively demonstrated?

The word is of Latin derivation, but the meaning is the same as in the Greek, denoting a learner, a pupil.

In the Gospels it designates both the large group of people who had interest in Jesus as a teacher and worker of miracles and that smaller group who severed certain ties in order to attend him and learn of him.

The book of Acts has the word some thirty times, always in the sense of a member of the Christian community. In no case is there anything to indicate sacrifice or suffering as the condition for bearing this cognomen. In the one instance where the verb form is used, in Acts 14:21, it denotes the making of converts.

Biblical usage, then, seems to suggest that the term may be applied both to a believer, a convert to Christianity, and to one who strives to measure up to the demands of Jesus Christ in terms of sacrificial devotion.

BIBLIOGRAPHY

A. B. Bruce. *The Training of the Twelve.* New York: Richard C. Smith, 3rd edition, 1930.

A. M. Fairbairn. *Studies in the Life of Christ.* London: Hodder and Stoughton, 14th edition, 1907. Pp. 130-148.

A. E. Garvie. *Studies in the Inner Life of Jesus.* New York: Armstrong, n.d. Pp. 236-252.

R. Newton Flew. *Jesus and His Church.* London: Epworth, 1938. Pp. 35-42.

Henry Latham. *Pastor Pastorum.* Cambridge, Eng.: Deighton Bell, 1910.

Robert P. Meye. *Jesus and the Twelve.* Grand Rapids: Eerdmans, 1968.

K. H. Rengstorf, "Mathētēs," TDNT, Vol. IV, pp. 415-461.

A. T. Robertson. *Epochs in the Life of Jesus.* New York: Scribners, 1920. Pp. 98-119.

Eduard Schweizer. *Lordship and Discipleship.* London: SCM, 1960.

David Smith. *The Days of His Flesh.* New York: Doran, n.d. Pp. 145-175.

James Stalker. *Imago Christi.* New York: Hodder and Stoughton, 1889. Pp. 263-280.

Chapter X

THE TRANSFIGURATION

"The Transfiguration is at once the commentator's paradise and his despair."

—G. B. Caird

"God, who commanded the light to shine out of darkness, hath shined in our hearts, to give the light of the knowledge of the glory of God in the face of Jesus Christ."

—The Apostle Paul (KJV)

FROM THE SYNOPTIC ACCOUNTS IT IS APPARENT THAT A CLOSE CON-nection exists between the developments at Caesarea Philippi and the transfiguration scene. Nothing intervenes in the record except some teaching on discipleship, which grows naturally out of the discussion between Jesus and the Twelve. Further, all three of the Synoptics have a time notice here that looks back to Caesarea Philippi. Matthew and Mark make it a six-day interval (Mt. 17:1; Mk. 9:2). Luke has "about eight days" (Lk. 9:28), which probably indicates that he is counting the days on which the two episodes occurred as well as the actual interval between them. This inclusive method of reckoning is not uncommon in the Scriptures.

The gap of approximately a week, with nothing inserted into it, by its very silence speaks loudly of the crushing effect of Jesus' pronouncements about his forthcoming death. To the disciples his words meant the dashing of the hopes they had built up around their concept of Messiahship. They could not adjust to a mission that included death, and for this very reason their minds were closed to teaching on resurrection such as Jesus had given. The proof of this lies close at hand, for when the Savior was coming down from the mountain a week later and admonished the three disciples to say nothing about what they had seen until the Son of man was risen from the dead, they wondered among themselves what the rising from the dead could mean (Mk. 9:9-10).

Before moving on to the transfiguration it is well to try to recapture the impact of the Caesarea Philippi incident. The topic of discussion was the identity of Jesus. "Who do men say that I am?" In kindness the disciples withheld the scurrilous things the Pharisees were darkly hinting, confining themselves to reports that he was John the Baptist, Elijah, Jeremiah, or one of the prophets. All these men had something in common: they belonged to the prophetic order. Certain features about Jesus seemed to put him in the same category. His words and works could be compared favorably with those of the leading prophets of Israel. Possibly something was being whispered among the people about his powers of analysis and penetration, such as his knowledge of Nathanael prior to their meeting (Jn. 1:47-48). He seemed to know what was in man (Jn. 2:25), much as Elisha could visualize his servant Gehazi's mission and confront him with his misdeed when he returned to stand in his presence (II Kings 5:19-27). Everyone knew of his denunciations of the evils of the time. Then there were those occasional words of prediction that dropped from his lips in true prophetic fashion.

But to Jesus the answers passed on by the disciples were not satisfying. After all, John the Baptist, the last of the prophetic order (Lk. 16:16), had recognized a qualitative difference between Jesus and himself (Mt. 3:14). So the Master pressed his disciples to supply their own answer to the question about his identity (but without putting words into their mouths). He was not interested in grooming reporters; he was preparing witnesses. He wanted men who had convictions about him that were unshakable. Judging from the narrative, there was no rush to respond, no chorus of replies. It is much easier to relate what others say about Jesus than to make a personal confession. Peter managed it and drew the Lord's commendation. This dual statement—the Christ and the Son of the living God—came from Peter, to be sure; but in the last analysis it was a revelation of the Father. The secret of the Lord is with them that fear him. Peter was permitted to know something that was hidden from Herod, from Pilate, and from a multitude besides.

The second phase of events on that day of conference stands

in sharp contrast except for the fact that it included Jesus and Peter. Once more the Master initiated the conversation and the disciple responded, but now the objective of the messianic mission is in the foreground. Peter protested violently. As he saw it, death was not at all befitting for God's anointed, and it was so unnecessary. But as Jesus explained, the man who had so recently been the vehicle of divine revelation was demonstrating by his protest against the cross that he was thinking now the thoughts of men. For the moment he was on the ground of the unregenerate. He could have no part with the Lord if he was prepared to reject the cross that his leader was ready to endure in the will of God. The man who was so right about the person of Christ was thoroughly wrong about his work. A disciple can be taught of God in one matter and yet by holding to preconceptions can be wrong in another.

The combined impact of the teaching about the cross and the rebuke administered to Peter was a heavy blow to the apostolic company. They were shocked, dazed, and utterly confused. It was to meet their need that Jesus, a few days later, was transfigured. This is made clear by the statement in Matthew 17:2 that Jesus was transfigured *before them* (Peter, James, and John). Further, both Matthew and Luke state that Moses and Elijah appeared to *them* (the disciples), despite the fact that these two spoke only with Jesus. Again, the heavenly voice was addressed to the disciples—"this is my Son." What happened on the mount was calculated to clarify something that must have been obscure up to that time. In speaking of what lay before him at Jerusalem, Jesus had not mentioned the name of God, had not cited a divine purpose or command. His only hint lay in the affirmation that he *must* go to Jerusalem. The disciples could have understood the saying to mean that, when he confronted this stronghold of Judaism, he would be overwhelmed by man and would go down to defeat at their hands. On the mount the three would come to know that their Master was ready for glory and that the death that was coming was purely voluntary, something he would accomplish, not something he would have to accept because of human opposition.

We are asserting that the transfiguration occurred for the sake of the disciples. Is it possible to affirm that it was for Christ's benefit? Some have thought that he needed it for his encouragement, seeing that he was faced with so much public opposition and with such dullness of comprehension on the part of his closest followers. But the narrative gives no hint of hesitation or weakness or discouragement on his part.

Campbell Morgan maintains that the transfiguration signified the attainment of perfection in the manhood of the Master, giving him the right of entrance into heaven. "Here at last, that humanity, perfect in creation, perfect through probation, was perfected in glory."[1] Again, "With regard to His mission, the transfiguration was the prelude to His death. It was the crowning of the first part of His mission, that of realizing perfect life."[2] The event could then be linked with the baptism, which Morgan likewise treats as an approval of the course of Jesus' life up to that time. It is significant for such a view that the divine voice is mentioned in both incidents. Undoubtedly the transfiguration meant much to Jesus, but it is nevertheless probable, from the various factors already noted, that it was chiefly an educative instrument for the benefit of the disciples. They did not need to be convinced of the divine sonship of Jesus. Peter had confessed that, and there is no indication of dissent. The need was for light on the mission of their Master, not on his person.

It may appear strange, in view of this need, that on the mount the most obvious thing was the revelation of the glory, with the clarification of Jesus' mission confined to conversation between him and two figures out of the past. But it should be borne in mind that the revelation of the glory was simply to the sight of the three disciples and was not interpreted, whereas the suffering aspect of the mission was spelled out in revelation of word. So the relevance to the Caesarea Philippi incident and to the need of the disciples is preserved.

THE SETTING

Information is scanty about the place. Matthew and Mark simply speak of it as a high mountain.[3] Mount Hermon answers well to this description and it has the advantage of being in the general region of Caesarea Philippi. A possible drawback is the mention of the presence of scribes at the healing of the epileptic

---

[1] *Crises of the Christ* (1936) , p. 229.

[2] *Ibid.*, p. 231.

[3] This in itself is calculated to arrest the attention of the alert reader, for an elevated place is often the scene of divine revelation, such as Sinai, Carmel, Zion, and the Mount of the Sermon (Mt. 5–7) .

boy (Mk. 9:14). But this could have occurred near Caesarea
Philippi rather than at the base of the mountain. The narrative
gives no help at this point. Another possible site with some tradition behind it is Mount Tabor, on the northern edge of the
plain of Esdraelon. But it could hardly be called a high mountain.
Furthermore, one would expect the Gospel writers to indicate
a journey from Caesarea Philippi to this area if this was indeed
the chosen spot.

Our sources do not say whether the transfiguration took place
during the day or at night, but several factors favor the idea
that it was a nocturnal scene. The sleep of the disciples points
in this direction, as does Luke's note that Jesus went to pray.
We know from other notices in the Gospels that he usually withdrew for prayer in the night seasons. Then there is the consideration that the descent from the mountain came on the following
day (Lk. 9:37).

As to the burden of Jesus' prayer on the mount, one can only
surmise. The need of steady purpose and strength to carry out
the divine commission laid upon him must have been present,
as well as a concern that the disciples would be enlightened
about the goal of his mission and accept it cordially. These
themes would naturally be present; neither excludes the other.

THE TRANSFORMATION

Matthew and Mark say that Jesus was transfigured, the passive
form of the verb serving to emphasize that what he experienced
was something granted to him by God the Father. Luke is content to say that the appearance of his countenance was altered.[4]
The mysterious change was not from without, as though some
giant spotlight became focused on him, but from within. His
countenance was affected first, then his garments. The "form of
God," which had been veiled through incarnation, was permitted
for this little while to shine forth, as it was seen by Saul of
Tarsus on the road to Damascus (Acts 9:3) and by the seer of
Patmos (Rev. I:16). What appealed to the sight of men as light
expressed the inward perfection that could be described in terms
of fullness of grace and truth (Jn. 1:14). We read that Satan
tries to transform himself into an angel of light, but there is

4 It may be that Luke avoided the technical word for the sake of his Gentile
readers, who might give it a pagan association such as the process whereby a
man sought to be absorbed into deity, as in certain mystery religions.

no correspondence between the outward guise he assumes for the purpose of beguiling the unwary and the inner diabolical reality (II Cor. 11:14). It is fitting that the word "transform" in this instance is not the same at all as the term used of Jesus.

MOSES AND ELIJAH

Since these two figures from the past could not manifest the form of God, their participation in glory on this occasion (Lk. 9:31) should probably be understood as due to the heavenly state of which they had been partakers for some time. Of all the men of former ages these two alone had experienced a revelation from God in which he caused a manifestation of himself to pass before them (Ex. 33:17-23; I Kings 19:9-13), and at the same place (Horeb, i.e. Sinai). Now they are on holier ground, in the presence of the incarnate glory. The prayer of Moses— "show me thy glory"—has its answer, and his longing is realized. Significantly, these two are not so preoccupied with the glory before them as to be lost in the wonder of that alone. They welcome the opportunity to enter into conversation with Jesus about something quite different, namely, the decease he was going to accomplish at Jerusalem (Lk. 9:31). It is important to notice how the place of death is spelled out, an obvious point of contact with the Caesarea Philippi narrative (Mt. 16:21).

Is there some special reason why these two and not others (such as Enoch, for example) should be chosen for this confrontation with the Savior? Many have concluded that they stand here in a representative role, Moses epitomizing the law and Elijah the prophets. If so, the Gospels may be said to testify to the truth proclaimed by Paul, that Christ died for our sins according to the Scriptures (I Cor. 15:3). "The law and the prophets" could be a convenient way of summing up the testimony of the Old Testament (Acts 26:22). This may well be a true explanation, even though the Markan account mentions Elijah before Moses and even though Elijah was not a writing prophet.[5] But there is surely a personal as well as an official reason for the presence of these men. Moses the lawgiver was also the lawbreaker. He needed that forthcoming death on Calvary as much as anyone else. Elijah, in the very heyday of his success as a prophet, turned and ran before the threats of Jezebel. His for-

[5] The mention of Elijah disposes of the popular notion that Jesus might be Elijah (Mk. 8:28).

giveness could not be final until that sacrifice had been made on the cross by the Son of man.

Further, these two had much in common with Jesus of Nazareth. Moses performed signs and wonders before Israel in the name of the Lord, but to little avail. The people were stubborn in their unbelief and failed to enter the promised land because of it. Jesus had a similar reception for his mighty works. And as Moses interceded for Israel in the midst of failure and threatened judgment, being willing to be cut off himself if they could be spared, so Jesus wept in compassion over Jerusalem. Elijah was a lonely prophet, even when surrounded by the throngs on Mount Carmel. Jesus, too, was in many ways a lonely figure, despite his popular following. He prayed alone, suffered alone, and died alone. The two had something in common respecting the close of their ministries. Elijah was supernaturally taken up for a glorious reception into heaven, as though anticipating the ascension of the Savior into glory.[6] As Elijah was able to bestow the power of his spirit on Elisha, so did the ascended Lord pour out his Spirit on his disciples.[7]

We are given no information as to how the disciples recognized Moses and Elijah, whether through hearing Jesus call their names or getting the identification from him afterward. It is even possible that they had a general mental picture of what the two men would look like from the data of the Old Testament. Since they had been disciples of John the Baptist, whose appearance seems to have been deliberately fashioned in imitation of Elijah, this would likely be of assistance in identifying one of the pair.

From Mark and Matthew comes the information that Jesus talked with the two men. Luke goes further and indicates the subject of the conversation. They discussed Jesus' forthcoming death at Jerusalem (Lk. 9:31), the very theme that had caused so much consternation at Caesarea Philippi. But as though to emphasize the unique character of this death, it is called an *exodus*. Granted that this could mean simply the end of life (it is so used in *Wisdom* 7:6, "For all men have one entrance into

---

6 Moses, too, was thought of as taken up. Note the title of the extra-canonical work, *The Assumption of Moses*.

7 It is significant that the names of Moses and Elijah appear together at the close of the Old Testament (Mal. 4:4-5). They may be in view also in Rev. 11:4-6. In Jewish eschatological thought they were combined. See W. C. Allen, *The Gospel According to St. Matthew* (ICC), p. 184.

life and a like exit," and in II Peter 1:15), yet there are two factors that suggest a deeper meaning. One is the statement that Jesus would *accomplish* this exodus, which is rather strange language for such an ordinary experience as death. The other is the fact that shortly after this, on the way down the mountain, Jesus spoke of his resurrection (Mk. 9:9). So it may well be that the word *exodus* in this setting is designed to point to death as a victorious event, despite its appearance of weakness and defeat, holding in itself the prospect of glorious resurrection. Israel's exodus was associated with victory over enemies, and was a step on the road to the fulfillment of God's promise to his people to bring them into the inheritance of their fathers. The presence of Moses at this scene on the mount may be added reason, in view of his role in the historic exodus from Egypt, for accepting this extension of meaning in the present instance.

Possibly it was the combination of the glory light and the sound of voices that caused the disciples to stir out of their sleep. Their weariness was forgotten in the sense of excitement that gripped them now. What strange things they were seeing and hearing! But it is uncertain that the conversation made the desired impact on them, in view of the fascination of the scene itself. The full import probably did not dawn on them for some time. Yet the fact that such dignitaries as Moses and Elijah were talking with the Master about the very thing that had been a stumbling block to them should have been food for thought.

PETER'S REMARK

Quick to react to this extraordinary situation, Peter sought to express his feelings. "Master, it is well that we are here; let us make three booths, one for you and one for Moses and one for Elijah" (Mk. 9:5). Two of the Evangelists add the comment that he did not know what he was saying. It was a spontaneous outburst. Yet there must have been something in his mind to call forth this particular statement rather than one of an entirely different kind. Perhaps Peter was under the impression that heavenly visitors might linger for some time, in which case a shelter should be provided for them as well as for the Lord. But in that case no attention is paid to a shelter for the disciples. It has been suggested that the mention of Jerusalem could have brought to Peter's mind the ominous prophecy of Jesus made a few days earlier about his death in that city. The offer to construct booths could reflect a determination on Peter's part to keep the Lord there, far from Jerusalem, so as to forestall, if possible, such a dreaded event.

More fruitful is the line of thought that underscores the word "booth" (it can also be rendered "tent"). Israel Abrahams comments, "The rabbinic parallels, often quoted in illustration of the 'tabernacles' of the transfiguration scene, are also eschatological and messianic."[8] The combination of the glory light, the appearance of the two distinguished figures from the past, and his own aspirations for Jesus as the Messiah of Israel could have led Peter, in a burst of enthusiasm, to declare by his comment that the setting up of the kingdom could not long be delayed. There is even a possibility that the feast of tabernacles (booths) was then being celebrated in Jerusalem. As that festival drew to a close, the messianic aspect of it, as distinct from its function as a memorial of Israel's sojourning in the wilderness (Lev. 23:42-43), was magnified. Recall how Jesus capitalized on this aspect when he attended the feast the year before (Jn. 7:37). He had been reluctant to go up to Jerusalem on that occasion when people were looking for him to declare himself as Messiah on their terms. It may be that Peter was calling for a celebration of the feast in just such a fashion as the multitude. Pious Jews were known to erect their booths even when they were far removed from Jerusalem and could not attend in person.[9] If this be the right understanding of the situation, then Peter had not yet learned to pattern his thinking in terms of Jesus' teaching at Caesarea Philippi. By his remark he made it apparent that he was not reacting to the mystery of the passion but only to the extraordinary spectacle he had seen.

THE CLOUD AND THE VOICE

As though in answer to Peter (for according to two of the Evangelists he was yet speaking), a cloud appeared and overshadowed the company, and a voice was heard from the cloud acclaiming Jesus as God's beloved Son and commanding the disciples as a group to listen to him. While it is true that on various occasions in the Old Testament the overshadowing was intended to spell out the truth of divine protection and care of the people

[8] *Studies in Pharisaism and the Gospels*, Second Series (1925), p. 52. Cf. Zech. 14:16.

[9] Heinrich Baltensweiler, *Die Verklärung Jesu* (1959), p. 43.

of God,[10] this is not the only meaning of the cloud, especially when accompanied by a voice attributed to God. Sometimes rebuke is conveyed, as in Numbers 14:10-12. God had already come to dwell with his people in the person of the incarnate Son (Jn. 1:14), but it was not yet the season for the eschatological dwelling.

Clearly Peter was being subjected to censure. What was wrong? In case he was thinking in terms of memorializing the vision of glory by the erection of booths as shrines, then he should realize that the inspiration ought not to be localized but carried in the heart wherever one goes. The vision was intended to inform and guide and energize, not to stagnate into a cultic observance. Further, the language of the disciple was distressingly misleading on the theological side. Whether he realized it or not, Peter was ostensibly putting Jesus on the same plane with these Old Testament servants of God ("one for you and one for Moses and one for Elijah"). That will not do. God spoke in the past to the fathers through the prophets, but now he has spoken through a *Son*. The difference must be understood and respected. Jesus is a prophet but more than a prophet.

Peter seems to have felt that the radiance on the countenance of the Savior was prophetic of the promised glory of the coming and kingdom of Messiah. This is supported by II Peter 1:16ff. While the glory could be interpreted in this way, it ought not to be put in the foreground so as to eclipse the importance of the exodus at Jerusalem. According to the conversation between Jesus and the two Old Testament figures, another feast must intervene before the final enactment of the feast of tabernacles. Christ, our Passover, to use Paul's term, must first offer himself in death. His victorious bearing of the cross will guarantee the final glory.

The import of the heavenly voice is along this same line. It bade Peter and his companions hear the Son—to hear him, that is, in the sense of heeding him. Peter had proposed building booths on the basis of a revelation of glory. Jesus had announced the building of a church based on a revelation of suffering and sacrifice. Peter had disputed with Jesus only a few days before. Now he is ranting thoughtlessly because he has caught a glimpse of glory that has appealed to him as the teaching about the cross did not. What he needs is to heed the word of his Master. Ap-

[10] David Daube, *The New Testament and Rabbinic Judaism* (1956), pp. 30-31.

parently Moses and Elijah received it and were engrossed in it. Why not the disciple and his fellows? Other revelations of the cross will come. Let these men be sure that they do not close their minds to the teaching. "Listen to him." This command comes with special force, due to its apparently close connection with the prediction given through Moses of the coming of a prophet to whom Israel must hearken (Deut. 18:15). As though to dramatize its fulfillment, Moses is withdrawn from the scene, so that the disciples see no man save Jesus.

The Command to Keep Silence

All the Synoptics make some allusion to this, whether to note the fact that the three disciples did not communicate to others what they had seen or to stress the basis for this restraint in the command of Jesus that nothing should be said until after his resurrection (Mk. 9:9). A similar prohibition was laid on the disciples after Peter's confession (Mk. 8:30), which seems to mean that his followers were not to herald him as the Messiah. Noting these and other cases, such as the silencing of demons and the insistence that some of the beneficiaries of Jesus' healings were not to make known what he had done for them, Wilhelm Wrede saw in this pattern of prohibition what he called the messianic secret.[11] He contended that the early church, when it became convinced after the resurrection that Jesus was the Messiah, felt the embarrassment that its own tradition of the public ministry of Jesus did not contain any clear indication that Jesus felt or asserted a messianic claim. So it proceeded to inject into the gospel story a series of prohibitions against declaring his Messiahship, in the hope that this would serve to explain why his messianic status had not been held among Jesus' followers prior to the resurrection. This strain is strongest in Mark's Gospel.

No doubt the theory exhibits considerable critical ingenuity, but it is not convincing. Are we really to suppose that the resurrection of Jesus, or belief in his resurrection, was capable in itself of creating the conviction that he was the Messiah? Did the people who believed that John the Baptist had been raised from the dead (Mk. 6:14) conclude that for this reason he must be the Messiah? We have no intimation that this was so. If the

---

11 *Das Messiasgeheimnis in den Evangelien* (1901).

early Christians developed a view of Jesus that included his Messiahship when as a matter of fact they had been given no reason to hold this view by their contact with him prior to the resurrection, then they were guilty of holding a different conception of their Master than he held of himself.

The most satisfactory solution of the riddle of the messianic secret lies in the recognition that Jesus could not allow the impression to get abroad that he was the Messiah because the popular notion of the Messiah was utterly different from that which he adopted for himself. He refused to pose as a political leader who could be expected to lead the nation to freedom and to a restoration of Israel's glory. His warning to the three not to disclose what they had witnessed on the mount reflects his awareness that if the recital of the glory of that scene were permitted, it would only encourage this false expectation regarding his mission and would blind his followers to the necessity of his death on the cross. This is reason enough for the private character of the transfiguration scene.[12]

HISTORICITY OF THE TRANSFIGURATION

Because nothing similar happened to Jesus at any time during his earthly career and because such a thing is foreign to human experience, the transfiguration as event has been called into question. Actually the solitary occurrence tends to accredit it. If other occasions were introduced, the suspicion would naturally arise that they were literary creations designed to magnify the person of Jesus.

It should be noted that all three Synoptics include the event. John does not, for his purpose seems to have been to include for the most part material that was not in the other Gospels. He pictures the glory of Christ in other than physical terms and as continuing as a permanent feature rather than breaking forth in a single episode. The eye of faith was required to apprehend this inner glory (Jn. 1:14).

Not only do all the Synoptics include the transfiguration; they all place it at a most strategic point in the record, making it a turning point in the ministry, so that everything that comes after it bears directly or indirectly on the conclusion of Jesus' earthly

---

12 Eugene Dąbrowski, *La Transfiguration de Jésus* (1939), p. 165.

course at Jerusalem. Without this record the narrative would be impoverished. It would lack cohesion.

A further witness to the transfiguration is to be found in II Peter 1:16ff., where the elements of place (holy mount), observers (we . . . eyewitnesses), the transfiguration itself (glory), and the voice of the Father testifying to his beloved Son are included. No mention is made of Moses and Elijah.

Yet it must be granted that the word "vision" occurs within the sacred record itself (Mt. 17:9), necessitating an examination of the possibility that something other than an external event is intended. The notion of a subjective vision can be dismissed, for it is wholly improbable that three men would have the same vision, self-induced, at the same time and place, and without any adequate explanation of what could have caused it.

The same word for *vision* is used at times in the book of Acts as the means whereby divine revelation was given to one of God's servants. A case in point is the experience of Peter on the housetop at Joppa (Acts 10:17). Another is the experience of Cornelius a short time before (Acts 10:3). It is further said that Peter was in an ecstatic state or trance (Acts 10:10), an item that does not appear in the accounts of the transfiguration. The conveyance of information through vision did not detract from its reality, and the experience did not lead to doubt but rather to compliance with that which was revealed. So nothing essential would be sacrificed if the transfiguration must be regarded as a vision given by God for the enlightenment of the servants of Christ. A final verdict on this question is difficult. Since the scene on the mount was witnessed *after* awakening from a heavy sleep, a presumption is created that the scene affected the disciples as a normal sensory experience rather than as something ecstatic.

A common method of treating the transfiguration in critical circles today is to regard it as a rewritten story of the post-resurrection ministry that has been read back into the pre-cross ministry of Jesus. It is thought that on this basis an adequate explanation can be given for the description of our Lord in terms of glory. C. H. Dodd probed this theory and concluded that there are strong reasons for rejecting it.[13] (1) The resurrection appearances took place against the background of separation. They were times of reunion. There is no suggestion of this in

13 *Studies in the Gospels* (1955), ed. D. E. Nineham, p. 25.

the transfiguration episode. (2) In the appearances Jesus always converses with the disciples, whereas in the transfiguration he is not represented as speaking to them at all. (3) Nothing in the resurrection appearances answers to the divine voice accrediting the Son. (4) In the appearances Christ suddenly shows himself, alone, to his followers, whereas in the transfiguration Moses and Elijah appear before the disciples. Jesus has been there all along. (5) There is no parallel in the appearances to the visible, luminous glory that characterizes the transfiguration and is so central to it.

Several items, the presence of Moses and Elijah, the cloud, and the allusion to the three tabernacles, have no place in the accounts of the resurrection appearances.

There are those who confidently label the transfiguration as myth because it presents Jesus in a guise that exceeds the category of the human. This terminology might be warranted, were it not for the fact that, even in situations where there is no aura of the supernatural in the trappings of the narrative, nevertheless Jesus shines forth from the narrative as one who, with all his humanness, exceeds the bounds of the human as we know it. The logic of the situation is to write "myth" over the whole of this unique life, but by doing so we would banish him from the arena of history and of relevance to our human needs. Few are willing to pay that price.

MEANING OF THE TRANSFIGURATION

What was this event intended to convey? It is reasonable to assume that the last reported utterance of our Lord prior to going up into the mount can be used to throw light on this question. He indicated that some were standing there who would not taste death before seeing the kingdom of God come with power (Mk. 9:1). The saying is admittedly difficult, but it seems to suggest that the transfiguration was intended as a foregleam of the glory of the Son of man as he would be in his consummated kingdom. This eschatological understanding of the event is sustained by II Peter 1:16ff., and it answers well as a corollary to the suffering of the Messiah that was discussed on the mount (Lk. 9:31; cf. Lk. 24:26; I Pet. 1:11). The glory in anticipation was designed to offset the perplexity and pain that the announcement of the passion had brought to the minds of the disciples.

Doubtless there are many additional values, for the transfiguration entwines itself so readily and so deeply into the texture of other phases of the career of Jesus in addition to death and resurrection—such as the baptism, the temptation, and the Gethsemane experience. Something of the vista that it opens to the gaze of the church is expressed by A. M. Ramsey:

> It stands as a gateway to the saving events of the Gospel, and is as a mirror in which the Christian mystery is seen in its unity. Here we perceive that the living and the dead are one in Christ, that the old covenant and the new are inseparable, that the Cross and the glory are of one, that the age to come is already here, that our human nature has a destiny of glory, that in Christ the final word is uttered and in Him alone the Father is well pleased. Here the diverse elements in the theology of the New Testament meet.[14]

In what way did the transfiguration leave its mark on the Son of man? Instead of developing a martyr-mystic complex as a result of the blend of Caesarea Philippi and the experience on the mount, Jesus continued to minister to the public much as he had been doing, and to his disciples even more than he had been doing, but in a mood of greater solemnity. He set his face to go up to Jerusalem (Lk. 9:53). It was a lonely path, for his disciples, including the three, followed him at a distance, afraid (Mk. 10:32).

BIBLIOGRAPHY

Heinrich Baltensweiler. *Die Verklärung Jesu.* Zürich: Zwingli, 1959.

G. H. Boobyer. *St. Mark and the Transfiguration Story.* Edinburgh: T. & T. Clark, 1942.

Joseph Blinzler. *Die neutestamentlichen Berichte über die Verklärung Jesu.* Münster: Aschendorff, 1937.

Eugene Dabrowski. *La Transfiguration de Jésus.* Rome: Institut Biblique Pontifical, 1939.

G. Campbell Morgan. *The Crises of the Christ.* New York: Revell, 1936.

A. M. Ramsey. *The Glory of God and the Transfiguration of Christ.* London: Longmans, Green, 1949.

Harald Riesenfeld. *Jésus Transfiguré.* Copenhagen: Ejnar Munksgaard, 1947.

14 *The Glory of God and the Transfiguration of Christ* (1949), p. 144.

CHAPTER XI

THE TRIUMPHAL ENTRY AND THE CLEANSING OF THE TEMPLE

"Something greater than the temple is here."
—Matthew 12:6

IN A STUDY THAT CONFINES ITSELF TO THE HIGHLIGHTS OF THE greatest life, no lengthy justification is needed for making a leap from the transfiguration to the closing week of the ministry in Jerusalem. In the same chapter in which he describes the transfiguration Luke goes on to say, "When the days drew near for him to be received up, he set his face to go to Jerusalem" (Lk. 9:51). It appears that the material that follows is put forward as belonging to a general movement toward the holy city and the consummation there. Much of this intervening data is part of what is generally known as the Perean ministry; but this may not be the best description of it, for Jesus seems to have spent a considerable part of this interval on the borders of Galilee and Samaria.[1] Mark's account is not as precise as Luke's, but is in general agreement in the sense that the sequel to the transfiguration is a ministry that took the Lord to Judea and across the Jordan and therefore in the direction of Jerusalem (Mk. 10:1, 17, 32). Jerusalem is cited as the objective of the journey.

The immediate precursor of the events we are to consider is the raising of Lazarus (mentioned only in John), which stirred official opposition and was followed by the retirement of Jesus

[1] N. B. Stonehouse, *The Testimony of Luke to Christ* (1951), ch. 6.

and the Twelve to a district beyond the Jordan. His final approach to the city was featured by the flocking of great crowds of people to get a glimpse of him, which may well be a testimony to the impact made on the whole area by the report of the raising of Lazarus. While it is true that the Galilean mission had been marked in its later stages by a waning in popular enthusiasm, largely occasioned by Jesus' refusal to accommodate his Messiahship to revolutionary demands (Jn. 6:66) and a corresponding increase in his preoccupation with the instruction of the disciples, it is clear that there was still a lively public interest in him which could easily be fanned to white heat. Early arrivals for the Passover were busy exchanging surmises with one another. "What do you think? That he will not come to the feast?" (Jn. 11:56).

One should not overlook in this connection the effect of the itinerating of the Seventy. Since these men were sent out after the transfiguration (Lk. 10), and since they were to minister in the places where Jesus himself planned to come, and since at least some of their time must have been spent in Perea, it is reasonable to conclude that the air of expectation and even excitement that pulsates through the narratives of Jesus' approach to Jerusalem owes something to the ministry of these forerunners.

It is at Jericho that the concourse of the multitude becomes noticeable. Bartimaeus the blind beggar hears the crowd sweeping by and makes his inquiry about its cause. It is at Jericho that diminutive Zacchaeus is obliged to climb a tree in order to see the noted visitor as he passes along. In the midst of all this ferment, Jesus is not changed. He is still the Healer (Lk. 18:42), still the Savior (Lk. 19:10).

The way Luke begins the following paragraph is significant. "As they heard these things, he proceeded to tell a parable, because he was near to Jerusalem, and because they supposed that the kingdom of God was to appear immediately" (Lk. 19:11). A nobleman is pictured as going into a far country to receive kingly power and then return. His servants received at his hands certain funds that were to be used in trading while he was gone. But the citizens hated him and sent word after him that they refused to have him as their ruler. The setting for the parable is the mounting wave of fervor and acclaim for Jesus as a national leader, but the content of the parable emphasizes the official hatred and opposition he faced. These elements jostle one another in the incidents that follow. By the way Jesus came into the city, he seemed intent on satisfying the ardent hopes of the multitude; but by what he proceeded to do in cleansing the temple he seemed to fly in the face of the opposition and invite by his conduct a deepening and hardening of the hatred of the rulers.

The term "triumphal entry" is traditional language, yet it is not altogether suitable, for such a description more adequately fits the second coming in glory. Yet, since the term has become sanctified by use, it is expedient to continue to employ it.

Clearly Jesus is responsible for this event. It was not urged on him by the disciples or forced on him by the multitude. The disciples seem not to have given much thought to it at the time. At least they did not realize the import of what was taking place (Jn. 12:16).

Preparation for the event involved the sending of two disciples to secure the colt that Jesus needed for a mount. It was tied at a crossroads area not far from Bethany. Along with the request for the use of the animal went a pledge that it would be returned when the Lord's need for it was ended (Mk. 11:3). The incident reflects an important element of leadership. Friends of Jesus apparently made known to him from time to time their desire that he avail himself of such facilities as they had to offer, whether it be the home of Martha and Mary, or the upper room in Jerusalem, or this colt. Jesus himself seems to have welcomed such help. Not only did it meet a real need in his situation, but it enabled his followers to feel that they were making a contribution to his cause. They were doing what they could.

With preparations now made, Jesus began the journey into Jerusalem from Bethany, somewhat less than two miles from the city. A crowd formed ahead of him and another followed (Mk. 11:9). Many were pilgrims bound for the feast, but according to John some of the people were with him when he raised Lazarus from the dead (Jn. 12:17-18). The return of the Lord to Bethany was enough to bring them out in considerable numbers. Jerusalemites, hearing of his approach, streamed out of the city to meet him.

The combination of the approaching Passover festival with its reminder of deliverance from Egyptian bondage long before, and the return of the prophet of Galilee, who seemed to hold the potential for a new deliverance of Israel from its enemies, created a tumult of excitement. A festive mood gripped the procession. Singing broke out spontaneously (Mk. 11:9-10). Use was made of the Hallel, especially that part which includes the cry "Hosanna" and the reference to "the festal procession with branches" (Ps. 118:25-27). Garments were spread in the way. Branches were broken off from nearby trees and were strewn in the path of the oncoming prophet of Nazareth, now treated as a conqueror. The use of palm branches (Jn. 12:13) may have a special message, for these were not only a token of rejoicing (Lev. 23:40; Neh. 8:15; Rev. 7:9), but they may have carried political significance, since they had been used at the feast of tabernacles when Judas Maccabeus' recapture of the temple from the Syrians was celebrated (II Macc. 10:7). Now another strategic moment had come in the life of the nation. Perhaps the hour for freedom was about to strike again.

Such thoughts were far from the mind of Jesus. Where the uphill road crested at the summit of the Mount of Olives and the holy city burst into view, he wept over it, breaking out into open lamentation (Lk. 19:41). This apparently did not dampen the spirits of the accompanying throng, though it must have puzzled those who were close at hand. Jesus was lost in his own thoughts. Before him was spread the city where he must yield up his life, yet he did not weep on this account. He wept out of sorrow and sympathy for the doomed metropolis. He could not force it to accept him and his message, but he loved it to the end. He was mindful of its tragedy even more than of his own impending agony.

How is one to evaluate this event? It creates perplexity because Jesus' initiative on this occasion seems out of keeping with his attitude toward popular acclaim earlier in his ministry. He had withdrawn from the multitude when they would force him to become their king (Jn. 6:15), and he had refused the suggestion of his brothers that he go up to the feast of tabernacles and show himself (Jn. 7:4-9). On several occasions he had asked people to refrain from telling others what he had done for them, dreading the notoriety and the resulting pressure to become the object of political hopes and ambitions. Yet now he seems about to play into the hands of those who would use him, if they could, for these very ends.

Can it be that Jesus wished to satisfy a certain element in his following? This is unlikely, for he would proceed to dash their expectations in a few days. Why should he create a false impression in their minds? To conclude that he staged this incident to bring consternation to his opponents is equally unsuitable. He had never acted out of such motivation before. Rather, this was distinctly a messianic act. As Jesus had elicited a messianic confession from the disciples, so he would have one from the multitude ("Son of David," Mt. 21:9). That the early church understood the situation in this light is apparent from the citing of Zechariah 9:9 in the accounts of Matthew and John. The prophet had summoned Israel to rejoice at the coming of her king, meek and riding on an ass. It is altogether possible that Jesus included this passage in his postresurrection instruction of the disciples (Lk. 24:27, 44-45).

If we are bothered by the aspect of publicity given to the messianic status by the Lord's action, in contrast to his previous conduct, it need only be said that in a few days he would make open confession of his Messiahship before the Sanhedrin (Mk. 14:62). The necessity for restraint was now past. It would be a grievous error, of course, to assume that Jesus' view of his Messiahship was that of the crowd. His teaching concerning his death immediately after this event (Mk. 12:8; Jn. 12:24) looks in an entirely different direction.

The true King of Israel had come to his own, but not as an earthly conqueror. He was not fulfilling the predictions of his final advent as Judge and universal Ruler. Here the citing of Zechariah 9:9 is crucial, for it speaks plainly that Israel's King on this occasion comes not in glory but in lowliness. The divine order established in Old Testament prophecy is not violated. The King must suffer before he exercises sovereignty. He is the Servant-King riding on to keep his engagement with death.

THE CLEANSING OF THE TEMPLE

What would Jesus do, now that he had set foot inside the holy city? This must have been the subject of much speculation by the people. Matthew tells us that all the city was shaken (Mt. 21:10), a reminder of a similar stirring when the Magi arrived to inquire about the birth of the King of the Jews. Then the city was troubled (Mt. 2:3).

There was no doubt in Jesus' mind and no hesitation in his movements. He went directly to the temple. When he glimpsed it from the crest of the Mount of Olives it lay before him resplendent in its dazzling beauty. But now he went to inspect it at close range, and what he saw was not pleasing.[2] Passover season was approaching, and already the large area just inside the temple walls, known as the court of the Gentiles, was alive with activity. Money-changers were busy serving those who wished to exchange their money for the official Tyrian coinage that was alone acceptable in payment of the half-shekel tax that went into the temple treasury. Merchants with sacrificial animals and birds were scattered here and there throughout the broad expanse of the court. The noise of huckstering filled the air, mingling with the cries of the animals.

This traffic was in the hands of the Sadducaic priests, with the avaricious Annas at their head. It was defended on the ground of convenience for the worshipers, since the animals were guaranteed to be fit for sacrifice. Care was taken to allow nothing of this sort beyond the barrier that separated this court from the higher, interior areas crowned by the shrine itself. Probably it was argued that since this outer court was open to the Gentiles, there was no harm in using it for such a purpose, seeing that such people were unclean anyway. In fact, they were called dogs because of this ceremonial (and often moral) uncleanness. Attempts have been made from time to time to condone this arrangement. For example, Israel Abrahams observes, "The sacro-sanctity of the inner courts would be, as it were, humanized by the secularisation of the more remote precincts."[3] Yet he grants that the system was liable to abuse and he is not prepared to blame our Lord for being scandalized. The temple authorities themselves must have felt a certain awkwardness in allowing the traffic, for it is difficult to see how this could go on without violating the cleanliness of the temple. Even the outer court was supposed to be off-limits for those with dusty feet and was not to be used as a thoroughfare.[4]

It is likely that protests had been made from time to time by sensitive souls, but the ears of the hierarchy preferred the confusion that spelled profit for them to any demands for reform. At any rate Jesus sensed that direct action was called

[2] According to Mark his inspection of the temple area was followed by withdrawal to Bethany, for the hour was late. Matthew and Luke place the cleansing directly after the arrival in the city. John has no report of the cleansing at this point, but describes the same or a similar act in connection with the beginning of the ministry (Jn. 2:13-22).

[3] *Studies in Pharisaism and the Gospels*, I (1917), 82.

[4] R. H. Lightfoot, *The Gospel Message of St. Mark* (1950), p. 62.

for; and he tackled the situation single-handedly, moving the whole mass before him until quiet reigned in the court.[5] If it be asked how he could possibly succeed in clearing out such a huge nest of commercialism unaided, several things need to be borne in mind. His reputation as a performer of signs and wonders made men cautious about opposing him. Further, with right on his side, it was difficult to resist the indignation that flamed from his eyes and sounded from a voice that brooked no opposition or delay. Zeal for God's house was consuming him. Again, this figure had just elicited a tremendous demonstration of enthusiasm from the masses as he entered the city. This would make even the authorities hesitant to oppose him.

The hypocrisy of these leaders is seen in the aftermath. With order restored, Jesus was able to use the court for teaching and for healing the blind and lame who were brought to him (Mk. 11:18; Mt. 21:14). When children began to sing his praises in the holy precincts, crying out, "Hosanna to the Son of David," the chief priests and scribes objected indignantly (Mt. 21:15). They could not bear to hear the praises of Christ in the very place where they had not found the hubbub of the merchants distasteful.

A direct result of Jesus' action in clearing out the temple court was a challenging of his authority by the rulers of the Jews (Mk. 11:27-28). In fact, it was the immediate cause of a series of exchanges with various groups that tried to challenge him in these closing days. This badgering of our Lord testifies to the extreme vexation felt in the highest circles of Jerusalem over what he had done. Efforts to discomfit and discredit the Master become a common occupation. Animosity is building up that will not rest until this obnoxious Galilean is put to death.

It is noteworthy to what extent the temple dominates the teaching of Jesus in this period. In connection with the parable of the wicked tenants he quotes a portion of Psalm 118 dealing with the rejected stone that becomes the head of the corner (Mt. 21:42). He goes on to state that this in turn means for the nation the loss of the kingdom of God. By its rejection of its rightful Messiah Israel loses its distinctive place in the divine economy. Interestingly enough, this is the very psalm used by the multitude as it sang the praises of the Son of David on the

[5] Such a prodigious feat has met with some skepticism. Klausner alleges, without any textual support, that Jesus had the help of his followers and some of the people (*Jesus of Nazareth* [1925], p. 315).

way to Jerusalem (Ps. 118:25-27; Mt. 21:9). Not only so, but
at this time Jesus solemnly checks the admiration of his disciples
for the beauty of the temple buildings by his prediction that it
will be torn down, stone from stone (Mk. 13:1-2).

At his trial a few days later, it was soon evident that the
incident of the temple-cleansing was still occupying the thoughts
of many minds. False witnesses declared that they had heard
the prisoner say that he would destroy this temple made with
hands and build another not made with hands (Mk. 14:58). The
language contains an echo of John's version of the cleansing
(Jn. 2:19), even though it shows a misunderstanding of Jesus'
meaning. His accusers knew that any threat against the temple,
which was so dear to the heart of all Jewry, would inflame the
Sanhedrin more readily than anything else.

It remains to review this act of Jesus in terms of his motivation. Why did he undertake it? Could it have been simply a
gesture of protest, an effort to bring reform to the center of
Israel's religious life? Such an objective could not be called unworthy, even though the abuses were likely to return in a short
time. Granted that the temple was marked for destruction, yet
in the meantime it should continue to function as a genuine
place of worship. After all, the followers of Jesus would be
making use of it in days to come (Acts 2:46; 3:1). But more
than this was surely involved.

Some incline to see in his act a dramatic acted parable of
the sweeping away of the old order of animal sacrifice in favor
of the new day of spiritual worship that was about to dawn (cf.
Jn. 4:21-24). The language of John's account of the cleansing
could be interpreted as hinting at such a development (Jn.
2:15-16). On the other hand, Jesus did nothing to challenge the
actual offering of sacrifices. He could still refer to the temple
as his Father's house (Jn. 2:16).

This emphasis on the demise of the sacrificial system, though
possibly present, is not the main thrust, at least so far as the
Markan account is concerned. This Evangelist informs us that
Jesus himself explained the situation in terms of two passages
from the prophets. The one (Isa. 56:7) contained God's affirmation that his house was to be called a house of prayer for all
the nations. The other (Jer. 7:11) contained a description of
what had happened to the temple in the latter days of the

southern kingdom before the captivity. It had become a den of robbers.

History was repeating itself. Corruption had invaded the holy place of God's habitation, not simply in the form of grasping commercialism but more importantly in terms of robbing God by desecrating his abode. But this situation is to be taken along with the central item in the word from Isaiah. Bad as the merchandising was, this in itself was not the major complaint. It is rather this, that by turning the court into a mart of trade the Jewish authorities had denied to the Gentiles the privilege of using the portion of the temple open to them. They could not go on into the interior courts, for this was expressly denied to them. A barrier with warning signs kept them confined to the outer perimeter. At the dedication of the first temple Solomon had recognized the right of the foreigner to enjoy access to the temple and to pray there (I Kings 8:41-43). Ostensibly this right was maintained. but practically it had been withdrawn by obstructing the one area the Gentile could use.

Jesus, then, is solicitous for the spiritual needs of these people who are not of the chosen nation. It should not escape the student that this incident is simply one aspect of a broadening prominence given to the Gentile in the Gospel tradition as the narrative moves on to the close of Jesus' earthly career. One can go back to Matthew 12 and find that in connection with the debate between Jesus and the Pharisees over the observance of the sabbath, our Lord affirmed that the functioning of priests in the temple on the sabbath was a technical violation, yet it passed unchallenged. He went on to claim that in his own person and mission there was something greater than the temple (Mt. 12:6). On the strength of this he continued to do good on the sabbath. Matthew goes on to support this by a quotation from Isaiah 42:1-4, where the Gentiles are seen as profiting from the ministry of God's servant. In this way the temple and the welfare of the Gentile are linked long before the closing days of the ministry in Jerusalem. But as the end draws near the Gentiles come ever more sharply into focus. Doubtless they are in view in Jesus' prediction of the preaching of the gospel in the whole world (Mk. 14:9), and they are there by open declaration in the Great Commission. The gospel must be proclaimed to all the nations (Mt. 28:19). Surely it is significant that in John's record, immediately after the report of the triumphal entry (it will be remembered that John does not have an account of the temple-cleansing at this point), we read of Greeks coming to the feast and desiring to see Jesus (Jn. 12:20). He was the hope of the Gentiles.

A further look at the two passages used by Jesus from the Old Testament reveals that the context of Jeremiah 7:11 contains a pledge by God to destroy his house in Jerusalem as he did the sanctuary at Shiloh. So the act of Jesus in clearing the court was not merely remedial. It was in a sense prophetic of the destruction of the temple as a righteous judgment of the Almighty. On the other hand, the context of Isaiah 56:7 does not deal with the status quo but looks on into the future. It is only in the age to come that in the truest sense God's house shall be called a house of prayer for all peoples. Lohmeyer notes that "Jesus bases His action on the idea of the eschatological holiness of the Temple. He makes preparation for it by removing everything which militates against that eschatological holiness."[6]

Jesus had come as King of Zion (Zech. 9:9) and as Lord to his temple (Mal. 3:1). He is the Stone rejected by the builders but destined to become the Head of the corner. Death is here, but so is resurrection.

> Why is Christ "greater than the Temple"? There can be only one all-embracing answer. It is because God's presence is more manifest in Him than in the Temple. On Him, not on the Temple, now rests the Shekinah.[7]

Surely our Lord, as he wrought that day in Jerusalem, was making inevitable the breaking down of the middle wall of partition, that Jew and Gentile should be one in him in the new temple of his body, even as by his sacrifice on the cross he would rend the veil so that both might have unhindered access to the God of all the earth.

BIBLIOGRAPHY

Israel Abrahams. *Studies in Pharisaism and the Gospels*. Cambridge, Eng.: Cambridge University Press, First Series, 1917. Pp. 82-89.
Alan Cole. *The New Temple*. London: Tyndale, 1950.

[6] Ernst Lohmeyer, *Lord of the Temple* (1961), pp. 38-39.
[7] Alan Cole, *The New Temple* (1950), p. 12.

R. H. Lightfoot. *The Gospel Message of St. Mark.* Oxford: Clarendon, 1950.

Ernst Lohmeyer. *Lord of the Temple.* Edinburgh: Oliver and Boyd, 1961.

T. W. Manson. *The Servant-Messiah.* Cambridge, Eng.: Cambridge University Press, 1953.

E. F. Scott. *The Crisis in the Life of Jesus.* New York: Scribners, 1952.

CHAPTER XII

THE UPPER ROOM

*"He brought me to the banqueting house, and his banner over
me was love."*

—Song of Solomon

AFTER SEVERAL DAYS OF TEACHING IN THE TEMPLE, INTERSPERSED
with controversy as he was challenged by various groups, Jesus
sought a place of quiet where he might be alone with the disciples before his passion. All the Evangelists report the meeting in the upper room; but whereas the Synoptists describe the
institution of the Lord's Supper, John omits this[1] and devotes
considerable space to a farewell discourse in which the Master
unburdened his heart to his own.

SETTING

Luke notes that with the approach of the Passover the chief
priests and scribes were seeking a way to put Jesus to death,
when unexpectedly they found an ally in one of the apostolic
band. Judas was ready to betray his Lord for an agreed sum of
money, and began looking for a favorable opportunity to carry
out his bargain (Lk. 22:1-6).

Under these circumstances, any private meeting of a prolonged
nature between Jesus and his disciples would have to be set up

---

[1] He has already given the essence of its meaning in connection with the
discourse on the Bread of life (ch. 6). Jeremias explains the omission as part
of a developing tendency in the early church to keep from unbelievers the
secret and precious things that belonged only to the saints (*The Eucharistic
Words of Jesus* [1955], pp. 72-87).

without the knowledge of Judas and be convened with great care, for Jesus was aware of his intentions. Peter and John were delegated to make the arrangements. They were to go into the city (during holy week the group spent the night on the Mount of Olives) and look for a man carrying a jar of water (Lk. 22:10). This apparently slender clue was quite adequate, because men did not ordinarily assume such a chore. Following their man, the two disciples located the house where Jesus was to eat the Passover with his followers. Their assignment was to make ready for the feast.

The friend who had made space available for this purpose remains unnamed, one of those obscure figures who rendered valuable service to our Lord during his earthly ministry and found satisfaction in doing so. To such the service carried its own reward. That room would be a hallowed spot from that day forth. Jesus had been there.

Speaking of living quarters in Jerusalem, Dalman observes, "The upper stories of the houses, especially the rooms erected on the flat roofs, are the 'upper rooms' of which the New Testament speaks. . . . They were not used as the usual family dwelling-rooms and could quickly be turned into guest-rooms."[2]

The owner provided the space, the disciples brought the items needed for the feast, but it was Jesus who contributed most. His presence and instruction turned a routine observance into an unforgettable experience (cf. Lk. 24:35). It was a foretaste of heaven (Lk. 22:16).

John tells us that when the group assembled, Jesus was gripped by the knowledge that his hour had come, the season for his departure from the world and his return to the Father. Yet he was not so preoccupied with this realization as to be oblivious to the men before him. Rather, his love for these who must remain in the world surged to a new height.[3]

STRUCTURE

Although the discourse is central to John's presentation, it is preceded by an account of the washing of the disciples' feet by the Savior (13:2-17) and is in turn followed by the great prayer

[2] *Sacred Sites and Ways* (1935), p. 281.

[3] The words "He loved them to the end" (Jn. 13:1) can equally well be rendered, "He loved them to the utmost" (cf. the use of the same expression at the conclusion of I Thess. 2:16).

of chapter 17. The order is suggestive. First the disciples are cleansed, then instructed, then prayed for. It may be that the pattern for these things was seen to reside in the arrangement of the ancient tabernacle in the wilderness. As one entered the enclosure he would encounter the brazen altar of sacrifice (cf. Jn. 1:29). As he moved toward the tabernacle building, he would come to the laver, where the priests washed themselves before going into the holy place to perform their ministrations (cf. the footwashing in Jn. 13). The holy place with its three objects presents correspondences to the upper room. In the table of the loaves of presentation one may see an adumbration of the Lord's Supper; in the golden candelabrum an intimation of the promised Holy Spirit in his capacity as Enlightener or Counselor; in the altar of incense a foregleam of the teaching on prayer conveyed by Jesus on this occasion. As a climax the most holy place, which admitted the high priest only, and that once a year, can be said to answer to the great intercessory prayer of our Lord on this occasion. What commends the credibility of this pattern is the large place given to Jewish matters in the Fourth Gospel, including the record of Jesus' frequent use of the temple, especially at festival time. Furthermore, the reader is given advance notice in 1:14 (literally, "and tabernacled among us") that this motif is likely to be amplified as the Gospel unfolds.

As to the discourse proper (Jn. 14–16), it has much in common with other farewell messages. Probably the most important of these outside the Scriptures is *The Testaments of the Twelve Patriarchs*, modeled on the aged Jacob's words to his sons prior to his death (Gen. 49). In these testaments each of the twelve sons of Jacob is represented as gathering his sons about him and addressing them by reviewing his life, adding items of counsel and warning, and concluding with predictions about the future. The same threefold pattern may be seen in Paul's address to the Ephesian elders (Acts 20), wherein he reviews his manner of life in their midst, encourages them to attend to the ministry given to them, and concludes with predictions about the worsening of conditions facing the church.

These same three strands are observable in the upper-room discourse, though they do not follow each other systematically as in *The Testaments of the Twelve Patriarchs*, but are intermingled. Jesus cites his own ministry in terms of his coming forth from the Father (Jn. 16:28), his example of love (15:12), his teaching (15:20, 22), his works (14:11; 15:24), and his rejection by the world (15:20, 23-24). His words of instruction and admonition fill much of the discourse, but it will be sufficient to allude to the new commandment of love (13:34), the necessity of abiding in him in order to have fruit (15:1-11), and the warning against failure in the time of testing (16:1, 4). His predictions on this occasion are numerous, including the treachery of Judas (13:21), the act of Peter in denying the Lord (13:38), desertion by the disciples (16:32), the coming of the evil one (14:30), persecution (16:2), the future ministry of the Spirit (14:26; 15:26; 16:7-11), his own death (15:13), his departure from the world to the Father (16:5, 28), and his return (14:3).

Farewell discourses do not ordinarily involve much interruption from those who are being addressed, but on this occasion there were factors such as the predictions regarding Judas and Peter, awareness of the sinister threat of action by the Jewish authorities against Jesus, his enigmatical way of speaking, and the disciples' feeling of apprehension as they faced the future without the immediate presence of their Leader. So they broke in on him·repeatedly, no less than seven times, as follows: the beloved disciple (13:25), Peter (13:36-37), Thomas (14:5), Philip (14:8), Judas not Iscariot (14:22), some of the disciples (16:17-18), and the disciples as a group (16:29). In this respect the upper-room discourse is akin to some of the others in this Gospel. Jesus was plagued by questions during his discourse on the Bread of life (ch. 6), his teaching at the feast of tabernacles (ch. 7), his address recorded in chapter 8 and the one associated with the feast of dedication (ch. 10).[4]

Still another observation on structure is in order, derived from C. H. Dodd's study of the discourse. He notes that there are two basic elements here, one of which is the employment of sayings by Jesus that are reported in the Synoptics, especially in teaching situations that arose shortly before the passion, which are presented in John's own fashion in his account. An example is the help to be expected from the Holy Spirit (Lk. 12:12; Jn.

---

4 C. H. Dodd notes a similarity between the upper-room discourse and those in the Hermetic literature, where oracular utterances by the teacher are followed by lack of comprehension and therefore by questioning from the pupil, which in turn leads to explication by the teacher (*Historical Tradition in the Fourth Gospel* [1963], pp. 319-320).

15:26-27). The other is the recapitulation of themes already touched on in the course of the Fourth Gospel.[5] The body of this Gospel is composed in the main of signs followed by discourses calculated to explain the signs. It is true that there is no sign performed in the upper room, for it is withdrawn from the world; but possibly we are intended to see something approaching a sign in the footwashing. Certainly it is followed by interpretation, as are the signs in the rest of the Gospel. There are several references to the works that Jesus had previously performed among the people, which would include the signs (14:10-12; 15:24; 17:4).

THE WASHING OF THE DISCIPLES' FEET

During the meal Jesus rose to perform a service for his followers that was wholly unexpected on their part. The men had walked through the streets of the city, which meant that their sandaled feet were dirty. Judging from Jesus' attitude toward externals, this in itself would not unduly concern him (cf. Mt. 15:20). But he was concerned with the spiritual condition of his followers. According to Luke 22:24, this time of holy fellowship was marred by disputation among them as to which of them should be regarded as the greatest. Jesus saw an opportunity of dealing with the problem in a way that they could never forget. The owner of the house, out of respect for Jesus' wish for privacy, had not only absented himself but also kept any servant from disturbing the gathering. A basin of water and a towel had thoughtfully been provided, but they remained unused. Men who are obsessed with a sense of superiority do not readily take the role of a servant. But the one who had taken the form of a Servant under God (Phil. 2:7) was quite prepared to take that same station in relation to men. He had been doing it, in fact, all along (Lk. 22:27). Out of a sublime consciousness that he was nearing the nadir of his majestic condescension and would then return to the Father (Jn. 13:3), he knew that he need not fear that the execution of a menial task would ruin his true dignity. And so he girded himself and began to make the rounds of his astonished followers.

From his own statements on this occasion the conclusion can be drawn that his act had both a theological and a practical

---

[5] *The Interpretation of the Fourth Gospel* (1953), p. 390.

significance. Peter, rebelling at first against the thought of accepting such a service from his Master, went to the opposite extreme of asking that his hand and head be included in the ablution, only to be told that one who had been bathed all over needed only to have his feet washed. Peter was clean in the sense that he had received the bath of regeneration (cf. Tit. 3:5; I Cor. 6:11). He learned that only his "walk" needed to be cleansed; his standing was not involved. His life had already felt the cleansing power of salvation (13:10).

Had Jesus stopped here, the most pressing need for the act would not be pointed out. So, on resuming his seat, he expounded this aspect, indicating that in washing the disciples' feet he had given them an example for ministering to one another in this way (13:14-15). To think of footwashing as a perpetual obligation for the church of all times and in all places is surely to miss the point. Such service is appropriate only where the actual physical need exists (I Tim. 5:10). The enduring obligation is that of mutual service among the saints whatever be its form. Footwashing is not something to be elevated into an ordinance alongside baptism and the Lord's Supper, for it does not point directly to Christ and his salvation as these do.

The Expulsion of Judas

While talking to Peter about this matter of footwashing, Jesus included the rest of the company as clean, but with one exception (13:10-11). The presence of Judas made the Savior troubled in spirit, and he went so far as to say to the group that one of their number would betray him (13:21). Consternation gripped the circle, as they looked at one another in dismay. At that moment Judas' face must have been a study. Perhaps he found it convenient to reach down and pick something off the floor. He was in a dangerous spot and knew he must remain cool. Jesus himself provided the way of escape for him by speaking to him before the others of a mission he must fulfill with all speed. Since this task was not specified, the company assumed that it had something to do with his duties as treasurer (13:29). John's comment that it was night when the betrayer set out is freighted with meaning, for his Gospel makes much of the contrast between light and darkness (1:5; 3:19; 8:12). Judas indeed was unclean, for he was still of the darkness, having refused to come to the light even though it was shining about him all the while.

THE NEW COMMANDMENT

Relieved by the departure of Judas, Jesus was now free in spirit to speak of the things that were upon his heart. He could not proceed in an atmosphere of treachery. Now he turns to instruct his own, and begins with the primacy of love as a new commandment (13:34). The Israelite had been charged to love his neighbor as himself (Lev. 19:18), so the command of Jesus was not new in every respect. But it had a new frame of reference, as fellow believer now takes the place of neighbor, not in the sense of supplanting the old obligation but rather of extending it to all who share the faith. By limiting the sphere to believers, Jesus is not excluding love for all men, but is simply stressing what must prevail among his followers.

The commandment is new also in that it has a new standard by which to measure itself—"as I have loved you." By demanding the love of neighbor as one loved himself, the old commandment moved in line with the spirit of the Golden Rule. However, the love of Christ goes beyond this, for it is a self-sacrificing love (15:12-14). It actually puts the good of another before consideration of self (Rom. 12:10). Remarkable is Jesus' observation that all men will recognize those who have love for one another as his disciples (13:35). It seems to tell us that despite his rejection, he had left an unforgettable deposit of love with the common people. They had seen it in his look. They had felt it when his hand rested on their diseased or twisted bodies. They had sensed it in his unflagging labors to reach the multitude and minister to the needs of men wherever he went. Such love cannot be successfully imitated. It must be imparted. The divine love must operate in the disciples of Jesus, not some pale reflection of it (17:26). And since the world will be able to recognize this love, clearly it must be love in action rather than a sentiment carried in the heart.

THE NEW PROVISION

We have seen what Christ expects. Now it is in order to examine what he provides. Various things enter into this legacy, the first of which is the promise that the disciples will have an abode in the Father's house (14:2). The Master knows that these men are distraught. They have heard that one of their number will turn out to be a denier, another a betrayer of the Lord. Their world seems in danger of falling apart. Jesus bids them anchor their hope to the glorious future. Whatever happens to them here cannot affect their title to that heavenly home. The place where they were sitting had been prepared for their coming by two of their number. Now Jesus is about to depart to prepare that other "upper room" for their arrival. From this one they will soon be leaving, but from that one there will be no going out. Yet even that place of blessing is not the real magnet, but rather the assurance that the Lord himself will be there.

A second provision follows logically. Jesus is the way to the Father (14:6). "No man cometh to the Father but by me." The wording is significant—"cometh," not "goeth." Jesus stands with the Father. That is his native right. He is the eternal Son, the one who alone is able to bring us to God (I Pet. 3:18).

Third, there is a special provision made available to the disciples when their Master is taken from them and they must carry on without him. It is the promise that if they will ask anything in his name, he will do it (14:13-14). He had made some great pronouncements on prayer before, but now he introduces a special basis for encouragement in the prayer life. Prayer made in the name of Jesus is the new norm. Their Lord and Master has the ear of the Father. They can have the same open reception if they will come in his name, by his authority, praying as he would pray, guided by the will of God and the desire to glorify him. Only on the basis of such praying can the greater works be expected to follow, performed through them by the one who has gone to be with the Father (14:12).

Fourth, the departure of the Son of God will not mean such a loss as the disciples imagine, for it will open the way for him to send that other Counselor, the Holy Spirit, to be in them and abide with them. Jesus goes so far as to say that his departure is to their advantage, since the Spirit cannot come unless he goes (16:7). Two special ministries are cited here, connected with the two titles Paraclete and Spirit of truth (14:16-17). The former has the meaning of Advocate (cf. I Jn. 2:1) and fits admirably with the emphasis on witness found here. As the disciples bear their witness to Christ they will have the powerful support and advocacy of the Spirit (15:26-27). Allied to this is the Spirit's ministry toward the world. As Dodd puts it, "The Advocate becomes a prosecuting counsel, and 'convicts' the world"[6] (16:8-11).

As the Spirit of truth this divine Helper will bring to remembrance the things Jesus has said (14:26), guide into all the truth, and show things to come (16:13). These elements of instruction, when fulfilled, were destined to play a crucial part in the framing of the New Testament.

Fifth, the Lord bestowed the legacy of his peace (14:27). Who can fail to marvel at that peace, maintained without nervousness or wavering at the most trying period of his life? Yet it was not something artificial, a sort of insulation that sheltered him from troubles. He was able to maintain his serenity despite a troubled spirit (13:21), however paradoxical that may seem.

Sixth, the disciples learned that their sojourn in the world could be an experience of bringing forth fruit unto God, even though their Master was no longer with them in the flesh (15:1-11). So far they had done little more than sit at his feet. Now they were to have the opportunity of showing themselves useful. While the specific nature of the fruit is not stated in so many words, it is hinted at by the fact that Jesus alternates the command to abide in him with the injunction to abide in his love (15:9). This may serve to bring the thought into line with Paul's teaching in Galatians 5:22, where he declares that the fruit of the Spirit is love. If this is correct, then this passage on fruitbearing is intended to be linked to the teaching on the new commandment, and it is no mere happenstance that in this same paragraph Jesus speaks about keeping his commandments (15:10). More than love may be in view; but if this is central, other fruitage will result (cf. I Cor. 13:4-7).

Seventh, the Lord sought to prepare his own for the tribulations that lay ahead of them (16:1-4). These men are to face persecution with their eyes open, not counting it a strange thing that they should be called on to suffer for Christ's sake. The hatred of the world could be expected to make them its target. Nothing more was needed for this than continued loyalty to him against whom the hatred and violence had first of all been directed (15:18-25). The servant is not greater than his Master. Yet these men could face this prospect of stern opposition with cheerfulness, for their Lord had overcome the world (16:33). He could speak of

6 *Ibid.*, p. 414.

ultimate victory with entire confidence even before the final storm broke around his head.

It would be wrong to see in the teaching of these chapters only a series of provisions by which the disciples, soon to find themselves bereft of their master, can manage to get along in his absence. Underscoring and penetrating everything else is the most dynamic factor of all—the sharing of the life of the Son, who in turn shares the life of the Father. It is first expressed here in the words, "In that day you will know that I am in my Father, and you in me, and I in you" (14:20) ; but the truth is repeated many times, especially in the great prayer of chapter 17. Father and Son come and make their abode with the believer during his earthly pilgrimage when he has not yet reached that abode set aside for him in the Father's house (14:23). Now we are in a better position to grasp the significance of Jesus' language when he speaks of his love, his joy, and his peace as given to his own. If these men are partakers of his life they are partakers of all that belongs to him, apart from his sinlessness. It remains to appropriate these gifts by faith.

THE GREAT PRAYER

Having opened his heart to his little company, Jesus now does the same to his Father in heaven. Several of the basic truths taught in the upper room now reappear clothed in the accents of prayer, including his relation to the Father, the relation of the disciples to him and to the Father, the character of the world and his triumph over it, and the need of realizing love and unity among the followers of the Son even as these qualities abound between the Father and the Son.

Though prayer is never a proper medium for preaching or for commenting on people's shortcomings, it is a fitting vehicle for instruction in the sense that much can be learned from it. Westcott is surely right when he says, "At the supreme crisis of the Lord's work they [the disciples] were allowed to listen to the interpretation of its course and issue, and to learn the nature of the office they had themselves to fulfill."[7]

The Lord Jesus prays for himself (17:1-5), asking that the Father will glorify him, for he has glorified the Father on the

---

[7] B. F. Westcott, *The Gospel According to St. John* (1896), p. 236b.

earth. This requested glorification is twofold, encompassing both the successful endurance of the cross and then exaltation to the Father's presence. Both aspects are seen as phases of glory (cf. Jn. 12:23-24).

As he goes on to pray for his people, Jesus has in view first his immediate followers (17:6-19), then future believers (17:20-26). His favorite description of the apostles recurs here—"those whom thou hast given me." When he spent a night in prayer before selecting this band of men, he was seeking to make sure that he had those whom the Father had chosen to give him. To these Jesus had manifested the Father, and they in turn had kept the word they received. No complaint is made about their dullness of comprehension or their littleness of faith, or their resistance to the teaching about the necessity of the passion. Jesus counted it a great thing that in contrast to their countrymen they had been willing to follow him. Furthermore, they are the Father's gift. Will the Son complain about the Father's choice? They believed the crucial item that Jesus was actually the Son of God who had come forth from the Father. They believed it when the nation refused to do so.

In praying for these men Jesus expressly excludes the world from his intercession (17:9). It would be a gross mistake to assume that this is a reaction against the world because of its rejection of him. Jesus is not showing resentment by this limitation. His coming had the world in view (Jn. 3:16-17). In a very real sense the world is in the background here, for the Master is confining his petition to the disciples because they are the means of reaching the world with the message of the gospel.

The prayer is one-third completed and still there are no actual petitions for his own, but now at length these begin to emerge. His first request is that the Father would keep (preserve) them (17:11). He himself had kept them during the days of the ministry (17:12), extending to them his shepherd care. Now he looks to the Father for the continuance of this oversight. Two reasons dictate the necessity for protection. One is the hatred of the world (17:14), of which Jesus had already spoken in the discourse. To endure this, the disciples will need the constant overshadowing of divine love and care. The other is the opposition of the evil one (17:15), which is a still greater menace because of his invisibility and subtlety.

Jesus is careful to note that he is not asking the Father to take these men out of the world. Such a course would leave the world without the witness it sorely needed. They must stay, but they can have the assurance of divine help in the midst of their difficult task. In this connection one may recall Jesus' forecasts about the trouble Peter was going to have (Jn. 13:38). He went so far as to say that Satan had asked for this leading disciple that he might sift him as wheat. The Master did nothing to insure that Peter would not be exposed to the situation that would bring about his downfall. Instead, he assured the disciple of his prayer to the end that Peter's faith would not fail (Lk. 22:32). "Kept by the power of God through faith"—that is the divine plan.

A second petition asks that the Father would sanctify the disciples in the truth (17:17). To insist that this means a request to make them holy men is to miss the force of the language. Certainly Jesus was desirous that they be holy men, but his prayer at this point looks to something that is fundamental to holiness. The meaning of the word *sanctify* must be gleaned from its use in verse 19, where "consecrate" is clearly the idea. Jesus did not say that he made himself holy, for he was that already. But just as he made sure that his own life was kept in line with the purpose of his coming into the world, so he prays that his followers will be set apart for their task of making him known. The word sanctify, then, does not stand in contrast to what is impure, but to what is natural or common. These men have been chosen and called. Their commission must be kept inviolate. It needs to be renewed in them constantly as a result of the Savior's prayer.

In the third petition the Lord prays that his own may be one (17:21-23; cf. v. 11). The nature of this unity is clearly indicated—"even as thou, Father, art in me, and I in thee." Jesus was on earth and the Father was in heaven (which does not deny his omnipresence). Likewise believers may be separated by great distances from one another and may belong to different branches of the church, but these factors need not disturb their essential unity in the Spirit (cf. Eph. 4:3). Yet the very fact that Jesus prayed such a prayer shows that the unity cannot be assumed to take care of itself. It needs cultivation by the saints.

The final request is that the men who are the Father's gift to the Son may be with him to behold his glory (17:24). It was essential to their call that they should be with him (Mk. 3:14). They were not always completely with him in spirit or understanding, but they continued with him in his testings (Lk. 22:28). They are the firstfruits of his mission in the world, and he insists that they belong with him in the life to come. Here we catch a glimpse of the warmth and depth of the Savior's love for the redeemed. He cannot bear to be without them, even though he will have the fellowship of the Father and the adoration of the angelic hosts (cf. Rev. 3:21).

To his beloved followers he will show his glory. What they discerned of it on earth arrested and thrilled them (Jn. 1:14). But they could hardly take in all the facets of that glory. This must wait until they are like him (I Jn. 3:2).

A study of the prayer reveals that the correspondences between the ministry of Jesus Christ and that of his servants are many and striking. Both are divinely sent, both are bearers of the word, both are set apart to manifest the name of God. The ministry is one, for it is his through theirs; and the goal is one, that the world may believe (17:21), and thereby the Father may be glorified.

BIBLIOGRAPHY

T. D. Bernard. *The Central Teaching of Jesus Christ*. New York: Macmillan, 1892.

A. B. Bruce. *The Training of the Twelve*. New York: Richard R. Smith, 1930.

C. H. Dodd. *The Interpretation of the Fourth Gospel*. Cambridge, Eng.: Cambridge University Press, 1953. Pp. 390-423.

A. E. Garvie. *Studies in the Inner Life of Jesus*. New York: Armstrong, 1907. Pp. 350-373.

F. B. Meyer. *Love to the Uttermost*. New York: Revell, 1888.

H. C. G. Moule. *The High Priestly Prayer*. London: Religious Tract Society, 1908.

Johannes Munck, "Discours d'adieu dans le Nouveau Testament et dans la littérature biblique," *Aux sources de la tradition chrétienne* (Mélanges offerts à M. Maurice Goguel). Neuchâtel: Delachaux et Niestlé S. A., 1950.

H. Leonard Pass. *The Glory of the Father*. London: Mowbray, 1935.

Marcus Rainsford. *Our Lord Prays for His Own*. Chicago: Moody, 1950.

David Smith. *The Days of His Flesh*. New York: Doran, n.d. Pp. 435-451.

H. B. Swete. *The Last Discourse and Prayer*. London: Macmillan, 1913.

John Watson. *The Upper Room*. New York: Dodds, Mead, 1892.

B. F. Westcott. *Peterborough Sermons*. London: Macmillan, 1904. Pp. 3-127.

Chapter XIII

GETHSEMANE

"Jesus never found relief in His Divinity from His human suffering. He took refuge in prayer."

—T. B. Kilpatrick

"Thy will be done in earth, as it is in heaven."

—Jesus of Nazareth

THERE ARE TWO FAMOUS GARDENS IN THE BIBLE: EDEN, WHERE THE first Adam failed, and Gethsemane, where the Last Adam wrestled in prayer and attained the victory and poise that carried him through the remaining hours of his earthly course. The name Gethsemane means "oil press." Here, where the olives were pressed, the Son of God endured his great soul travail.

The short journey out from the city and across the brook Kidron has sometimes been compared to that which David took when Absalom's revolt had made his position in Jerusalem precarious (II Sam. 15:23). Jesus' rejection was nigh at hand, but he was not fleeing from it. He sought the quiet of the garden for a final prayer vigil. Often, John tells us, he frequented the place with his disciples. We are reminded of Jesus' words in his lament over Jerusalem, "How often would I have gathered thy children together." Surely the needs of the people must often have been before him in those previous seasons of prayer. But now he comes to pray for his own need. To the Christian pilgrim no spot in all Palestine is more sacred than this. The veil that hides the intimate prayer life of the Savior is pulled aside for us just a little. From what we see, we can appreciate his criticism of hypocrites who

189

love to pray long prayers in public with studied repetition. It was all so foreign to the genuineness of the spiritual communication he maintained with the Father.

As we approach this anteroom to Calvary, we note first the part played by the disciples. The bulk of them were instructed to sit near the gate. They were not to be idle, for according to Luke 22: 40, Jesus bade them pray. Yet it was not prayer for him, but for themselves, that they might not enter into temptation. To the inner circle of the three, however, Jesus gave the special privilege of remaining somewhat closer to him as he went on ahead to be alone. To them he confided his heaviness of soul and told them to watch. They had been witnesses of his glory on the mount; now they would be witnesses of his sufferings, a kind of preview of Calvary. This was the third occasion on which they were allowed to be with Jesus. Is it possible that the importance of the privilege was beginning to fade a bit in their minds? Was it an old story now, so that they did not sense how desperately the Lord needed them? We know that it was his habit to slip away from the Twelve and spend time alone in the open, usually before the break of day. But here we have a very human touch. Now Jesus wants the presence and sympathy of these men, much as Paul urged Timothy to make every effort to come to him soon at Rome, where the apostle was a prisoner facing certain death.

Could the Lord expect much from this trio? They were loyal but confused and depressed. With the previous announcements Jesus made to his disciples about his impending death, there is no suggestion in the narratives that there was any sympathetic response from these chosen followers. He was very much alone. He had been alone when he faced the rigors of the temptation. Since then he had taken these men to himself and had trained them, schooling them in his teaching and seeking to share his mind with them. But they were of little help. Their lack of physical participation is a token of their lack of spiritual understanding and sympathy with Jesus' announced intention of accepting death. The very aloneness of our Lord, however, is some measure of preparation for the ordeal of the cross, when he must be forsaken even by the Father for a season.

With a soul sorrowful unto death, in sharp contrast to his exultation when the Seventy returned and he lifted his heart to the Father with joy in the Holy Spirit, Jesus turned away from his companions. When he returned and found them sleeping, he wondered that they could not watch for one hour. This may or may not be any clue as to the length of time he spent. The language suggests a considerable period spent in prayer, but the disciples had failed to stand by. In noting their failure the Savior says, "The spirit indeed is willing, but the flesh is weak." It is generally thought that by these words the Lord was giving an explanation of the failure of the disciples and putting the best construction on their failure. A few hours before, he had commended them as those who had continued with him in his testings (Lk. 22:28). Now they have failed to give support even in terms of physical watchfulness.

Coming the third time and finding the three once more in the grip of slumber, the Lord told them to sleep on and take their rest. In the midst of such a tense situation, it is very unlikely that these words were intended in a caustic sense. It was rather that little time was available for any purpose, whether watching or sleeping. They may as well finish out their rest.

The aftermath of the disciples' failure is sadly revealed in Peter's blundering with the sword. When the lights appeared in the garden and the little group was surrounded, Peter could think of only one thing. He must use force and save his Master from capture, or at least do what he could. Lashing out wildly, he succeeded only in taking off the ear of a servant, for his aim was poor. It is worth noting here that there is something of a parallel with the transfiguration incident. There Peter was out of turn with his word; here he is out of turn with his deed. In both cases there is a background of failure to stay awake. The time for watching and praying is before the test reaches us. When that comes, the hour is too late for praying, and we are unprepared to meet the test. Peter's act in drawing the sword was foolish, partly because it misrepresented the spirit and purpose of Jesus and his mission, and partly because it accomplished nothing. His act did not prevent the seizure of his Master. Peter had not yet grasped the truth that the weapons of our warfare are not carnal.

We turn now from the disciples to the Lord himself and his agony. He is in the garden to pray. Four recorded prayers of Jesus are especially notable. Two are fairly long—the prayer he taught the disciples and the longer prayer recorded in John 17. These are much studied and often used. But we ought not to forget the short ones, the prayer for forgiveness breathed out on the cross and this petition in the garden. Sometimes Jesus prayed more for the benefit of others than for his own need, as in John 11:41-42 prior to the raising of Lazarus. But Jesus and his own predicament constitute the burden of the garden prayer. It is an incomparable utterance, because it lays bare at once the awfulness of the situation Jesus faced and the powerful controlling force of his commitment to the Father. The whole incarnation is epitomized in the words, "Thy will be done" (Mt. 26:42; cf. Jn. 6:38; Heb. 10:9). In the repetition of the prayer we are to sense the inexpressible burden, the intolerable weight of a situation from which he sought relief. In a less drastic situation, the apostle Paul also prayed three times that the thorn imposed on him might be taken away. He, like Jesus, came to rest in the will of God and in that found peace, though the circumstances had not changed.

Jesus' prayer has two parts: a request and an acceptance of the divine will. The request was for the removal of the cup. Along with it went the determination to abide by the will of the Father. The prayer was essentially the same, three times offered. It is a powerful demonstration that we may have reiteration in prayer without having vain repetition. A. B. Bruce has ventured the opinion that the three prayers are in a sense different, for they represent three stages in the attitude of Jesus. The first prayer was simply the unburdening of Jesus' heart, as he sought relief. The second was a solemn facing of the cup and what it stood for, with all the pain and bitterness it would bring. The third was the stage in which victory was secured, in which victory the Savior was able to rest, with no resistance to the divine will, but rather an abandonment to it.[1]

At one point in his wrestling, according to Luke, there appeared an angel to strengthen him. As Carter remarks, "He was pleased to permit His Human nature to be so prostrate, so abandoned to its own weakness, as to need a creature's sympathy and a creature's aid."[2] The renewed strength is immediately poured into yet more earnest prayer (Lk. 22:43-44).

What was the cause of the soul distress? Jesus used two words, *hour* (Mk. 14:35) and *cup* (Mk. 14:36). He wanted the hour to pass and the cup also, if in any way they could be avoided and still the will of God be done. It is natural to connect the word "hour" with the use of it in John's Gospel, where it is consistently employed with reference to the death toward which Jesus moved steadily, relentlessly, all through his ministry. The hour speaks of the inescapableness of the cross, even as the cup speaks of the element of suffering which must be the lot of the Son of man. Scrip-

---

[1] A. B. Bruce, *With Open Face* (1896), pp. 294-295.
[2] T. T. Carter, *The Passion and Temptation of Our Lord* (1867), p. 49.

ture knows of three cups: the cup of the Lord, filled with suffering, as in this passage; our cup as believers, which is one of blessing
(I Cor. 10:16); and the cup of sinners, which is filled with the
wrath of God (Jer. 25:27; Rev. 14:10). The three cups answer
well to the three crosses planted on Golgotha.

The Gethsemane experience is not easy to interpret, for although soul distress and prayer are involved, things that are common enough to our lot, yet there is a mystery here for which there
is no parallel in human life to give light. It is not surprising that
explanations of the cup should differ with various interpreters.
That the cup is in some way associated with Jesus' death almost of
necessity follows from his allusion to the cup in the upper room.
There it is viewed as a gracious gift of his life for others; here it
must be appreciated somewhat differently, for the point is not
any repudiation of the plan to provide the gift, but what has to be
faced is the colossal difficulty in providing it.

The lowest level of interpretation makes the cup to be the fear
of death. According to Hebrews 2:15, the fear of death is a strong
factor with human beings, holding many in its grip throughout
life. Yet here is one point where we rightfully expect our Lord to
rise above any craven preoccupation with the dread of dying. It
would be a strange paradox that saints should be able to draw
from Christ the inspiration and strength to die bravely and un-
complainingly for his sake, yet he himself be found quailing before the experience of death. We cannot help recoiling from any
such view of the matter. One who could fearlessly and single-
handedly drive the merchandising throng from the temple and
calmly come back to Judea in spite of threats of stoning is not
one to turn weak and timid at such an hour as now faced him.

Another view sees in the cup the fear of Jesus that he was going
to die prematurely, there in the garden, so would not be able to
finish his course and give his life upon the cross. Many pressures
were upon him. This was the hour of Satan, when the powers of
darkness ringed our Savior about and beset him like a flock of
vultures. This viewpoint seeks support in the fact that the cup
does not always mean the cross, since Jesus told the sons of Zebedee that they would drink his cup, and yet only one of them died
for his sake, the other living on to an old age and dying a natural
death. Appeal is also made to Hebrews 5:7, which speaks of Jesus
and says, "Who in the days of his flesh, when he had offered up
prayers and supplications with strong crying and tears unto him
that was able to save him from death, and was heard in that he

feared" (KJV). This viewpoint is generally associated with the idea that the chief pressure upon Jesus in the garden was Satan, who was seeking to kill him then and there.

We shall take up these arguments one at a time and see what they amount to. First, as to the cup and the sons of Zebedee, we may grant the point that "cup" need not necessarily refer to death; but we should avoid making an improper use of this point. The cup may well signify the cross for Jesus and suffering for his sake so far as others are concerned, namely, those who, like Paul, seek to be conformed to his death. Our identification with Christ does not make our suffering redemptive. His cup remains unique even though in a sense it may be shared.

The use of Hebrews 5:7 needs to be examined also. Undoubtedly this verse has a relevance to the garden experience, but it is wrong to take the words "in that he feared" and make them mean that he feared he was in danger of missing the will of the Father. The word for "fear" in that passage is not a verb but a noun, and it means simply piety or reverence. There is no proof from Hebrews 5:7 that Jesus feared an immediate death in the garden and sought deliverance from that. The death that is in view is the death of the cross.

We should beware also of overpressing the part of Satan in the garden trial. We should remember Jesus' words spoken in the upper room: "The ruler of this world is coming. He has no power over me" (Jn. 14:30). We could hardly expect that Satan, who had been so successfully resisted in the temptation and throughout the ministry, would now be able to muster such power against Jesus as to be irresistible. Furthermore, Satan was at work along other lines entirely, having put it into the heart of Judas Iscariot to betray Jesus. This was much the more desirable course for Satan to pursue, for it would mean that when Jesus was led out to die, he would go with the stigma upon him of having been declared worthy of death by the highest court of his own nation. A death in the garden could not begin to give Satan as much satisfaction as the ignominious death of Calvary. The possibility remains, to be sure, that Satan could have been working along more than one avenue of approach.

The view under consideration is ruled out anyway by John 18:11, for there, *after* the struggle in the garden, Jesus still speaks of the cup as something with future reference. "Shall I not drink the cup which the Father has given me?"

A third attempt to understand the cup sees in it the fear of

Jesus that in the events of the next few hours he himself would
be the occasion for increased human guilt. Because of him Judas
would become a remorseful suicide, an abandoned, derelict soul
cast out into the eternal void. Because of him some members of
the Sanhedrin would find their sleep disturbed for many a night
by an uneasy conscience. Because of him Pilate would go, tor-
mented, to an untimely end. The nation Israel, in seeking his
death, would take to itself the curse of bloodguiltiness, and would
pay its debt in terms of a demolished temple, a wasted city, and a
ruined national life. All this was too much for the gentle spirit
of the Son of man. It unnerved him. He could not face it. The
view has a certain attractiveness, but it cannot stand. Jesus had
predicted the suffering and fall of Jerusalem and had done so in
some detail in the presence of his disciples. He had wept over the
holy city. Yet there is no suggestion at that time, when all this
was vividly before his vision, that he gave way to any such agony
as befell him in the garden. Furthermore, Christ had been a divider of men all along. The die was not being cast that night. It
had been cast long before for everybody concerned, with the possible exception of Pilate. At no other point in his earthly career
did Jesus venture any suggestion that he shrank from his course
because to pursue it to the end would involve so many people in
the guilt of rejection. He merely sealed the doom for which they
themselves were responsible. They failed to come to him because
they loved darkness rather than light.

The final explanation for the cup, which alone gives promise of
throwing light on the dark mystery of the garden experience,
contends that what convulsed the Savior was the fear of separation from God due to becoming the sin-bearer for men. He had
long contemplated from afar what this would mean to him, but
now the hour was upon him and it was overwhelming. He began
to gaze into that cup and discern its awful contents. He had gladly
companied with sinners and gloried in it, but now he was to be
counted a sinner, standing in the sinner's place, bearing the sinner's curse. The darkness of Gethsemane's night presaged the
blackness that would enshroud Golgotha. The awfulness of the
prospect before the Savior began powerfully to affect him. It was
an utterly new experience. Strange terms are used to describe it—
his perplexity, his amazement, and then his agony, with his soul
writhing in the torment of having to be identified with sin, that
thing he hated most of all, for it was so foreign to his nature. In
line with this, we note that the one reference made by Jesus in a

specific way to Isaiah 53, made just before going to the garden, singles out this very aspect of his sufferings: "For I tell you that this scripture must be fulfilled in me, 'And he was reckoned with transgressors' " (Lk. 22:37). When to this is added the realization on his part that death in the place of sinners would entail separation from a holy God (cf. Mt. 27:46), the cup must indeed have seemed too bitter to drink.

The impulse to escape became a passionate urge, a desperate cry—"Let this cup pass from me." The reality will be worse than the anticipation. *I cannot endure it. Is there no other way?* Right here is where Satan's part comes in. Read again the last two verses of John 14. The RSV puts it thus: "I will no longer talk much with you, for the ruler of this world is coming. He has no power over me: but I do as the Father has commanded me. . . ." Note the description of Satan as the ruler of this world. We recall in this connection also Luke 4:13, "And when the devil had ended every temptation, he departed from him until an opportune time." That time has now arrived. Jesus is horrified by what he sees in the cup. Satan will seize this moment of shrinking and weakness. He will renew his offer of a throne of glory, with all the kingdoms of the world ready to serve the Master. Perhaps Jesus will see now the wisdom of accepting so generous an offer at so low a cost. Thus Satan can snatch an eleventh-hour triumph. It is harder for Jesus to resist now than at the beginning, for this is zero hour. Some of his disciples, at least, are armed. He has many friends in Jerusalem. Plenty of pilgrims will rise to lend a hand, for the memory of the triumphal entry is still fresh.

But the Son of God cannot, will not, do this thing. Blocking the way is the will of his Father, and he has bowed before that will all his days. He cannot refuse it now. He must embrace it as never before and find in the sweet will of God the blessed antidote to the bitterness of the cup. The will of God is never so precious as when it costs dearly to embrace it. Abraham found it so on Moriah's hill. So did Jesus amid the deep shades of Gethsemane.

There is no doubt about it, Gethsemane was the Savior's preparation for Calvary. On the cross he yielded up his body as a sacrifice for sin, but here in the garden he anticipated that hour by yielding up his will, the very kernel of his existence. Conquered were his dread and aversion. He was ready to die. It is notable that in the upper room Jesus confessed to having a troubled soul (Jn. 13:21). The same mood, deepened and more tragic, was upon him in the lonely hours of his prayer-wrestling in the garden. But when he stepped forth into the flickering light of the torches of his captors, he had such composure that they fell back in wonder and dismay. Through the trying hours that followed until his eyes closed in death, that outward calm remained with him, sustained by the deep peace of a soul that was perfectly attuned to God. "A Cross once gladly accepted ceases to bring pain."[3]

BIBLIOGRAPHY

A. B. Bruce. *With Open Face*. London: Hodder and Stoughton, 1896.

T. T. Carter. *The Passion and Temptation of Our Lord*. London: Joseph Masters, 1867.

A. M. Fairbairn. *Studies in the Life of Christ*. London: Hodder and Stoughton, 1907.

F. W. Krummacher. *Suffering Savior*. Chicago: Moody, 1947.

A. Kuyper. *His Decease at Jerusalem*. Grand Rapids: Eerdmans, 1928.

K. Schilder. *Christ in His Suffering*. Grand Rapids: Eerdmans, 1938.

3 James Black, *Dilemmas of Jesus* (1924), p. 159.

THE ARREST AND TRIAL

"He died because in the ecclesiastical council He claimed to be the Son of God and the Messiah of Israel, and because before the world-wide tribunal He claimed to be Christ a King."

—A. Taylor Innes

OUR SOURCES BECOME MUCH MORE COMPLETE AND DETAILED AS THEY deal with the closing events of Jesus' earthly life, leading Martin Kähler to observe that the Gospels are accounts of the passion with introductions. There have been plenty of signs along the way pointing to the outcome: Jesus' predictions of his sufferings, tension with Jewish leaders during the last few days, and then the defection of Judas.

Jesus knew that the seclusion of Gethsemane was only a brief interlude of freedom from the tightening circle of opposition. His last words to the disciples made mention of the coming of the betrayer with the result that he himself would be delivered into the hands of sinners (Mk. 14:41).[1] His command to arise and be going is the same as he used regarding the departure from the upper room (Jn. 14:31). The meaning is plain. He is not proposing flight from danger but is leading his followers to confront it.

THE ARREST

Hardly had Jesus spoken than the quiet of the garden was broken by the sound of advancing feet. The darkness was pierced

---

[1] The words "It is enough" are of uncertain meaning. Conceivably *apechei* could refer to Judas—"He has been paid in full"; but it is strange that Jesus would allude to the financial side of the betrayal at a time like this, and strange also that he would make such a comment before actually speaking of the betrayal as imminent.

198

by torches held high to disclose the whereabouts of the Galilean. Clearly the betrayer had not come alone. With him was a great multitude, many of them armed. The Sanhedrin had its representatives, chief priests and scribes and elders (Mk. 14:43). These stayed in the background, yet Jesus recognized them as chiefly responsible (Lk. 22:53). Another segment of the multitude was made up of officers employed by the Sanhedrin to keep order in the temple area (Jn. 18:3). The same term is used of those who were sent to take Jesus at an earlier time (Jn. 7:32) and later to apprehend Peter and John (Acts 5:22). These men, who are probably to be distinguished from the Levites charged with care of the temple precincts, were under the authority of captains (Lk. 22:52), who were out in full force this night. Rarely had the temple police received so important an assignment.

Accompanying them was a cohort of soldiers from the Roman garrison quartered in the castle of Antonia at the northwest corner of the temple area.[2] They are carefully distinguished from the temple police (Jn. 18:3). Probably there was an understanding between the Sanhedrin and the Roman authorities that when disorder threatened, these troops would be made available. They figure in the trial of Jesus (Mk. 15:16).[3]

It seems strange that there should be such a large number of men, armed and ready, sent out to apprehend a man who was not known for his belligerence, one surrounded only by a small band of disciples. The authorities did not fear the immediate followers of Jesus, but they were taking no chances. They had a certain dread of his person, induced in part by their failure to get him into their power up to this time (Jn. 7:32) and particularly because of the way he had swept everything before him in clearing the temple.

Attention focuses now on the betrayer. The first move is his. But John's account adds a significant item not contained in the Synoptics, to the effect that before Judas identified him Jesus stepped forward to ask of the advancing throng, "Whom do you

2 A cohort at full strength consisted of 600 men. However, the word was also used for a *maniple* or detachment of 200 men. The smaller number would have been adequate for this occasion.

3 Because John's account does not actually say that the soldiers were Romans, and because of certain problems in the narrative on the supposition that they were Romans (such as the conducting of Jesus to the house of Annas rather than to Roman authorities), Josef Blinzler conjectures that the cohort belonged not to the Roman but to the Jewish military (*The Trial of Jesus* [1959], pp. 67-68).

seek?" When they explained that they were seeking for Jesus of Nazareth, he replied, "I am he." The effect was electric. They fell to the ground as though paralyzed. W. D. Davies accounts for this reaction by saying, "As Jesus reveals who he is by pronouncing the Divine Name his opponents draw back; they are overwhelmed by numinous awe in the presence of the Divine."[4]

Now it was the turn of Judas to act, so as to fulfill his assignment to identify Jesus. Because many of the soldiers were not familiar with him and because of the darkness, it was felt that a sign from Judas was necessary. Jesus' self-identification made this superfluous, but the betrayer felt bound to carry out his bargain. Matthew and Mark indicate that he overplayed his part, embracing the Master with feigned eagerness and repeatedly showering kisses upon him. John, it seems, could not bring himself to report such a prostitution of the token of affection. He adds a significant word, however, saying that Judas "stood with them" (the captors of Jesus). It is an eloquent statement marking the second decisive step in Judas' downfall. The first was his decision to oppose Jesus even though he remained in his company (Jn. 6:70). Now he stands no longer with Jesus but with the Jews who are seeking his life. He has found his proper position. But in the end he is seen neither with the disciples nor with the Jews. At last he is alone and unable to bear himself, so he takes his own life (Mt. 27:3-10). The devolution of a soul is complete.

Only once is the technical term for "betrayer" used of Judas (Lk. 6:16). Otherwise a very general term is employed, indicating one who delivers something or someone. It is actually the same term used of the Father's gift of the Son as the Savior (Rom. 8:32) and of the Son's self-giving (Gal. 2:20). As Westcott puts it, "His act is regarded in relation to the Lord's Passion, and not to his sin."[5] How remarkable is this restraint in speaking of one who had failed so terribly. Honest men knew well enough their own weakness and refused to point the finger in scorn.

No sooner had Judas stepped out of the way than hands were extended from all sides to lay hold of the Son of man. It was too much for Peter to bear. Whipping out a sword, he tried to stem the tide by lunging at the man nearest him, who happened to be a servant of the high priest. Off came an ear, which Jesus made haste to restore. In the moment of peril to himself he is still solicitous for the welfare of others. He could not endorse this wild dis-

---

[4] *Invitation to the New Testament* (1966), p. 394.
[5] *The Gospel According to St. John* (1896), on 6:64.

play of force, which was wholly misguided. There are those, however, who find a measure of contradiction in the narrative. Had not Jesus himself bidden his followers arm themselves that very night (Lk. 22:36)? It may not be easy to explain his counsel; but this much can be said, namely, that the comment of the Master to the effect that two swords would be sufficient shows that he did not intend that the disciples should use them. Most of the group remained unarmed. It is likely that Jesus sought to teach his followers that a new period was opening for them, one filled with opposition and trial. The swords could serve to symbolize the need for preparedness to face the new situation.

Indeed, Jesus deplored the show of armed might by his captors. He was being sought as though he were some sort of brigand. No hand had been laid on him during his public teaching in the temple. But now things are different. "This is your hour, and the power of darkness" (Lk. 22:53). Finally, the hour of sinful desire coincided with the hour of divine determination. This was man's day, and he foolishly interpreted it in terms of his own strength rather than of divine permission.

On the way to Gethsemane Jesus had indicated the outcome of his seizure as far as the disciples were concerned. It would fulfill the Scripture, "I will strike the shepherd, and the sheep will be scattered" (Mk. 14:27; cf. Zech. 13:7). By stepping forward and offering no resistance, Jesus was able to afford opportunity for the disciples to flee, and they were quick to take advantage of it.

Peter, however, did not go far. Reproaching himself with the reminder that he was pledged never to desert his Lord, no matter what others would do, he slipped back and mingled with the throng as it made its way to the city. Our accounts indicate that during the night, as Jesus was being examined before Caiaphas, Peter faced a trial of his own in the court of the high priest's house. By interweaving the two episodes the Evangelists emphasize that the servant is not greater than his Master and that the disciple cannot stand in his own strength.

THE ECCLESIASTICAL TRIAL

According to John's narrative, Jesus was first taken to Annas, the father-in-law of the high priest Caiaphas (Jn. 18:13).[6] This

6 The official relationship between the two men is difficult to make out, since Acts 4:6 calls Annas the high priest and Luke 3:2 seems to accord them a joint high-priesthood.

brief confrontation no doubt gave satisfaction to one who had long desired to get Jesus into his power. It also provided an interval during which members of the Sanhedrin could be summoned from their homes for a nocturnal meeting. The fact that this account is peculiar to the Fourth Gospel suggests that John himself may have witnessed these preliminary proceedings (cf. Jn. 18:16).

Somewhat confusing to the reader is John's apparent reference to Annas as the high priest (Jn. 18:19), whereas in the same context (Jn. 18:24) he states that after the examination Annas sent Jesus to Caiaphas the high priest. The confusion is somewhat relieved by the realization that one who held this office could be designated by the title even after giving way to a successor.[7] Though Annas had not exercised the duties of this office for some fifteen years, he continued to be a powerful figure in the priestly hierarchy.

His interrogation of Jesus concerned his disciples and his teaching (Jn. 18:19). Since he had no desire to involve his followers, Jesus remained silent on this subject, and so far as his teaching was concerned he was content to make the observation that such an inquisition was unnecessary. After all, his teaching had not been carried on in secret, but openly in synagogue and temple, so that its character was well known. If Annas hoped to elicit from him an admission that could be used against him at the forthcoming trial, he was disappointed.

By this time the Sanhedrin had been assembled, or at least a quorum of its membership; and into their midst Jesus was led, bound, and made to stand before this august body. Caiaphas, as high priest, presided. The first order of business was to call witnesses. Jesus had no counsel, nor were there any witnesses on his behalf. Whether such were not available or whether they were deliberately not sought, we are uninformed. Mark insists that the large number of witnesses against the Lord worked to the disadvantage of his opponents, since they were false witnesses whose testimony did not agree. It seemed for a time that a good case might be made out against him on the ground of a blasphemous utterance to the effect that he would destroy the temple.[8] But the

---

[7] Josephus (*Antiquities* xviii.2.2) does this with Annas, whom he calls Ananus.

[8] The wording of the charge in Mark 14:58 shows resemblance to the words of Jesus recorded in John 2:19, but he had not indicated that he would destroy the temple. Hence the accusation was false at the vital point of responsibility for damage to the house of God.

witnesses could not agree on exactly what he had said, so their testimony had to be thrown out, especially since Jesus, by his silence, refused to confirm anything (Mk. 14:61).

Faced by a stalemate, Caiaphas displayed his customary resourcefulness by taking the initiative in demanding from the prisoner a reply to this question, "Are you the Christ, the Son of the Blessed?" (Mk. 14:62). At this point Jesus discarded his reticence. His "I am" affirmed his messianic status, but he was not content to stop here. To this item of revelation he appended a prophecy of future vindication. He would be seen as the Son of man coming with the clouds of heaven (Mk. 14:62).

This was all Caiaphas needed. By tearing his robe at the top he indicated that he had personally come to a decision concerning the prisoner. This man stood condemned by his own declaration. He was guilty of blasphemy. The others concurred, condemning him to death, and expressed their horror at his impiety by turning to physical abuse, in which the guards who had arrested him joined (Mk. 14:65).

How much of the late night hours were passed in this way is not certain; but the records state that in the morning "the whole council held a consultation" (Mk. 15:1), which led to the removal of Jesus to the Roman governor. Mention of the whole council has led some to think that only a quorum acted during the night and that their decision was affirmed by the full court, which met now in the early morning for the purpose of making legal the action that had been previously taken. This may be so, although Matthew indicates that the whole Sanhedrin had been meeting to hear the case during the night (Mt. 26:59).

But is the account of the Jewish trial historical? Some scholars have expressed doubt on this score. They are able to point to the fact that Jesus was put to death by crucifixion, a Roman practice, rather than by stoning, which was the prevalent Jewish method. But all that is needed to account for such a death is action by the Roman authorities. It is further pointed out that the basis for a verdict against Jesus was suspicion of political activity dangerous to the empire, whereas the accounts of the Jewish trial point to issues that seem quite irrelevant to such a charge.

Some additional ground for rejecting the Gospel accounts has been claimed because their reports of the procedure at the Jewish trial are out of line with regulations laid down in the Mishnah. This collection of orally transmitted laws was drawn up in the second Christian century. One of its tractates, known as *San-*

hedrin, deals with the procedure of the Great Sanhedrin in trying capital cases. Numerous discrepancies appear when these
regulations are compared with the Gospel accounts. For example,
capital cases were not to be tried at night, and a verdict of conviction must not be reached on the same day as the trial. Again,
a death sentence could not be passed anywhere except in the
regular meetingplace, the Hewn Chamber. These and many
more requirements were violated at the trial of Jesus. So if one
were to take the Mishnah as the standard, he could easily conclude
that a trial such as the Evangelists report simply could not have
taken place. Therefore it can be written off as a fabrication, unless one were to conclude that the breaches of the code establish
the unfairness of the Sanhedrin in arriving at a negative verdict
in Jesus' case. This latter course has not infrequently been taken
by Christian writers.

The difficulty in evaluating points of procedure by comparing
the Gospel accounts with the Mishnah is this, that when the
Mishnah is compared with other Jewish sources, whether rabbinic
writings or Josephus, which lie closer to the time of the Gospels
than it does, the unreliable character of the *Sanhedrin* tractate
clearly appears. On the basis of a careful study, Herbert Danby,
the editor of the widely used edition of the Mishnah, comments as
follows: "The Mishna fails to agree with the earlier accounts of
the Sanhedrin because the historical Sanhedrin had ceased to exist, and the Sanhedrin which it did know, on which it based its
description, was a purely academic institution, having purely
academic powers and purely academic interests. It had no national territory to govern, only a national literature to expound."[9]
George Foot Moore estimates the matter similarly: "The inquiry
whether the trial of Jesus was 'legal,' i.e., whether it conformed
to the rules in the Mishnah, is futile because it assumes that those
rules represent the judicial procedure of the old Sanhedrin."[10]

If the Sanhedrin had in mind from the start, as apparently it
did, to take the case to Pilate, it is inconceivable that it would
have transgressed its own rules so flagrantly as to invite rejection
by the governor on grounds of unlawful procedure.

Furthermore, as Blinzler points out, there is no hint that the

9 "The Bearing of the Rabbinic Criminal Code on the Jewish Trial Narratives in the Gospels," JTS, 21 (Oct. 1919), 75.
10 *Judaism,* II (1946), 187, n. 5.

early church ever raised the issue of irregularities in the Jewish trial.[11]

Another approach to the Jewish trial questions the accuracy of the Gospel writers on the ground that their records do not reflect the actual historical situation but are colored by the antagonism the Christian community increasingly felt toward the Jews as the two confronted each other during the second half of the first century. This bitterness is read back into the Gospel narratives; it accounts for the attempt to pin responsibility on the Jews. Any blame attached to the latter group is reduced to a minimum by this outlook. "A decision that he should stand trial on a charge of seditious activities was arrived at with the connivance or concurrence of the holders of highest Jewish office." This is as far as Paul Winter will go in admitting Jewish responsibility.[12] But Winter's picture of relations between Jesus and the Pharisees during his ministry is altogether too rosy. It ignores the evidence of the Gospels to the effect that there were repeated clashes and even attempts on the life of the Master.[13]

It is quite understandable that Jewish scholars should rankle under the charge that their people mistreated Jesus of Nazareth. The temptation is great to make anti-Semitism the culprit, alleging that the real fault lies in reading back later tensions between Christians and Jews into the record of Jesus' life. But this cannot be regarded as successful. "The inclination, frequently to be observed, to condemn as unhistorical or at least suspicious everything in the passion story which throws an unfavorable light on the Jews, has to be met with the question: 'Whence, then, came the boundless anti-Semitism attributed to primitive Christianity if the Jews had little or nothing to do with the death of Jesus?"[14] From the very first, exponents of the new faith accused the Jewish nation of putting Jesus of Nazareth to death (Acts 2:23, 36; 3:15; 4:10; 7:52; cf. I Thess. 2:15). This they could not have done unless there were a basis in fact, which points directly to the action of the Sanhedrin (see Acts 4:10 on this). But of course this has nothing to do with anti-Semitism, for those who made the charge were themselves Jews. They were simply calling

11 Blinzler, op. cit., p. 144.
12 Winter, On the Trial of Jesus (1961), p. 135.
13 See C. F. D. Moule, The Birth of the New Testament (1962), pp. 40-41, 95-96.
14 Blinzler, op. cit., pp. 42-43.

their fellow countrymen to repentance. That the Evangelists were guilty of bias in picturing the responsibility of official Judaism is not borne out by a study of their records. Matthew mentions the condemnation only incidentally, Luke says nothing about it, and finally John does not even include an account of the Jewish trial.[15] So the emphasis, instead of growing, decidedly diminishes so far as the trial is concerned.

An effort has been made in another direction to relieve the Jewish people of substantial onus in the condemnation of Jesus. The claim is advanced that there were two Sanhedrins in those days, one of a religious nature, the other political in the sense that it was the creation of the government and served its interests. Zeitlin tries to make out a case for the existence of this political body, asserting that it is meant wherever there is a reference to its being *summoned*.[16] The religious Sanhedrin was not summoned, because it had regular times of meeting. The conclusion drawn is that Jesus must have been condemned by the political Sanhedrin, which did not truly represent the nation but was friendly with the Roman authorities. Any evidence for two Sanhedrins, however, is inferential rather than documentary. Neither Josephus nor the New Testament mentions two bodies. And as Danby observes, "This dual system, a sort of 'House of Convocation' side by side with a national parliament, each working independently of the other, seems especially out of place in the Jewish constitution. The Jews' outstanding claim to national distinction was the theocratic nature of their government, in which civil and religious matters were everywhere interpenetrating, and for all practical purposes identical."[17] Montefiore dismisses the theory by saying, "It is too problematic and hypothetical to be discussed here."[18]

If for any reason one is disposed to regard the Gospel accounts of the Jewish trial as slanted and is therefore desirous of confirmation from an extrabiblical source, he will be interested in a letter that Mara bar Sarapion wrote to his son, who was away from home studying. The letter is generally dated shortly after the fall of Jerusalem. After mentioning the mistake of the

---

15 *Ibid.*, p. 125.

16 Solomon Zeitlin, *Who Crucified Jesus?* 2nd edition (1947), pp. 68-83. A more elaborate presentation of this position is given in an earlier work by Adolf Büchler, *Das Synedrion in Jerusalem* (1902).

17 *Op. cit.*, pp. 74-75.

18 C. G. Montefiore, *The Synoptic Gospels* (1927), p. 358.

Athenians in killing Socrates and of the citizens of Samos in burning Pythagoras, Mara continues: "Or what did it avail the Jews
to execute their wise king, since their kingdom was taken from
them from that time?" He explains the last statement by adding,
"The Jews were slaughtered and driven from their kingdom, and
live dispersed everywhere." Blinzler judges that the expression
"wise king" indicates a knowledge of Jesus' teaching and also of
his alleged messianic dignity.[19] The testimony of this man is particularly important because he does not write from the Christian
standpoint, but is a Stoic and a worshiper of the gods.

A crucial point in the whole discussion on the trial of Jesus is
the right of the Sanhedrin to carry out the death penalty. The
one passage that bears directly on this is John 18:31. "Pilate said
to them, 'Take him yourselves and judge him by your own law.'
The Jews said to him, 'It is not lawful for us to put any man to
death.'" John's statement receives support from a passage in the
Palestinian Talmud as follows: "Forty years before the destruction of the temple they took from Israel the right to inflict capital
punishment."[20] Juster sought to discount this, contending that it
is only an inference from a statement in the Babylonian Talmud
(*Abodah Zarah* 8b) that forty years before the destruction of the
temple the Sanhedrin left its meetingplace there. Since it was
held that only in the temple could a verdict be reached in capital
cases, this departure was regarded as tantamount to a loss of the
right to inflict capital punishment.[21] But in taking this ground
Juster seems to have overlooked the fact that the item contained
in the Palestinian Talmud is a *baraitha*, which puts it before
A.D. 200 and hence earlier than the Babylonian Talmud.[22] Consequently its testimony should not be ignored.

A frontal attack on the accuracy of John 18:31 was made by the
German scholar Hans Lietzmann in his essay *Der Prozess Jesu*,
published in 1931, in which he depended heavily on Juster. His
arguments have often been repeated in discussions on this subject.[23] Three of these are of special interest to students of the
New Testament and will be noted here. First, there is the right
of the Jews to put to death even a Roman who penetrated the

[19] *Op. cit.*, pp. 36, 38.

[20] *Sanhedrin* I, 18a.

[21] J. Juster, *Les Juifs dans l'empire romain*, II (1914) , 133, n. 1.

[22] G. D. Kilpatrick, *The Trial of Jesus* (1953) , p. 17.

[23] See, for example, "The Competence of the Sanhedrin," by T. A. Burkill
in *Vigiliae Christianae*, X (1956) , 80-96.

barrier that separated the court of the Gentiles from the inner area of the temple. Josephus reports Titus as saying to the Jews during the siege of Jerusalem, "Did we not permit you to put to death any who passed it, even were he a Roman?"[24] This is a remarkable example of the lengths to which the Romans were prepared to go in recognizing the right of the Jews to maintain their own religious laws and customs. However, its very uniqueness makes it unsuitable as a negation of John 18:31. Sherwin-White well expresses this unsuitability. "But if the Sanhedrin had the general right to execute offenders against the religious law, this special concession would not have been necessary."[25]

A second alleged instance has to do with the death of Stephen. The presence of the Sanhedrin is noted (Acts 6:15) as well as the use of witnesses (Acts 6:13; 7:58). Schlatter understands the imposing of the death penalty on the basis of an "agreement by which Pilate gave a free hand to the Jewish authorities in Jerusalem to suppress the Jewish Christian community."[26] But Luke avoids saying that the Sanhedrin carried out the death penalty. He contents himself with the use of the indefinite subject "they" throughout the whole paragraph (Acts 7:54-59). Blinzler's judgment seems better here, namely, that "before judgment could be passed the proceedings were forcibly interrupted by the Jews present."[27] Feelings against Stephen were running high and finally burst through all restraint, resulting in the stoning.

The third incident relates to the death of James, the brother of Jesus, as reported by Josephus (*Antiquities* xx.9.1). In the interval between the death of the Roman governor Festus and the arrival of Albinus his successor, the younger Ananus, who was high priest at the time, saw an opportunity to act against the Christians. He brought James and certain others before the Sanhedrin, accused them of transgressing the law, and gave them over to be stoned. This created offense among many in Jerusalem, resulting in a deputation going out to meet Albinus and informing him of the action, including the charge that Ananus had acted without authority in convening the Sanhedrin for his purpose, since he lacked the governor's consent. Shortly there-

---

[24] *Jewish War* vi.2.4.

[25] A. N. Sherwin-White, *Roman Society and Roman Law in the New Testament* (1963), p. 38.

[26] A. Schlatter, *The Church in the New Testament Period* (1955), p. 87.

[27] *Op. cit.*, p. 162.

after, King Agrippa replaced Ananus. The anger of Albinus over the information he received suggests that he resented the action taken without his authorization. Granted that the death penalty was assessed on this occasion by the Sanhedrin and carried out, yet the action was palpably illegal, so the incident can hardly be used to counter John 18:31.

One of the most recent and certainly one of the most able contributions to the discussion is that by Sherwin-White. He notes that the power of capital punishment was one of the most jealously guarded of the powers of government. The one exception was the case of the free communities "which for past services to the Roman State were made independent of the authority of Roman magistrates in local administration, and enjoyed unrestricted jurisdiction over their own citizens."[28] The history of the Jewish community in Palestine under the Romans and even before fully justifies the remark that "turbulent Judaea is the very last place where we would expect any extraordinary concessions."[29]

A reasonable solution to the whole problem is "that the Sanhedrin was allowed in the procuratorial period a limited criminal jurisdiction, both for police purposes in the Temple area and for the maintenance of the Jewish law."[30] Apart from this, John 18:31 may be safely regarded as expressing the status quo.

Before moving on to the Roman phase of the trial, we should note that some scholars have advanced the opinion that the meeting of the Sanhedrin did not constitute a trial but only a hearing, an interrogation, in order to gather information that could be submitted to the Roman governor when the case was taken to him.[31] The difficulty with this approach is that it runs counter to the testimony of Mark 14:64 to the effect that the Council unitedly "condemned him as deserving death." In such a setting, the verdict surely has the force of an official sentence. Using the same word "condemned," Matthew states that it was this decision that drove Judas, in remorse, to renounce his action and proceed to take his own life (Mt. 27:3).[32]

---

28 *Op. cit.*, p. 36.

29 *Ibid.*, p. 37.

30 *Ibid.*, pp. 41-42.

31 E.g. O. Cullmann, *The State in the New Testament* (1956), pp. 45-46.

32 If some doubt arises as to how information such as Judas' appearance before the Sanhedrin could come into Christian hands, and for that matter the needed information about Jesus' appearance before that body, Jesus himself

THE TRIAL BEFORE PILATE

Early in the morning (Jn. 18:28) the whole Sanhedrin brought Jesus before Pilate (Lk. 23:1). The place was the Praetorium (Jn. 18:28), which should mean the palace of Herod the Great to the west of the temple area, where the Roman governors usually resided when they were in the city. However, John provides a further detail that raises some uncertainty. The spot where Pilate had his judgment seat set up is called *lithostrōtos*, meaning an area paved with stones (Jn. 19:13). Modern excavations at the Castle of Antonia adjacent to the temple have disclosed a section paved with large stones, which seems to answer well to the situation pictured by the Evangelists. It is possible that at feast time Pilate thought it wise to be with the Roman garrison.[33] If this was the location, only a few minutes would have been required to bring Jesus before him.

We must look to Luke for a statement of the charge.[34] They were three in number: perverting the nation, opposing the payment of tribute to Caesar, and making himself out to be Christ, that is to say, a king (Lk. 23:1). The first was vague (though Pilate thought seriously enough of it to repeat it—Lk. 23:14), the second was untrue (Mk. 12:17), and the third was ambiguous. Probably the first and third were closely related. Except for the introduction of the term "Messiah" (Christ) there is no relation to the charges brought at the religious trial, and even this term is given a frame of reference by a use of the word "king" that is calculated to suggest to Pilate's mind something quite different from the concept of Messiahship that Jesus entertained. While the title "king" could serve to indicate the ground on which the Sanhedrin had condemned him (blasphemy in claiming that he was the Messiah directly associated with God), it could also be given such a turn as to suggest a purpose to head a revolutionary movement designed to secure the Jews' independence from Rome.

---

need not be ruled out. This could have been a part of his postresurrection teaching. Other possibilities are Joseph of Arimathea and Nicodemus, both members of the Council. Acts 6:7 opens up still another possibility.

[33] C. H. Dodd, *Historical Tradition in the Fourth Gospel* (1963), p. 108.

[34] In reporting the trial, Matthew follows Mark rather closely, making some additions; Luke is the only one to give the full list of charges, and he seems especially concerned to call attention to Jesus' innocence; John gives help at the crucial points of the nature of Jesus' kingship and the cause of Pilate's final surrender of the prisoner to be crucified.

The Jewish leaders hoped to impress Pilate with Jesus' criminality on this score and so to gain an immediate hearing, something they could not hope for on the basis of a charge of blasphemy. They admitted their desire to put the prisoner to death but confessed they lacked the authority to do this (Jn. 18:31).

It is difficult to say how much Pilate knew about Jesus, but in any event he could not take lightly the implication that this man could be a threat to the Roman position in the land. Josephus pictures conditions twenty years or so before this. "And so Judaea was filled with brigandage. Anyone might make himself king as the head of a band of rebels whom he fell in with, and then would press on to the destruction of the community." [35] The prisoner might be a guerrilla chieftain or someone more influential and dangerous. So Pilate was concerned to inquire if he were the king of the Jews (Jn.18:33). Having refused to align himself with an independence movement (Jn. 6:15), Jesus could assure Pilate that he was not a king with political ambitions. The proof lay close at hand, his refusal to summon his followers to fight for him when he was arrested in the garden (Jn. 18:36). Pilate seemed satisfied with this explanation. He may have already verified this through the report of the cohort commander.

This conversation took place within the Praetorium. When the two reappeared before the Sanhedrin, which had now been augmented by a multitude of other persons (Lk. 23:4), many accusations were leveled at Jesus. His refusal to answer any of them astonished the governor (Mk. 15:5), but it was no source of astonishment to those familiar with the prophetic Scriptures (Isa. 53:7).

The crowd refused to rest content in Pilate's statement that his examination had convinced him that Jesus had committed no crime (Lk. 23:4). Rephrasing the original charge about perverting the nation, they claimed that he stirred up the people by his teaching, implying it was revolutionary and disloyal, "from Galilee even to this place" (Lk. 23:5).[36] It was true that the final journey from Galilee to Jerusalem was marked by a cultivation of the crowds rather than the near-secrecy that characterized other visits.

One word, at least, caught the ear of the governor. This man had been in Galilee. That meant that he belonged to the jurisdiction of Herod Antipas, who was then in the city. An idea

[35] *Antiquities* xvii.10.8.
[36] Cf. the note in Alford's *Greek Testament* on Luke 9:52.

was born in Pilate's mind. Why not send the prisoner to Herod?
It is probable that he felt reasonably sure that Herod would
judge him innocent of the charges. After all, if Jesus were such
a menace to the state as his accusers tried to maintain, Herod
would surely have ferreted him out long ago and dealt with
him.[37] This is the Herod who had put John the Baptist to death.
Though he had not seen Jesus, he had heard of his miracles and
was all set for a demonstration, especially since he was in a position to send a good report to Pilate if this prophet cooperated.
But he was doomed to disappointment. This playboy prince, who
was more interested in entertainment than in the administering
of justice, was destined to get nothing from Jesus other than
dignified silence. A miracle just now might save his life, but he
had not come to perform tricks for the amusement of courts.
Disappointed, Herod's soldiers put on a show of their own, with
Jesus as the pilloried victim. The quarrel between Herod and
Pilate, whatever it may have been,[38] was patched up that day.
But as far as Christian tradition was concerned, Herod had
placed himself among the enemies of Jesus (Acts 4:27).

With the disposal of the case tossed back at him, Pilate could
only affirm his original insistence of the innocency of the accused,
backing it up now with the observation that Herod had found
no crime in him. But the wolves were beginning to howl again,
so the governor cast about for some expedient. He was thinking
of a beating to teach Jesus to stay out of further trouble, followed
by release (Lk. 23:16), when the crowd before him began to
swell noticeably. The populace had turned out to demand their
annual Passover favor from Pilate, the release of a prisoner. This
gave the governor an idea, which he acted on without reflection,
one that got him into deeper trouble. Aware as he was that the
motive behind the bringing of the Galilean prophet to him by the
Sanhedrin was their envy of his popularity, Pilate thought he
saw a way out of his awkward situation. Surely the crowd, if
given a choice between Jesus and Barabbas, would not hesitate
to ask for Jesus (Mt. 27:17).

Pilate failed, however, to reckon with two important considerations. If Jesus was popular, so was Barabbas. He was regarded
as a hero, one who dared to take part in an uprising. In doing so,
he had committed murder. Perhaps he had killed a Roman soldier
or two. Jesus had refused to take a stand against Rome. The

---

[37] Blinzler, *op. cit.*, p. 196.
[38] Luke 13:1 may provide a clue.

other item Pilate failed to take into account was the determination of the Sanhedrin. When they saw that there was a possibility that Jesus might be called for by the crowd, they took no chances, but fanned out through the press of humanity, passing the word to the rank and file that if they knew what was good for them they would ask for the release of Barabbas. In a few moments the situation was well in hand. Cries went up all over the square demanding the release of Barabbas. People were not interested in challenging the judgment of their own leaders.

The release of Barabbas did not in itself necessitate the condemnation of Jesus, but Pilate, caught by surprise, showed ineptness in asking the crowd for guidance. What should he do, then, with Jesus, this one who was supposed to be King of the Jews (Mk. 15:12)? The shouts grew deafening, demanding that he be crucified. Pilate's protest of the prisoner's innocency was weak and ineffectual now. It was a case of one against a howling multitude.

Not infrequently the question is asked, What had become of the people who welcomed Jesus with such enthusiasm a few days before when he rode into the city? Had they shown their fickleness by shifting ground? This may have been true of some who had been sobered by learning of the action of the Sanhedrin against their hero. But in large part the crowd was probably made up of people who lived in Jerusalem, who were accustomed to ask the yearly favor of the governor and who had learned to conform to the wishes of the chief priests and elders.

The crowd had Pilate on the run and they sensed it. Their countrymen had made this despised Roman back down two or three times before, and it pleased them to think that they were about to put something over on him now. At this point, with a shrug, Pilate was about ready to give up; but he wanted to make it plain that his sense of justice could not endorse death for the prisoner. So he called for a basin of water and washed his hands to symbolize that he was free of bloodguiltiness in this matter. Matthew, ever on the alert to add a feature that would fix responsibility on the Jewish nation, adds that the people responded to Pilate's claim of innocence by assuming the burden for themselves and their children (Mt. 27:25).

Now, at length, Pilate ordered the scourging that he had talked about. It was done inside the Praetorium and was carried out in a spirit of amused contempt by the soldiers. This time they had a *king* to deal with. Very well. Why not give him the royal treatment, with robe and crown, after lacerating his back with the cruel scourge that tore into the flesh? Following the physical abuse and the mockery, Pilate brought him out once more, hopeful that the sight of a figure so mauled and so helpless would stir sentiments of pity and make possible, after other measures had failed, the release of the accused.

But Pilate was a poor psychologist. "He failed to take into account the common principle that when you have wrongfully injured a man you hate him all the more. . . . The people were infuriated by the sight of the innocent, unmurmuring Sufferer whom they had thus mangled. They cannot bear that such an object be left to remind them of their barbarity, and with one fierce yell of fury they cry, 'Crucify Him, crucify Him.' "[39]

Exasperated, Pilate fired back at the crowd, "Take him yourselves and crucify him, for I find no crime in him" (Jn. 19:6). This was a taunt, for he knew the Jews could not do this. It was his way of saying that the blame belonged to them if this innocent person were going to die.

The Jewish leaders hastened to assure Pilate that from their standpoint the prisoner indeed deserved to die. "We have a law, and by that law he ought to die, because he has made himself the Son of God" (Jn. 19:7). Since neither word has the definite article, the phrase could well have been taken by Pilate to mean, "a son of a god."[40] This superstitious Roman, already disturbed by his wife's dream (Mt. 27:19), is now shaken by the fear that this strange, quiet personage before him is really an immortal god in human form. Hence the anxious query posed to Jesus, "Where are you from?" But the question was met with silence. When Pilate prodded the prisoner with the reminder that he had better talk, seeing that he was dealing with one who had power to release and power to crucify, Jesus countered firmly with the observation that there was a higher power. Caiaphas knew something about that higher power even if Pilate did not. Therefore he had the greater sin.

For the second time the discussion was getting into areas where Pilate had no competence (cf. Jn. 18:37-38), so he cut short the dialogue and once more indicated to the throng his purpose to release Jesus, only to be staggered by an unexpected counterblow. "If you release this man, you are not Caesar's friend; every one who makes himself a king sets himself against Caesar." The words

[39] Marcus Dods, *The Gospel of St. John*, II (1895), 307.
[40] C. H. Dodd, *op. cit.*, p. 114.

pierced the governor like a dart. They constituted a threat to his position. The expression "Caesar's friend" was a technical term. This title "was an honor reserved for loyal senators, prominent knights, and meritorious administrators. It assured its holder a brilliant career."[41] The loss of this title, as Stauffer goes on to show, could be disastrous for one's career. Especially with Tiberius as his superior, a man of suspicious and demanding temperament, Pilate did well to fear that a review of his administration might prove his undoing. The tug of war with the Sanhedrin had come to an abrupt end. He brought Jesus out from the Praetorium, took his place on the judgment seat, and with a disdainful wave of the hand toward the prisoner, announced, "Here is your King!" (Jn. 19:14). It was sarcasm pure and simple. Such a king and such a people! Again the oft-repeated demand was lifted that Jesus be crucified, and was met by the scornful question, "Shall I crucify your King?" Pilate had so insistently linked the word "king" with the prisoner, taking it from their own complaint (Lk. 23:2), that the Jews were sick of hearing it and went so far as to say, "We have no king but Caesar." Yet this sell-out was the logical conclusion of all that had gone before.

> The opponents of our Lord, unable to find a way of action for themselves on their own lines, fell in with the Sadducean policy of Caiaphas—a policy which, however hateful to themselves, yet made itself dominant by proving itself alone efficacious. There is this additional tragedy, then, in the final close— that the Pharisees, for the sake of slaying the Lord, foreswore the creed which had been their glory and their life, and allowed themselves to be found crying in Pilate's Hall, "We have no king but Caesar."[42]

The trial was over. All that remained was the formal verdict delivered from the *bēma*. Jesus must die by crucifixion.

An aftermath of the trial belongs to the crucifixion. It was the practice of the Romans to announce the reason for the execution of a person, particularly if the circumstances were somewhat unusual.[43] So the inscription put up by Pilate's order did more than identify the victim. It gave a reason for the execution. The basis for the verdict was clearly of a political nature. Jesus had

41 Ethelbert Stauffer, *Jesus and His Story* (1960), p. 133.

42 H. S. Holland, *The Philosophy of Faith and the Fourth Gospel* (1920), p. 192.

43 Cf. Suetonius *Caligula* 32.

been judged guilty of sedition, though he disavowed any kingly ambitions of a worldly sort. Pilate had been crowded into a corner and forced to render this verdict, though his heart was not in it. Now he has the last word, saying to the world that this Jesus is the King of the Jews, the very thing they had denied during the trial.

In summary, the representatives of Israel and the representative of Rome had pronounced against Jesus of Nazareth, although on very different grounds. Jew and Gentile had conspired to put him to death. They must share the blame (Acts 2:23; 4:27).

And what of him who endured such contradiction of sinners against himself? His bearing throughout has been majestic. No Roman could have shown more stoical fortitude. No Jew could have exhibited such perfect obedience to the will of God.

BIBLIOGRAPHY

Josef Blinzler. *The Trial of Jesus.* Westminster, Md.: Newman, 1959.

T. A. Burkill, "The Competence of the Sanhedrin," *Vigiliae Christianae,* 10:2 (July 1956), 80-96

Oscar Cullmann. *The State in the New Testament.* New York: Scribners, 1956. Pp. 24-49.

Herbert Danby, "The Bearing of the Rabbinical Criminal Code on the Jewish Trial Narratives in the Gospels," JTS, 21 (Oct. 1919), 51-76.

C. H. Dodd. *Historical Tradition in the Fourth Gospel.* Cambridge, Eng.: Cambridge University Press, 1963. Pp. 83-120.

M. Goguel. *The Life of Jesus.* New York: Macmillan, 1949. Pp. 483-530.

Leonard Goppelt. *Jesus, Paul and Judaism.* New York: Nelson, 1964. Pp. 84-90.

A. Taylor Innes. *The Trial of Jesus Christ.* Edinburgh: T. & T. Clark, 1905.

G. D. Kilpatrick. *The Trial of Jesus.* New York: Oxford, 1953.

Frank J. Powell. *The Trial of Jesus Christ.* Grand Rapids: Eerdmans, 1954.

K. Schilder. *Christ on Trial.* Grand Rapids: Eerdmans, 1939.

A. N. Sherwin-White. *Roman Society and Roman Law in the New Testament.* Oxford: Clarendon, 1963. Pp. 24-47.

James Stalker. *The Trial and Death of Jesus Christ.* London: Hodder and Stoughton, 1894. Pp. 1-109.

Ethelbert Stauffer. *Jesus and His Story.* New York: Knopf, 1960. Pp. 121-134.

Henry Wansbrough, "Suffered under Pontius Pilate," *Scripture,* 18 (July 1966), 84-93.

Paul Winter. *On the Trial of Jesus.* Berlin: Walter de Gruyter, 1961.

Solomon Zeitlin. *Who Crucified Jesus?* New York: Harper, 1942. Pp. 68-83, 144-171.

Chapter XV

THE CRUCIFIXION

> "His Cross, so far from being to Him a bitter disappointment, was the hour in which there flamed up into glory the spirit, purpose, passion of His life."
>
> —George H. Morrison

> "The Cross of Christ is man's only glory or it is his final stumblingblock."
>
> —Samuel M. Zwemer

APPARENTLY JESUS RECEIVED THE VERDICT OF DEATH IN SILENCE. FOR him there was no appeal to Caesar. Unlike Paul, he was not a Roman citizen. Moreover, he was ready to die, for his hour had come.

THE JOURNEY TO CALVARY

Before long the prisoner was on his way to the place of execution, surrounded by soldiers, with many of the Sanhedrin following them, besides a crowd of people possessed of a morbid curiosity to see the Galilean die. It was customary for a condemned man to be burdened with the cross on which he was to suffer—not the whole of it but the crossbar to which the hands were fixed at the execution. The upright beam was left in the ground. It speaks well for the physical stamina of Jesus that after sleepless hours and bodily abuse, not to mention emotional strain, he was able to bear his cross through the streets and somewhat beyond the wall of the city. As the procession was going out the gates, his strength gave way (Mt. 27:32). Who was to carry the cross now?

217

The Romans were masters of the country, and in a case like this they did not hesitate to press people into service (Mt. 5:41). Looking around, they sighted a certain man, Simon of Cyrene, coming into the city, and ordered him to pick up the wooden beam and fall in behind Jesus the rest of the way.

Along the route of travel stood mourning women, lamenting that the Nazarene who had gone about doing good was now facing the terrible death of crucifixion. It is rather paradoxical that this reaction should be superimposed on the scene of passionate insistence on his death by the Sanhedrin, seconded by the crowd outside the Praetorium. Yet the same contrast may be seen a few years later when angry men stoned Stephen in the same area and others, grief-stricken, picked up his body and took it away for burial (Acts 7:57-58; 8:2).

Jesus turned the lamentation back on those who expressed it. They and their city needed it more than he. Dire things were coming upon it, as he had predicted to his disciples (Lk. 21:20-24) and to others as well (Mt. 23:38). His epigram put it neatly. "For if they do this when the wood is green, what will happen when it is dry?" (Lk. 23:31). He himself is the green tree, filled with the life of God. If he must suffer, what will be the fate of those who have no fruit and are ready for destruction?

The traditional site of the crucifixion is a point outside the city to the west of the temple area, where the Church of the Holy Sepulchre now stands. A competing location, called Gordon's Calvary, lies to the north of the city. Golgotha (Mk. 15:22) is the Aramaic name for the spot, meaning a skull. The Greek equivalent is *kranion* (Lk. 23:33), which has come over into English through the Latin as "cranium." However, an older Latin term, *calva*, meaning "bare head" or "skull," accounts for the word Calvary in the King James Version of Luke 23:33. Uncertainty surrounds the meaning of the word Golgotha. Possibly it refers to the shape of the hill, skull-like in formation. Even if the resemblance were only faint, the very fact that this was a place of execution could easily suggest a connection and lead to the use of this word.

As to the time of the crucifixion, John says it came at about the sixth hour (Jn. 19:14), which means around noon. On the other hand, Mark places it at the third hour (Mk. 15:25), which would be about nine in the morning. Admittedly the problem is difficult because the manuscripts of Mark seem to unite behind this reading. It may be significant, however, that Matthew, who so often

follows Mark, lacks this time notice, as does Luke, suggesting
that this item could have come into the text of Mark at a very
early stage of its transmission. It is worthy of note also that the
statement about the crucifixion repeats what has been said at the
beginning of the previous verse, which is awkward. So internal
evidence is not favorable to the Markan reading. There are
advantages, too, in adopting the noon hour, for this would allow
more adequate time for all that had to transpire during the trial
before Pilate, including the trip to Herod, and it helps to explain
Pilate's astonishment that Jesus was dead by the middle of the
afternoon (Mk. 15:44). One could be expected to survive after
three hours whereas six hours was quite another matter. On the
other hand it can be argued that if the darkness came at the
sixth hour, an earlier time must be assigned to the crucifixion
to make room for the things that occurred prior to the darkness.

The Crucifixion

Even for a callous age, crucifixion was a cruel punishment. The
Romans adopted the practice from the Carthaginians and limited
its use mainly to slaves and rebels. Thousands of Jews lost their
lives in this fashion during and after the siege of Jerusalem.[1]
Amazing in their objectivity, the Gospel writers are content to
state the fact of crucifixion without going into detail or playing
upon the sympathy of their readers. An attempted reconstruction
of what took place has been supplied by Bishop.

> The executioner laid the crossbeam behind Jesus and brought
> him to the ground quickly by grasping his arm and pulling him
> backward. As soon as Jesus fell, the beam was fitted under the
> back of his neck and, on each side, soldiers quickly knelt on
> the inside of the elbows. Jesus gave no resistance and said
> nothing, but he groaned as he fell on the back of his head and
> the thorns pressed against his torn scalp.[2]

Then followed the driving of the spikes and the lifting up of the
body onto the upright beam. With the nailing of the feet, the
operation was concluded. The only movement of the body left
to the victim was to lift oneself a short distance by pressing on the
nails at the feet.

In view of the awful suffering that crucifixion imposed, it is not

[1] Josephus *Jewish War* v.11.1.
[2] Jim Bishop, *The Day Christ Died* (1957), p. 311.

surprising that there should have been a guild of women in Jerusalem who added a touch of mercy to the scene by offering a stupefying drink to all who had to undergo the ordeal. They offered this relief to Jesus before he was placed on the cross, but he refused the wine mingled with myrrh (Mk. 15:23). He wanted to meet death in the full possession of his mental powers. Had he taken the drink, we could not have had the clear-cut statements from his lips during those last hours that are recorded in the Gospels.

Two criminals were executed along with Jesus, but only in his case is an inscription mentioned. The others were common criminals; he was extraordinary. His advertised offense consisted in being King of the Jews. To the Roman mind this suggested Zealot sympathies; to the Jewish mind it suggested a (false) Messiah; to the Christian mind it suggested the Lord of glory whom sin-blinded men had failed to recognize (I Cor. 2:8).

According to custom the clothing of those who were crucified became the property of the soldiers involved. When the various items belonging to Jesus had been parceled out to the four men, his tunic remained. Being seamless, it did not invite partition. Therefore the soldiers cast lots for its possession, unconsciously fulfilling Scripture with marvelous precision (Ps. 22:18). If Mary had made the tunic with her own hands and was watching what went on, it meant that the sword was pressed a little deeper into her heart (Lk. 2:35).

The work of the soldiers was done. All that remained was to watch and wait. Jesus had his own thoughts, and they come to expression at intervals as the seven sayings from the cross. Observe the symmetry of these sayings. They begin with a broad perimeter, the circle of his persecutors, move on to one who was in the act of shifting from opposition to adherence, then concentrate on the two who were the dearest on earth to him, and finally narrow down to the Father and himself in the last four words. These sayings from the cross are priceless because they interpret for us the sufferings of Jesus and his reaction to them.

"Father, forgive them; for they know not what they do" (Lk. 23:34). The prayer should be heard against the background of the outcrying against him. In his cantata, *The Seven Last Words*, Dubois brings together the cries of the multitude before Pilate—"crucify him"—and the prayer of Jesus coming through at intervals, so as to give a striking contrast. Usually victims of crucifixion filled the air with screams and curses. In this case some word of

righteous indignation might have been expected such as Je
uttered when struck by an officer in the presence of Annas (Jn.
18:23). But no, there is only a prayer for others. Jesus had taught
love for enemies. Now he exemplifies it by interceding for those
who had a part in placing him there—the soldiers for inflicting
torture without compunction, Pilate for giving him over to death
to save his own position, the Sanhedrin for their determination to
destroy him, the nation for not receiving him, and for all in
every time and place whose sin conspired to bring him into the
throes of death.

Are we to suppose that the prayer for forgiveness was a virtual
setting aside of divine justice? No, it simply meant that when
these who had joined in putting Jesus to death had the chance
to hear the gospel preached to them, they would have an option.
If they found their hearts convicted, they could have forgiveness.
If they crucified the Son of God afresh, they would do it with their
eyes open and would have to bear the solemn consequences.

Jesus pleaded the ignorance of those who united in slaying him
(cf. Acts 3:17). Ignorance does not mean that men are excusable,
but it does mean that they are forgivable (I Tim. 1:13). Pentecost was part of the answer to the prayer, Paul was another part,
and there still is no end to the answer (Eph. 4:32).

The prayer was grounded on the serene confidence that what
was happening on the cross had everything to do with God's
reception of sinners. Jeremias comments, "We have in this prayer
an implicit interpretation of Jesus' death. For Jesus offers it in
place of the expiatory vow: 'May my death expiate all my sins',
which a condemned man had to say before his execution."[3]
Having no sins of his own, Jesus was not content to glory in this,
but interceded for sinners in word even while he mediated for
them in the act of dying in their stead.

No small part of the suffering of the cross belonged to the
realm of the spirit. Who can measure the distress that attaches
to being repudiated, counted an outcast, treated like an animal?
Human dignity was trampled. Nakedness sharpened the sense of
shame. It is likely the Romans, to avoid offending the sensibilities
of the Jews, allowed a loin cloth for the victim, but this was all.
The sight of Jesus hanging there, helpless and exposed, brought
out the worst in the bystanders. To understand it, one must
realize the long frustration that dogged the Jewish leaders as they

---

3 J. Jeremias, *The Central Message of the New Testament* (1965), p. 48.

had watched the Nazarene growing in popularity and influence and felt themselves unable to stop him. To them he was a bold innovator, a nonconformist, a blasphemer. Now at last he was getting his just deserts. They had to vent their feelings of satisfaction. And so they mocked.

The rulers of the Jews, the members of the Sanhedrin who had condemned him, now challenged him to save himself and show that he was Christ, the King of Israel, by coming down from the cross (Mk. 15:32). They did not know that such a demonstration would make impossible the saving of others, and for their salvation he had come. The challenge could not be accepted.

Having nothing else to do, the soldiers took up the taunt (Lk. 23:36). Those who passed by stopped long enough to add their participation. Since the Passover season had arrived, people were very conscious of the allegation that Jesus had designs on the temple. It had been charged at the trial before the Sanhedrin that he had threatened to destroy it. Picking this up, the passing throng derided him. Surely one with such power could find a way to come down from the cross (Mk. 15:29-30).

This general participation in the mockery suggests that the person of Christ, especially his high claims, together with his unsullied holiness and quiet dignity, brought to the surface the worst that was in the depths of the human heart. "They hated me without cause" (Jn. 15:25). One recalls here the famous saying of Archbishop William Temple, "Why anyone should have troubled to crucify the Christ of Liberal Protestantism has always been a mystery."[4] Man was in revolt against the God-man.

As in life and ministry, so in death, Jesus was inevitably the center of attention. Even one of the brigands who was being crucified, repeating the mockery he had heard from the crowd, lashed out at him. "Are you not the Christ? Save yourself and us!" (Lk. 23:39). It was the language of sarcasm rather than of faith. The other brigand, who apparently had joined in the reproach at first (Mk. 15:32), now experienced a change of heart. What produced it we are not told. Perhaps it was the prayer for forgiveness. For this man to believe that Jesus would yet come in his kingly power (Lk. 23:42), when nearly everyone was writing him off as a messianic pretender who was only getting what he deserved, reveals tremendous faith.

Already, while still on the cross, the uplifted Christ was be-

4 *Readings in St. John's Gospel* (1950), p. xxiv.

ginning to draw men to himself, as he had promised (Jn. 12:32). He offers immediate salvation ("today") that leaves nothing to be desired ("with me in Paradise"). As Alexander Whyte put it, the thief "took heaven, so to speak, at a leap that day."[5]

Among the spectators at Golgotha were several women who had faithfully followed the Master from Galilee and had ministered to his needs. John notes that three of them drew near to the cross, perhaps the better to hear what Jesus spoke from time to time. One of these was Mary his mother. No doubt she had a twinge of envy for a moment at the thought that a complete stranger would be sharing Paradise with her son and she could not. She had known much of joy and sadness in her lifetime: the joy of mothering the Savior of the world, of watching him grow and marveling at the things he said, of seeing him begin his ministry auspiciously—but the sadness of witnessing the people of Nazareth turn against him that bitter day in the synagogue, of finding her children sharing this resentment and lack of faith. Torn between allegiance to them and devotion to Jesus, she had a difficult role. But now, after much struggle and heartache, she has resolutely taken her place with her firstborn, cutting herself off from the rest of the family, if need be.

Jesus noted her presence now and divined what it meant. She was willing to pay a price to identify herself with him in the hour of his trial. Seeing the beloved disciple nearby, Jesus committed Mary to his care (Jn. 19:27). As he had honored his mother in life, according to the commandment, so in the hour of death he provided for her. In all probability the beloved disciple had a home in Jerusalem (Jn. 19:27; cf. 18:15). He now had a second mother to care for, and his first act was to remove her from the scene that she might be spared any further distress of soul.

All the Synoptists mention the strange phenomenon of the darkness that settled over the whole land (or earth), lasting for three hours. It seemed that nature was uniting with man in forsaking the Lord. But the deeper truth is that even God had forsaken the Sufferer, as evidenced by the cry that finally rose from his lips, "My God, My God, why hast thou forsaken me?" These are the opening words of Psalm 22, a Scripture portion especially pertinent to the suffering that Jesus was now undergoing. What irony faces us here—Christ, the great teacher on prayer and the one who has given the world such an example of a life of prayer,

---

[5] *Bible Characters*, Fourth Series (n.d.), p. 156.

now finds prayer futile! The only answer that begins to solve this enigma is the truth of the sheer holiness of God that cannot bear to look upon sin with favor. Just now his own Son needs him desperately, yet he cannot do anything but detach himself, for the Son is being made sin (II Cor. 5:21). This was the awful experience that Jesus had anticipated in the garden the night before, which had brought him such anguish. Now he was treading the winepress alone.

The important thing is that in this crisis Jesus cried to God at all. When the first Adam introduced sin into the world, he ran away from God when he sensed the separating power of that sin. But Christ will make the gates of Paradise echo with the strength of his cry out of a heart that desires above everything else God's holy presence. There is no failure of confidence (my God, my God). By thus enduring the curse of sin, Christ makes it certain that all who trust in God through him will be able to claim the promise, "I will never leave thee nor forsake thee."

Only at this late stage in his suffering did Jesus express his own sense of physical distress. Even then he made no actual request for help, but simply stated a fact. "I thirst" (Jn. 19:28). Someone has called it "a smothered sob of pent-up human agony." From time to time the claim is made that John's Gospel presents a docetic Christ, one without a genuine humanity. Yet it is in this Gospel only that this mark of true humanity is recorded. One cannot miss the paradox here. The bestower of living water (Jn. 4:10; cf. 7:37) is aflame with thirst. Christina Rossetti has expressed it well: "He . . . thirsted Who the world's refreshment bore."

Close at hand was a vessel containing some of the sour wine used by the soldiers. John tells us that unnamed persons dipped a sponge into the container and lifted it to Jesus' mouth. A measure of strength flowed momentarily through his exhausted body, enabling him to utter with a loud cry, "It is finished" (Jn. 19:30). The form of the verb is such as to suggest that Jesus had reference to the whole sweep of events that were now culminating in the cross. He was the Lamb slain from the foundation of the world, the agent of God in creation, the theme of many prophetic utterances, the incarnate Son, the ministering Servant. Though misunderstood, opposed, rejected, betrayed, abused and abandoned, he had borne it all patiently; and now he had endured the cross, despising the shame. He had become the Savior in fact, not merely in name and promise. The victim proclaims himself the victor.

All that remained was the final word of committal. "Father, into thy hands I commit my spirit" (Lk. 23:46). He was going home. By using this passage from the Psalms (31:5) Jesus honored the word of God, dying by it even as he lived by it. There on the cross, with its shame of nakedness and darker shame of alleged criminality, he wrapped about himself as a shroud the words that David had used long before. But he did not use them unchanged. He added that word of address, tender and intimate, that regularly marked his communion with the Almighty—the word Father (cf. Mt. 11:25; Jn. 17:1). And he omitted something, the words "Thou hast redeemed me," for they did not apply to him or his situation.

The ordeal of the cross is now past. The Son of God is ready to yield up his spirit. He has laid down his life as he said (Jn. 10:18).

As though in response to Jesus' final breath, the great veil before the holy of holies in the temple was torn from top to bottom (Mk. 15:38).[6] Early Christian speculation read this portent as a sign that the corrupt priesthood was exposed and judged,[7] or that the purpose of God now moved out to include the Gentiles.[8] But sober exegesis is more likely to conclude that the truth intended here is "that through the death of Jesus the way to heaven is made manifest."[9] Certainly the teaching of Hebrews 6:19; 10:19-20 looks in this direction. The isolation of Jesus on the cross from both man and God is seen as ended. Jesus becomes our forerunner within the veil.

This was the climax of a day that had brought strange things to pass, so that even the Roman soldiers about the cross were filled with a sense of awe. The centurion who commanded them could not refrain from exclaiming, "Truly this man was the Son [or a son] of God" (Mk. 15:39). This must be understood in the light of pagan ideas, and it does not rank with the attitude of

[6] For an account of this and other supernatural phenomena in connection with the crucifixion, one should consult *The Six Miracles of Calvary* (1928) by William R. Nicholson.

[7] A Christian interpolation in *The Testament of Levi* 10.

[8] A similar interpolation in *The Testament of Benjamin* 9.

[9] Gösta Lindeskog, "The Veil of the Temple," *Coniectanea Neotestamentica*, 11 (1947), 132-137. Lindeskog thinks that a possible secondary motif may be the abolition of the Jewish cult.

the penitent thief; but nevertheless it testifies to a deep impression made on rough men by the bearing and words of Jesus, supplemented by the darkness and the earthquake.

These soldiers who had figured in the crucifixion at the beginning were called on for the final task of insuring that the sufferers did not linger on into the sabbath and thus profane the holy day (Jn. 19:31). After breaking the legs of the two brigands to hasten their deaths, they turned to Jesus and found that the same treatment was not needed in his case, so they refrained. John saw in the preserving of the bodily structure a fulfillment of the saying, "Not a bone of him shall be broken" (Jn. 19:36). Regarding this quotation from Psalm 34:20, Dodd observes, "There is evidence that this psalm was held to contain the promise of the resurrection of the body. To the evangelist therefore it would suggest the promise of Christ's resurrection." [10]

One of the soldiers for some reason, whether from resentment at being denied the pleasure of breaking the legs of Jesus or from a sudden wanton impulse, pierced the side of the Savior with his spear (Jn. 19:34) .[11] The issue of blood and water has led to much physiological speculation, but this was probably far from the thought of the writer. His interest was almost certainly theological, as I John 5:6 attests. The blood is that of the Lamb of God now sacrificed for the sins of the world. The water is the symbol of new life through the Son, mediated by the Spirit (Jn. 7:37-39) .

Here ends the story of the crucifixion. What are we to make of it? There are those who feel uncertain about the details, on the ground that the writers may have yielded to the temptation to embellish the simple facts with imaginative additions.[12] Granted that this is a human tendency in narration, yet the crucifixion

---

[10] *Historical Tradition in the Fourth Gospel* (1963) , p. 131.

[11] This is a key item in the attempt by Hugh J. Schonfield (*The Passover Plot*, 1965) to explain the career of Jesus. His idea is that Jesus through a study of the Old Testament felt that he must suffer for the nation (Isa. 53) , so he planned a pseudo-death, including the staging of the triumphal entry, the baiting of the rulers of the Jews, the persuading of Judas to betray him, the cry of thirst on the cross, which should serve as a signal for a henchman to give him drugged wine. Because of the oncoming sabbath he felt sure he would be taken down from the cross in an unconscious condition and thus escape death. But the spearthrust proved deadly, so the whole plan went awry. Death was not followed by resurrection. How the author of this book could imagine that Christianity could spring from such a background is an enigma indeed.

[12] John Knox, *The Death of Christ* (1958) , p. 18.

accounts leave out so much we would like to know that it is probably more in line with the truth to charge the writers with restraint rather than with elaboration. They have been content to let the facts speak for themselves. We feel the facility of words most strongly when the imagination is involved in such a way as almost to transform the fancied into the real. But we feel the poverty of words most keenly when the crucially real has been most faithfully depicted. A margin remains that cannot be expressed. It can only be felt after, to be sensed by those spirits who have immersed themselves in the real.

In the death narratives the citing of considerable Scripture as fulfilled by the crucifixion may seem suspicious, for it could mean that events were fabricated in order to fit ancient prophecies.[13] But once again the restraint of New Testament writers in their use of the Old Testament needs to be recognized. Dodd has pointed out that these men,

> for all their anxiety to discover fulfilments of prophecy, and all their ingenuity in doing so, do not attempt to exploit the *whole* corpus of Messianic prediction. . . . The whole conception of the Messiah as king, warrior and judge, the ruthless vindicator of the righteousness of God, is absent from the Church's presentation of the Jesus of history, though imagination working freely upon the prophetic *data* might easily have constructed a quasi-historical figure having these traits. There has been some principle of selection at work, by which certain sides of the Messianic idea are held to be fulfilled, and others are set aside. What was that principle of selection? Surely the simplest explanation is that a true historical memory controlled the selection of prophecies.[14]

Jesus' Predictions of the Passion

The Gospel writers have not confined themselves to statements by the prophets of old. They introduce predictions of the passion by Jesus himself. Early in the ministry, it seems, he intimated that he would be taken away from his disciples, leading them to fast (Mk. 2:20). A more definite prediction emerged during the days at Caesarea Philippi, stating that he would be rejected by the rulers of the Jews and would be killed (Mk. 8:31; cf. 9:12). According to Luke 9:31, Jesus spoke with Moses and Elijah re-

---

13 *Ibid.*, p. 20.
14 C. H. Dodd, *History and the Gospel* (1938), p. 61.

garding his "exodus" at Jerusalem while he was on the mount of transfiguration. During the months that followed there were two occasions on which he spoke to his disciples about his forthcoming death (Mk. 9:31; Mk. 10:33). In the latter passage more details are given than before, including his condemnation by the rulers, the handing over to the Gentiles, and such items as the mockery and scourging. Mark 10:45 deals with the death in a more theological way, calling it a ransom for many. In Luke 13:33 we have a statement in which Jesus speaks of himself as a prophet who must die at Jerusalem. During holy week, much of his teaching was directed toward the theme of his rejection by the nation. Especially pointed is the teaching in the parable of the vineyard, in which the tenants put to death the son and heir of the owner of the vineyard (Mt. 21:33-41). At the supper in Bethany Jesus commended the woman who anointed him with costly ointment, saying that she had anointed his body beforehand for burial (Mk. 14:8). At the Last Supper he explained the cup as signifying his blood, which was to be poured out for many (Mk. 14:24).

A quick review of these passages shows that the predictions are mainly to the disciples and seem to date from the Caesarea Philippi situation. Mark 2:20, on the other hand, is earlier and is addressed to a general group. On both counts it is understandable why this latter prediction should be somewhat veiled and lacking in details. Yet the wording "taken away" points unmistakably to removal by those who are hostile to Jesus, and this is supported by the reference to the resultant fasting by his disciples.

The Fourth Gospel makes its own contribution to this theme, including Jesus' references to his "hour," his description of himself as the Good Shepherd who would lay down his life for the sheep (Jn. 10:11), and as a grain of wheat that must fall into the ground and die, resulting in a great harvest (Jn. 12:24).

These anticipations of the death have not gone unchallenged. One approach is to dismiss them as statements put into the mouth of Jesus by the early church. They are considered as "prophecy after the event."[15] But if the evidence of the Gospels is to be accepted at all, it should be clear that strong opposition developed against Jesus at an early period and increased as his ministry advanced. Plans were laid to do away with him. Jeremias comments, "The assertion of the Gospels that Jesus reckoned

---

[15] On this method of dealing with material in the Gospels, see the present writer's article, "Gemeindetheologie: the Bane of Gospel Criticism," in *Jesus of Nazareth: Saviour and Lord* (1966), ed. Carl F. H. Henry, pp. 159-173.

with the possibility of a violent death has the strongest historical probability behind it." [16] The same writer goes a step further. "If Jesus reckoned with his violent death, then he must have had thoughts about the meaning of that death." [17] Since the Servant theology which is detectable in these predictions was a declining emphasis in the church at the time the Gospels were written, it is highly improbable that we are to look upon Jesus' explanations of his death as the view of the church read back into his own consciousness. [18]

THE MEANING OF THE CROSS FOR JESUS

What, then, was the significance of the cross for our Lord? For one thing, he viewed it as *necessary*. This necessity lay in the divine plan rather than simply in the rise of opposition (Mk. 8:31; 10:45). [19] It belonged to the testimony of the prophetic Scriptures (Lk. 24:44-45). It shaped the outlook of Jesus. He confessed that he had come to die (Mk. 10:45).

Lest it be thought that this necessity was thrust upon the Savior against his will or was accepted passively, it is well to go a step further and emphasize that the cross was his *desire*. He felt pent-up and hampered until it was accomplished (Lk. 12:50). He accepted it gladly, not because he could take pleasure in the experience itself but because it was the Father's will. If he wanted to see the harvest, he must go down into death (Jn. 12:24). Out of love he was prepared to lay down his life for his friends (Jn. 15:13).

The cross was *central* to his most exalted experience (the transfiguration) and to his time of deepest distress (Gethsemane). It dominated his consciousness of *time*, for he thought and talked about his "hour." Before that hour came, no hand could be successfully lifted against him (Lk. 13:31-33). When it came he could cry, "It is finished."

The death of Jesus on the cross meant so much to him that he made it his *memorial*. Whatever he may have thought about

16 W. Zimmerli and J. Jeremias, *The Servant of God* (1957), p. 100.
17 *Ibid.*, p. 101.
18 Vincent Taylor, *The Cross of Christ* (1956), pp. 15-16.
19 Old liberalism erected a false necessity, supposing that Jesus expected to be received by the nation but had to accommodate himself to the prospect of death as time went on. In this view, the Gospel writers have harmonized two diverse elements by making it appear that he came with the intention of dying.

the value of his teaching and of his mighty works, he insisted that the partaking of the symbols of his body and shed blood should be the definitive act that served as a means of remembering him.

Occasionally the query is raised, How could the eternal Son of God die? There is no more difficulty here than in the fact of his birth, for if he could be born into this world, then he could also die. As Mozley reminds us, "The Logos could be said to have been born and to have suffered and to have died because He had taken that human nature to which such experiences belong."[20]

BIBLIOGRAPHY

Jim Bishop. *The Day Christ Died*. New York: Harper, 1957.

W. M. Clow. *The Day of the Cross*. London: Hodder and Stoughton, n.d.

James Denney. *The Death of Christ*. New York: Armstrong, 1903.

R. H. Fuller. *The Mission and Achievement of Jesus*. Chicago: Allenson. Pp. 50-78.

John Knox. *The Death of Christ*. New York: Abingdon, 1958.

F. W. Krummacher. *The Suffering Saviour*. Chicago: Moody, 1947.

T. W. Manson. *The Servant-Messiah*. Cambridge, Eng.: Cambridge University Press, 1953. Pp. 80-88.

G. Campbell Morgan. *The Crises of the Christ*. New York: Revell, 1903. Pp. 275-344.

Leon Morris. *The Cross in the New Testament*. Grand Rapids: Eerdmans, 1965. Pp. 13-179.

William R. Nicholson. *The Six Miracles of Calvary*. Chicago: Moody, 1927.

Michael Ramsey. *The Narratives of the Passion*. London: Mowbray, 1962.

K. Schilder. *Christ Crucified*. Grand Rapids: Eerdmans, 1940.

James Stalker. *The Trial and Death of Jesus Christ*. London: Hodder and Stoughton, n.d.

Ethelbert Stauffer. *Jesus and His Story*. New York: Knopf, 1960.

Vincent Taylor. *The Cross of Christ*. London: Macmillan, 1956.

---

[20] J. K. Mozley, *The Doctrine of the Incarnation* (1949), p. 81.

Chapter XVI

THE RESURRECTION

No man saw Jesus rise from the dead; only a few saw him risen; but all men are affected by his resurrection in one way or another.

"Blessed are those who have not seen and yet believe."

—Jesus of Nazareth

NEITHER PILATE NOR THE SANHEDRIN, IT SEEMS, HAD MADE ANY plans to give Jesus anything that would resemble an honorable burial. However, the Jews would certainly have acted to see that the body was interred, if only to avoid defiling the land, as required by Deuteronomy 21:23. But the decision of Joseph of Arimathea to ask permission of Pilate to take the body precluded any step by the Jewish authorities. His tomb was near at hand, making interment possible before the beginning of the sabbath. Whether he planned to shift the body elsewhere at a later time or to leave it there indefinitely is not disclosed. Whatever his intentions, the tomb was not needed for long, and was soon to be restored to him by the action of a higher power.

Little place is given to the burial in the Christian tradition, which attests its almost complete overshadowing by what happened on the first day of the week. Yet it does have its own niche in the statement of the gospel (I Cor. 15:4), because it links the death and the resurrection of the Savior, attesting at once the reality of the death and the factuality of the resurrection.

Apart from Joseph and Nicodemus, the only visitors at the tomb noted in the records were women who had accompanied

Jesus from Galilee (Lk. 23:55). They planned to return after the sabbath with spices for the body, so it was important to them to get the location of the tomb well in mind.[1] When Joseph, no doubt with help, rolled the great circular stone into place before the door of the tomb and departed, silence settled down on the spot until the arrival of a guard that the Sanhedrin had requested of Pilate. These were Roman soldiers, as may be seen from two features of the narrative: the sealing of the tomb, which was an official governmental act (Mt. 27:66), and the responsibility of these men to the governor (Mt. 28:14). Members of the Sanhedrin, hardly able to believe that they had finally gotten rid of the thorn in their sides, recalled that there was a report that the Galilean had talked about rising from the dead after three days (Mt. 27:63; cf. Mt. 12:40). Just to be on the safe side, they wanted the tomb guarded. To make a plausible case before Pilate they warned that the disciples might come and carry off the body. They may have had other fears that remained unexpressed. It was those fears that were realized, posing a new problem to their unbelief.

THE EMPTY TOMB

No human eye saw the Lord Jesus Christ rise from the dead. It was as unobserved as his conception in the womb of the Virgin Mary. But just as surely as that conception led to birth and the life that followed, so the silent emergence from the tomb ushered in the risen life of Christ with all its manifestations.

As long as the Savior did not appear to the Jews to discomfit them, they could tolerate the fact of the empty tomb and try to explain it away. Matthew describes how the hierarchy dealt with the problem, namely, by bribing the guards to say that while they slept, Jesus' disciples came and stole the body (Mt. 28:12-14). There is a touch of humor here, for sleeping men are hardly in a position to know what goes on.[2]

If the report of the empty tomb brought such consternation

---

[1] This circumstance makes implausible the view of Kirsopp Lake that the women returned to the wrong place and found an empty tomb, thus leading to the (mistaken) belief that Jesus had risen from the dead (*The Historical Evidence for the Resurrection of Jesus Christ* [1912]).

[2] Considerable interest attaches to the discovery during the last quarter of the 19th century of an inscription at Nazareth probably dating from the reign of the emperor Claudius. In the inscription an imperial warning is given of dire punishment for those who remove corpses. Some scholars see in this the

to the Sanhedrin that they could not think straight, it was equally disturbing to the disciples when they heard it from the women who had gone to the spot early on the first day of the week. Even though they were able to add to their report of the empty tomb (with the stone rolled away) angelic testimony that the Lord was no longer among the dead but was alive (Mk. 16:6; Lk. 24:5), the disciples remained incredulous. The report seemed to them nothing but an idle tale (Lk. 24:11).

However important the empty tomb may be as evidence for the resurrection, the fact remains that it was not convincing to the original followers of Jesus. Clearly they were not expecting the Master to rise from the dead. This has its own value, for it clears them of any suspicion of fabricating a report of resurrection. So little convinced by it were two Emmaus disciples that they started home in a despondent state of mind, even though they had the information that some of their own number had verified the report by visiting the spot and finding the tomb unoccupied (Lk. 24:13-24).

It is true that the empty tomb served in some measure to prepare the way for the risen Lord's self-revelation to his own, judging from the account in John 20:1-10.[3] Peter and the beloved disciple, alarmed by the fears of Mary Magdalene that unfriendly hands had taken the body of Jesus, rushed to the tomb and found the grave clothes in such perfect order that this explanation had to be ruled out. The body was not there, but the clothes were in the exact position they would occupy when they contained the body. This induced faith in the beloved disciple; but it was not shared with the others, apparently. He was content to keep his thoughts to himself, lest he become the object of ridicule along with the women.

Without the certification of the empty tomb early Christian preaching about the resurrection would have been lame and halting. But it proceeded in the serene confidence that no one could contest this fact. Pagans in faraway Athens could mock at Paul's declaration that a man had risen from the dead (Acts

---

acceptance by Roman officialdom of the Jewish tale of the theft of the body of Jesus, and look upon it as an attempt to stifle the young Christian movement at its supposed source (Nazareth), in the hope that religious peace would return to a nation that was tempestuous enough without this added ferment. For further discussion see H. J. Cadbury, *The Book of Acts in History* (1955), pp. 117-118.

3 Luke 24:12 appears to be unauthentic, an addition to the text based on the passage in John.

17:32), but not so the chief men in Jerusalem. They had to watch the infant church grow daily before their eyes because of the proclamation of the risen Savior, and could do nothing to stop it, for they had themselves been unwilling witnesses of the empty tomb (Mt. 28:11-15).

THE APPEARANCES

If the morning hours of the first day of the week were charged with confusion about the empty tomb, by evening a different atmosphere prevailed. The two Emmaus disciples, after their encounter with the risen Lord, rushed back into the city and burst in on the Eleven with their tidings, only to discover that they were not the first to see him, for he had appeared to Peter (Lk. 24:34). Hardly had the new arrivals told the story of their experience with the risen Lord than he himself appeared in the midst. The very suddenness of his coming, together with the fact that the doors were locked (cf. John 20:19), so startled those present that they were ready to think they had seen a spirit (Lk. 24:37). Ministering to their fears, Jesus showed them his hands and feet, that they might identify him from the marks of his suffering. Even then they could hardly bring themselves to believe. The cross had been so cruelly real and their grief had been so deep. To remove all doubt, Jesus took a piece of broiled fish and ate it in their presence (Lk. 24:42-43).

All this suggests that the primary purpose of this initial appearance to the Eleven and the others who were present was to convince them that he was the same Jesus they had known in days gone by, the one who had suffered on Calvary, the one who had died and had been buried. Death had now been robbed of its prey. Here was their leader standing in their midst, in what appeared to be the same body in which he had suffered. They were seeing him, touching him, and listening to his voice. Gradually there dawned upon these men the amazing truth that Jesus had indeed burst the bonds of death. "Then the disciples were glad when they saw the Lord" (Jn. 20:20). Their radiance of joy was not due alone to delight at seeing him alive again but also to the conviction his renewed fellowship with them conveyed, namely, that their own sins and mistakes, their dullness and their desertion, had all been forgiven and put away.[4] Jesus actually

---

[4] A. Schlatter, *The Church in the New Testament Period* (1955), p. 7.

wanted to be with them after all that had happened, and in this realization their hearts were comforted. He had sought them out as freely and voluntarily as he had in the old days when he called them into his service.

To a modern reader the fact that the appearances were limited to Jesus' followers may seem to curtail their value as certifying the fact of the resurrection.[5] But it is doubtful that the disciples themselves felt any embarrassment on this score. In the course of his message to Cornelius and his friends, Peter frankly acknowledged that the circle of witnesses was limited to Jesus' followers. "God raised him on the third day and made him manifest; not to all the people but to us who were chosen by God as witnesses, who ate and drank with him after he rose from the dead" (Acts 10:40-41).

Paul elevated the appearances into a constituent part of the gospel message when he declared that the *kerygma* included not only the death of Christ, his burial, and his resurrection, but his appearances also (I Cor. 15:5ff.). They were indisputable demonstrations that he had risen and become the Lord of life.

Several explanations can be given for the private character of the appearances. (1) Jesus had stated publicly that the nation that had rejected him would not see his face again until it was ready to welcome him (Mt. 23:38-39). (2) Faith is not necessarily created by a display of miraculous power. Jesus had warned that even the rising from the dead would not convince those who refused to accept the testimony of Scripture (Lk. 16:31). (3) A faith that rests on evidence but lacks the element of glad acceptance is not faith at all in the biblical sense. Genuine faith is always voluntary and spontaneous. (4) As Westcott was fond of pointing out, the resurrection appearances were disclosures of a new order. They involved resurrection life in which the world has no share. It would be unnatural and unfitting to manifest this new life to unbelievers. (5) Restriction of the appearances to believers left room for their testimony to the world as to what they had seen and heard. The Lord had been preparing the disciples for just this kind of ministry. Why should he deprive them of it by manifesting himself to the nation in his risen state? This was not in his plan.

---

5 However, as G. E. Ladd notes, those to whom Jesus appeared were not believers in his resurrection until he revealed himself alive ("The Resurrection of Jesus Christ," in *Christian Faith and Modern Theology* [1964], ed. Carl F. H. Henry, p. 282).

One may say in this connection that if the resurrection story were fiction, we could well expect it to contain accounts of appearances to Pilate, the Sanhedrin, and others. Its restraint at this point marks it off from the apocryphal literature that grew up around this theme.

A second problem confronting the student of the resurrection appearances relates to the nature of Christ's body. Some of the things said about it, such as the eating of food and the possibility of being touched (Lk. 24:39-43), point to a substantial bodily structure. On the other hand the sudden appearance and equally sudden disappearance (Lk. 24:36, 31) involve the supposition that the body possessed other qualities marking it off as in some sense different from the organism Jesus had during the days of his flesh. It could now pass through solid material; it could vanish and reappear. In at least one passage notice is taken of the fact that Jesus appeared in a different form from that which he manifested on other occasions (Mk. 16:12).[6] The reference alludes to the Emmaus pair rather obviously, and was probably introduced to explain how two people who had known Jesus could fail to recognize him until his familiar act of breaking the bread.

These two sets of facts concerning the body of the risen Lord are not necessarily contradictory. The first set conveys the truth that the risen Lord has the same body in which he suffered, and thereby serves an evidential function. The second set emphasizes the fact that the resurrection makes a difference, for Jesus has already begun to be glorified. He is now equipped for the life of the "far above all." He already belongs to the heavenly realm, and the new features of his bodily organism are prophetical of that new order of life associated with resurrection. In this connection, it should not escape our notice that Jesus himself was fully aware of the new situation brought about by his conquest of death. On at least one occasion he referred to teaching he had given his disciples "while I was still with you" (Lk. 24:44). Evidently he was no longer with his own in the same way as prior to the crucifixion. His appearances were separated by intervals that extended at times to several days' duration.

Much can be learned from the appearances of Jesus to various individuals. The basic truth emphasized in all of these is that Jesus continues to minister to the needs of his people in the way

---

[6] This reference belongs to the so-called long ending of Mark, which appears to have been added to what Mark wrote; but the addition came at an early time and probably contains some reliable tradition.

that is most helpful to them and also most instructive to other believers.

Notable is the fact that the Lord did not restrict his appearances to the apostles, thus safeguarding the spirit of democracy and equality in the church. Actually he showed himself first to a woman, rewarding the faithfulness of Mary Magdalene, who had served him with loving devotion during the ministry, had been at the cross, and was the first to reach the tomb (Mk. 16:9; Jn. 20:11-18). Jesus disclosed himself to her in what has been called the greatest recognition scene in all literature. In a flash her tears of grief became tears of joy. Instinctively she reached out to grasp him. When he had to rebuff her for holding him (as we have seen, he was not with his own on the same permanent basis as before the cross), he erased her disappointment by commissioning her with a message for the disciples. For her benefit as well as theirs he spoke of his followers as his brethren. Even his ascension could not cancel that relationship (Jn. 20:17).

Another person who received special attention from the risen Lord was Simon Peter (Lk. 24:34; I Cor. 15:5). This man shared Mary's grief over the death of Jesus, but in addition his heart was anguished by the sense of abysmal failure because of denying his Lord. The self-reproach must have been well-nigh unbearable. Jesus knew this, and moved to meet the need. Beyond the fact that the two met on the first day of the week, we have no information at all. It was a secret affair, too personal and too precious to be made common property, for sin is individual and so is the forgiveness of sin. The public pardon and restoration came later in the presence of Peter's fellows (Jn. 21). It is not too much to say that the prominence of Peter in the early church is a confirmation of the resurrection of Jesus, for without these dealings of the risen Lord with him he would have lacked the inner confidence and peace to continue, and he would not have had the consent of his peers to resume his role of leadership among the Twelve.

Thomas represents another kind of need. Absent when the Lord appeared to the other disciples on the evening of the first day of the week, he remained skeptical about their assertions that they had seen him. He was not prepared to say what or whom they had seen, but as for himself he could only be convinced by seeing the marks of suffering and feeling them with his hand. When the Savior appeared a week later he used the very terms Thomas had used as he invited the doubting disciple to assure himself.

Whether or not Thomas accepted the invitation to touch hands and side we do not know; but his doubt was swept away, swallowed up in a magnificent confession of the Master's deity and lordship (Jn. 20:28).

The general rule about appearing only to believers was set aside in the case of James (Jn. 7:5; I Cor. 15:7), but he was a chosen vessel as was Paul. Apparently this confrontation came somewhat later than those we have mentioned. Perhaps the events connected with the poignant meeting between the patriarch Joseph and his brethren formed something of a pattern for this meeting. The risen Son of God was able to leave behind him on earth a family united in faith. James' adherence seems to have influenced the other brothers and sisters to join the fellowship of Jesus' followers (Acts 1:14).[7]

In view of the private character of the appearances, it is not strange that Jesus should have used these occasions to continue his instruction of the Eleven. Their minds had been filled with confusion by his allusions to the necessity of his death and resurrection during the closing months of the ministry. Now that his forecasts had been confirmed by the events themselves, a different attitude prevailed among his followers. With eagerness these men hung upon his words as he took them through the Scriptures pointing out the relevant passages in Moses, the prophets, and the psalms bearing on his person and mission. Luke's account is particularly concerned with this aspect of Jesus' postresurrection ministry (Lk. 24:27, 44-47). The fruit of this period of instruction was gathered at Pentecost and in the days that followed, as the preachers of the word appealed to the correspondence between the prophetic Scriptures and recent events involving Jesus of Nazareth. It became a consistent part of the church's message to declare that his death and resurrection were "according to the Scriptures" (I Cor. 15:3-4).

This same phrase has been made the title of a book by C. H. Dodd, in which the author has shown that the New Testament writers manifest a common understanding of the Old Testament, a discriminating use of *testimonia*, an appreciation of the contextual demands of various statements, and a combination of diverse passages "so that they interpret one another in hitherto unsuspected ways."[8] Dodd is prepared to grant that the impulse

---

[7] The word "brethren" is capable of including sisters, just as the word in modern usage includes both men and women in the fellowship of the church.

[8] *According to the Scriptures* (1952), p. 109.

behind this handling of the Scriptures must have been the influence of Christ himself.[9]

The willingness of the disciples to wait for the full enduement of the Spirit at Pentecost, despite the fact that they had already had some experience in preaching (the sending out of the Twelve, Mk. 6:7-13) and despite the fact that they now had a superlatively wonderful message to tell, shows what a humbling experience it was to converse with the risen Savior and receive direction from him.

CRITICISM AND THE RESURRECTION

It is not our purpose here to examine all the various theories that have been propounded by those who do not receive the testimony of the Gospels concerning the resurrection but must try to explain in some fashion the rise of faith in the resurrection as the keystone of the early church.[10] Suffice it to say that the very diversity of these theories testifies to the weakness of all the attempts to explain the origin of the Christian church apart from the resurrection. The only way the complete transformation in the disciples can be accounted for, as well as their success in preaching the resurrection in the very place where their Master had been crucified, is to take the Gospel records seriously in what they tell us about the empty tomb and the appearances.

The stumbling block here is the miraculous character of the event, so men have tried to devise an explanation that would avoid this obstacle and yet manage to provide a fairly plausible basis on which to build the rise and growth of the Christian community. Probably the best attempt along this line is the notion that the hold of Jesus Christ upon his followers was so strong that they could not surrender to the thought that he had gone down to defeat. "The appearances were not external phenomena but were merely the goals of an inner struggle in which faith won the victory over doubt."[11] But to hold this view one must suppose that the early Christians were not content to describe their

---

9 *Ibid.*, p. 110.

10 For a survey of older critical theories, a useful book is *The Resurrection of Christ* (1920) by J. M. Shaw; for more recent points of view one may consult *The Theology of the Resurrection* (1965) by Walter Künneth or *Acquittal by Resurrection* (1964) by Markus Barth and Verne H. Fletcher.

11 Johannes Weiss, *Earliest Christianity*, I (1959), 30.

visionary experiences but decided to make them concrete by extending them as contacts with the living Christ on a physical basis. Thus it is impossible to escape a measure of falsification in the documentary sources of our faith, which is a heavy price to pay for the retention of resurrection in a nonbodily form.

We must try to understand, however, the straits into which historians find themselves forced when they are confronted by the alleged fact of the resurrection of Jesus. Their science obliges them to suppose a certain uniformity both in the universe and in human society. The emergence of a man from death does not conform to the pattern of what is common to man, and for this reason it lies outside the realm of historical verification.[12] This is the background for the contention that the resurrection is mythological. The only shred Bultmann will retain is the almost cavalier observation that Jesus rose into the *kerygma* or gospel proclamation of the church. A physical resurrection is ruled out on the basis of the uniformity of operation of natural law.

The one who approaches the resurrection simply as a historian is therefore not prepared to give cordial assent to the proposition that has often been advanced by Christian apologists to the effect that the resurrection of Christ is the best-attested event in all of ancient history.

But one cannot afford to overlook the fact that the witness of the apostles was not to an idea or a dogma, but to an experience they shared in common with other believers. *And this experience lay in the realm of history.* This experience came to them in spite of their unbelief, their lack of expectation. So history *does* surround the resurrection, even though no human eye observed the emergence from the tomb. The modern disbeliever in the resurrection, motivated by philosophical and scientific scruples, asserts that Jesus *could* not rise, whereas the followers of Jesus were prone to think he *would* not rise. The latter group nevertheless came to an early and unanimous conviction that he had risen. They were governed by stubborn fact, not shackled by theory. It is well to reflect that "for the biblical witnesses, and probably for their first listeners and readers as well, there is no difference between the *factuality, reality, actuality* of the crucifixion and of the resurrection events. They possess the same historicity."[13] One could well be skeptical about reports of the resurrection of

---

[12] T. A. Roberts, *History and Christian Apologetic* (1960), p. 160.
[13] Barth and Fletcher, *op. cit.*, p. 11.

man as we know him, but the report of the resurrection of Jesus Christ deserves to be considered in a separate category, for the event reported belongs to the consummation of a life that was unique. That uniqueness was experienced in the setting of ordinary existence in Palestine, which makes it all the more wonderful.

It will not do to claim that the reports of Jesus' resurrection stem from the commonly held belief in bodily resurrection that characterized Judaism, or that these reports are grounded on resurrections effected by Jesus during his ministry. The difference is monumental, for in his case we are not dealing with mere resurrection followed eventually by a return to death. Instead, death had no more dominion over him. He was alive for evermore.

No doubt there are difficulties connected with the resurrection narratives. The order in which the appearances occurred, for example, is not so clear as to be undisputed.[14] It should not disturb us that the various Evangelists introduce variety in details, for this is true of their records of the ministry as a whole. Broadus rightly says, "The sacred writers do not treat their Lord's resurrection as a doubtful point, needing to be established by their statements, but as an unquestionable fact."[15] What Sabatier wrote about the variations in the three accounts of Paul's encounter with the risen Lord (Acts 9; 22; 26) applies equally well to the resurrection narratives. "It is obvious to any unprejudiced mind that they were *undesigned*. . . . They are discrepancies of precisely the sort that one always finds existing in the most faithful repetitions of the same narrative. . . . They cannot in any way affect the reality of the event in question."[16]

One of the specific areas in which variation occurs is the geographical location of the appearances. Mark's Gospel creates expectation of a meeting between the risen Lord and the disciples in Galilee (Mk. 16:7), but there are no appearances recorded except in the long ending (Mk. 16:9-20). It is quite likely that if the original ending had survived, it would describe one or more meetings in the north. Matthew's Gospel indicates that Jesus appeared to certain women in the Jerusalem area and bade them tell the disciples to meet him in Galilee (Mt. 28:10); then it

14 However, the order in which the ten appearances are placed by James Orr (*The Resurrection of Jesus* [n.d.], pp. 155-156) seems defensible.

15 John A. Broadus, *Commentary on the Gospel of Matthew* (1886), p. 583.

16 A. Sabatier, *The Apostle Paul* (n.d.), p. 59.

goes on to record a meeting there with the Eleven (Mt. 28:16).
Luke's account mentions appearances in the Jerusalem area only—
to the Emmaus pair (Lk. 24:13-21), to Simon Peter (Lk. 24:34),
to the disciples as a group (Lk. 24:36ff.). This localization of the
appearances to the Jerusalem area tallies with Luke's interest
in Jerusalem at various points in his record, but he does not deny
that appearances occurred elsewhere. John places the appearances
both in Jerusalem (to Mary Magdalene, 20:11ff.; to the disciples
when Thomas was absent, 20:19ff.; when he was present, 20:26ff.)
and in Galilee (the rendezvous at the lakeside, ch. 21).

In view of the command to the disciples to meet the Lord in
Galilee, at first sight the delay in their departure seems strange.
What occasioned it? The most natural explanation is the occurrence of a series of appearances by the risen Lord in or near
Jerusalem. Then what occasioned the ultimate departure of these
men for Galilee? Apparently it was the cessation of the appearances in the Jerusalem area.

It is not difficult to understand why appearances should take
place in the neighborhood of Jerusalem, for it was here that
Jesus suffered, it was here that the disciples lingered, and it was
here that they were destined to commend the message of the
risen Christ to the nation. It is not so easy to ascertain the reason
for appearances in Galilee. Schlatter ventures the following suggestion. "The Event of Easter caused the disciples to break away
from old Israel. The resurrection narratives in Matthew and Mark
bring this out by removing the disciples from Jerusalem and by
joining them to Jesus in Galilee away from the Jewish Church."[17]

In the opening chapter of the book of Acts Luke states that
the appearances were spread over a forty-day period (Acts 1:3).
This is of some importance because it enables us to see how the
Lord could have met with his followers both in the area of
Jerusalem and in the familiar surroundings of Galilee. That Jesus
returned from the north is evident from the fact that Luke puts
the final appearance at Bethany in connection with the ascension
(Lk. 24:50).

WHAT THE RESURRECTION MEANT TO CHRIST

It is idle to imagine that we have the data to probe the mind
of Christ so as to establish in any complete sense the significance

---

[17] *The Church in the New Testament Period* (1955), p. 13.

of this great event in the consciousness of our Lord himself, but the materials available afford us at least a glimpse.

(1) The resurrection established the truthfulness of Jesus. On numerous occasions (Mk. 8:31; 9:9, 31; 10:34, etc.) he had intimated that his death would be followed by resurrection, even going so far as to fix the interval between the two events.[18] As a sportsman would say, he called his shot, then proceeded to make it good. Some scholars have contended that Jesus indeed spoke of his glorious coming in the future, but that the church made this general prediction into two, the one applying to the resurrection, the other to the return. But since the predictions of the return are very indefinite—one cannot know the day nor the hour, but in such a time as one does not expect, the Son of man comes—it is difficult to see how the church could have understood those predictions as having anything to do with the resurrection, which is regularly pictured as following on the death. Luke 13:32, for example, commends itself as an utterance that must go back to Jesus himself, and it mentions the third day. Furthermore, it is awkward indeed to suppose that the predictions of Christ's return in glory had any influence in shaping either the forecasts of his resurrection or the accounts of the appearances, for the reason that the return of the Savior was pictured as something that would be characterized by dazzling glory and tremendous power, whereas the appearances of Jesus did not manifest these characteristics. It was only in the visions of the ascended Lord that this element of splendor and majesty became evident (Acts 26:13; Rev. 1:14).

There was no confusion in the mind of Jesus between his resurrection and his return. Kümmel notes several items that "confirm the fact that Jesus really reckoned with an interval between his resurrection and the parousia."[19] One of these must suffice for our purpose. At the Last Supper Jesus said to his own, "Truly, I say to you, I shall not drink again of the fruit of the vine until that day when I drink it new in the kingdom of God" (Mk. 14:25). Kümmel is justified in commenting, "The prediction that Jesus will drink no more wine until he drinks it new in the Kingdom of God has a meaning in fact only if the Kingdom of God is not expected in the *most immediate* future and if the

[18] The seeming disparity between "after three days" and "on the third day" is not a grievous problem. Any part of a day could be counted as a day. Both Peter and Paul convey the standard tradition of the Jerusalem church on this subject, using the terminology of the third day (Acts 10:40; I Cor. 15:4).

[19] W. G. Kümmel, *Promise and Fulfilment* (1957), pp. 64-83.

disciples are to come together for meals for some time without their departed Lord."[20]

(2) The resurrection vindicated the claim of our Lord to be sent of God. In this great event the Father bore witness to the Son. He had already attested him by mighty works and wonders and signs (Acts 2:22), but even so the nation of the Jews refused him. Then God exhibited his mightiest work by raising Jesus from the dead, reversing the verdict of man (cf. Acts 4:10-11). It is probably the resurrection that is chiefly in mind in the item "vindicated in the Spirit" that forms a part of the creedal statement of I Timothy 3:16. Those who brought about the death of Jesus were no doubt of the opinion that they had exploded his claim to be the Son of God, for there was no help for him in the dark hours at Calvary. But he knew, as the church came to know, that by resurrection he was proclaimed Son of God with power (Rom. 1:3)

(3) The resurrection testified to the success of his mission. At his birth he was proclaimed the Savior, but he died in weakness and ignominy at the hands of his enemies. The cross seemed to make mockery of the notion that those who looked to him in faith had a new relation to God. Yet Jesus was confident that he had finished the work God had given him to do. Paul expressed it well when he wrote, "We are now justified by his blood" (Rom. 5:9). But the resurrection served notice on all that this redeeming mission had in fact been successfully carried out. Jesus was raised on account of our justification (as Rom. 4:25 should probably be translated), to make it plain that a new relationship had been set up by the cross for all sinners who were willing to come to God through him.

(4) The resurrection gave Jesus title to glory. Peter speaks of the sufferings of Christ and the glories to follow (I Pet. 1:11). The first of these was the glory of emerging triumphant over suffering and death (Lk. 24:26). Other glories would ensue.[21]

(5) The resurrection proclaimed Jesus to be the universal Lord. Students of Scripture are familiar with the fact that this title is used sparingly, whether on his own lips or in the record of the

---

20 *Ibid.*, p. 77.

21 It is granted that even the cross is capable of being considered as a glorification; this is the special contribution of the Fourth Gospel (Jn. 12:23-24). Usually, however, the cross stands in contrast to what followed in the experience of Jesus.

Evangelists, prior to the resurrection; but from that event it comes into its own as the truly appropriate way of designating him. "Jesus is Lord" seems to have been the first creedal formulation of the infant church (Acts 2:36; 10:36; Rom. 10:9; I Cor. 12:3). The records of Jesus' appearances echo with this word and reveal the homage that it evoked among the disciples (Lk. 24:34; Jn. 20:25, 28).

Affirming that all authority was his in heaven and earth he directed his own to go forth and make disciples of all nations (Mt. 28:18-19), and in this role he gave evidence of something more than overall control of the operations of the church by directing the service of each individual follower (Jn. 21:15-23). Now that he had finished his earthly course the Savior was not willing to permit the unfinished task, the proclamation of the gospel, to proceed in some uncertain, haphazard way, dependent on the whim and wisdom of men. He had chosen and trained his witnesses. Now he sent them forth, and they proved far more obedient and far more fruitful in his absence than in his presence.

In conclusion, it should be emphasized that the resurrection must be kept in the place of preeminence along with the cross, or else Christianity loses its distinctiveness. The resurrection is the corollary and complement of the incarnation. It is not viewed by the writers of the New Testament simply as the last in a series of miracles that dot the ministry of Jesus, for they do not describe it in these terms. It stands alone and apart as the mighty demonstration of the power of God breaking into human life and history "in these last days."

The question of Jesus' Messiahship was the central issue around which inquiry and controversy revolved during the days of his flesh. Few among the leaders of Israel were willing to acknowledge his claims, and as far as they were concerned his death made the acceptance of his Messiahship impossible. Under these circumstances, the fact that the apostles could make numerous converts right in Jerusalem, till even a great company of the priests became obedient to the faith (Acts 6:7), shows how powerfully the truth of the resurrection laid hold of the minds of the men of Israel. They had seen messianic movements rise and then fade away, but this one refused to evaporate. The unfolding centuries have seen it become the faith of hundreds of millions who have put their trust in the living Lord.

BIBLIOGRAPHY

Hugh Anderson. *Jesus and Christian Origins.* New York: Oxford University Press, 1964. Pp. 185-240.

Markus Barth and Verne H. Fletcher. *Acquittal by Resurrection.* New York: Holt, 1964.

Daniel P. Fuller. *Easter Faith and History.* Grand Rapids: Eerdmans, 1965.

Walter Künneth. *The Theology of the Resurrection.* St. Louis: Concordia, 1965.

G. E. Ladd, "The Resurrection of Jesus Christ," in *Christian Faith and Modern Theology,* ed. Carl F. H. Henry. New York: Channel, 1964. Pp. 263-284.

William Milligan. *The Resurrection of Our Lord.* London: Macmillan, 1901.

G. Campbell Morgan. *The Crises of the Christ.* New York: Revell, 1903. Pp. 345-384.

C. F. D. Moule. *The Phenomenon of the New Testament.* Naperville, Ill.: Allenson, 1967. Pp. 4-15.

H. C. G. Moule. *Jesus and the Resurrection.* London: Seeley, 1893.

James Orr. *The Resurrection of Jesus.* Cincinnati: Jennings and Graham, n.d.

A. Michael Ramsey. *The Resurrection of Christ.* Philadelphia: Westminster, 1946.

K. H. Rengstorf. *Die Auferstehung Jesu.* Witten: Luther Verlag, 1954.

William C. Robinson, "The Bodily Resurrection of Jesus Christ," *Bulletin of Columbia Theological Seminary,* 50:3 (July 1957).

A. Schlatter. *The Church in the New Testament Period.* London: S.P.C.K., 1955. Pp. 4-14.

J. M. Shaw. *The Resurrection of Christ.* Edinburgh: T. & T. Clark, 1920.

W. J. Sparrow-Simpson. *The Resurrection and Modern Thought.* London: Longmans, Green, 1911.

W. M. Smith. *The Supernaturalness of Christ.* Boston: Wilde, 1944. Pp. 187-228.

Ethelbert Stauffer. *Jesus and His Story.* New York: Knopf, 1960. Pp. 143-153.

H. B. Swete. *The Appearance of Our Lord After the Passion.* London: Macmillan, 1915.

Merrill C. Tenney, "The Historicity of the Resurrection," in *Jesus of Nazareth: Saviour and Lord,* ed. Carl F. H. Henry. Grand Rapids: Eerdmans, 1966. Pp. 135-144.

B. F. Westcott. *The Revelation of the Risen Lord.* 6th edition, London: Macmillan, 1898.

CHAPTER XVII

THE ASCENSION

> *"He ascended into heaven."*
>
> —Apostles' Creed

> *"We feel and grasp its fitness, its necessity, as the one possible sequel of the Resurrection. We handle the firm texture of contemporary truth in the narrative, in which the extreme economy of attendant wonders is a sure sign of the absence of mythical alloy."*
>
> —Bishop Handley Moule

IN A SURVEY OF THE HIGHLIGHTS OF THE GREATEST LIFE EVER LIVED on earth, one could no doubt justify the omission of any consideration of the ascension on the double ground that it scarcely appears in the Gospel accounts and that it is so largely overshadowed by the resurrection. Even the two statements of the event are suspect, for one of them occurs in the long ending of Mark, almost universally now regarded as unauthentic (Mk. 16:19), and the other (Lk. 24:51) shows up only in the Received Text, being absent from early textual witnesses that would be expected to contain it.[1] In dealing with the latter passage, Hort made the illuminating comment, "The Ascension apparently did not lie within the proper scope of the Gospels, as seen in their genuine texts: its true place was at the head of the Acts of the Apostles, as the preparation for the Day of Pentecost, and thus

[1] The recently discovered P[75] has the words in question, "and was carried up into heaven," but this does not greatly change the situation. If the words were originally in the text, it is hard indeed to explain how they would have been dropped.

the beginning of the history of the Church."[2] Only in Acts 1:9-11 do we have a description of the event, followed by allusions to Jesus' exaltation (which may be said to presuppose the ascension) both in Acts and in the Epistles.

However, the resurrection alone does not leave us wholly satisfied, for the Christ who appears to his own is to a considerable degree detached from his followers. He is not with them on the same terms as before. Yet he lingers for these times of contact which serve to prepare the disciples for their future work. Clearly the Lord is in a transitional state, seeming to belong more to heaven than to earth. Something is required to bring his earthly ministry to a conclusion and give him the exalted station that is recognized by the church from its very inception. A. W. Argyle writes, "Belief in the empty tomb, the resurrection of our Lord, and His appearances in His risen body, necessitate belief in His ascension. For it is certain that the body which came back to earth from the dead at some time left the earth."[3]

PROBLEMS

In part the difficulties in dealing with the ascension are textual, as already suggested. Whereas the reference to the ascension in Luke 24:51 is not well attested, the embarrassment is just the opposite in the opening chapter of Acts, where the event is mentioned twice (Acts 1:2, 9-11). J. H. Ropes has questioned the originality of the words "he was taken up" in Acts 1:2 on the ground that they are an addition supplied by a very early editor,[4] and further that they fall under suspicion since the ascension would then be mentioned before the appearances. It could be, however, that Luke wished to give advance notice of the ascension before describing it in Acts 1:9-11, though the order is admittedly awkward.

As far as Luke 24:51 is concerned, even if the shorter reading be insisted on as genuine, it should be granted that the text gives

2 F. J. A. Hort, *The New Testament in the Original Greek* (1881), Appendix, p. 73.

3 "The Ascension," ET, 66:8 (May 1955), 240.

4 He supports this by noting a certain amount of textual disarray in the verse. *The Beginnings of Christianity*, ed. Jackson and Lake, III (1926), 256-261.

a broad hint of the ascension, for it states, "He parted from them," something that is said in connection with no other appearance. The following verse makes it evident that the disciples did not expect any further self-disclosure of the risen Lord to them. So the ascension is implied in the close of Luke's Gospel.

But this very fact creates another difficulty, for in chapter 24 Luke has put several appearances into the record, one after the other, beginning on the day of resurrection, with no suggestion that this final meeting at Bethany was at a later time. On the other hand, in the Acts he asserts that the ascension took place at the end of a forty-day period during which Jesus appeared to his own (Acts 1:3). It may be that when Luke came to write part two of his work (Acts) he felt the need of making clear that not all the postresurrection appearances were on one day, just as he clarified the event of the ascension, which he had only hinted at in the close of the Gospel. It is also possible that during the interval between the writing of the Gospel and the penning of the Acts more precise information reached him about the events between the resurrection and the ascension.

There is still another complexity that demands attention, namely, the question whether there was one ascension or two. The event Luke describes in Acts 1:9-11 was witnessed by the Eleven, but there is a strong possibility that the ascension to which Jesus referred when talking with Mary Magdalene (Jn. 20:17) was a separate occurrence. The Lord seemed anxious to depart to the Father and did not want to be detained. He was not yet prepared to show himself to the disciples, since he had a prior obligation to present himself to the Father who had sent him. Support for this possibility emerges from what Jesus asserted to the Eleven when he showed himself to them in Galilee: "All authority in heaven and on earth has been given to me" (Mt. 28:18). This seems to imply contact with the Father, on such a basis as the ascension, on resurrection day. Furthermore, according to John 7:39 it is the glorified Jesus who makes possible the gift of the Spirit, so the breathing on them and the granting of the Spirit on the evening of that first day (Jn. 20:22) strongly suggests that he had been glorified in the sense demanded by the right to make such a request.

Our conclusion should probably be, therefore, that an ascension took place on the morning of resurrection day, unobserved by man, followed after an interval of forty days by the Lord's visible departure from the earthly scene.[5] It is this latter event that Christians usually have in mind when they speak of the ascension. Surely there is something eminently fitting in the fact that Luke the historian, the man who was concerned with the factual basis of the faith and who had traced out all things accurately (Lk. 1:3), should be the one to provide an account of this historic event.

A final observation should be made respecting the problem aspect of the ascension. As compared to the resurrection, it is only occasionally referred to as an event after Luke's account in the first chapter of Acts (Eph. 4:10; I Tim. 3:16; Heb. 4:14; I Pet. 3:22), and fails to appear explicitly in most of the great christological passages where the redemptive acts of the Savior are presented in sequence (I Cor. 15:3ff.; Rom. 8:34, etc.). The reason for this is that biblical writers in the main prefer to use the language of exaltation rather than ascension, since it is a more inclusive term and has more theological content, especially from the standpoint of the authority now vested in the risen Lord (see, for example, Acts 2:32-33). The ascension is viewed as a preparatory step, no doubt, to the present glorified state of the Savior and his heavenly work, but is swallowed up by the greater importance of that which is consequent to it.[6]

It should be observed also that there is no single term employed for the ascension to the exclusion of others. Just as the resurrection could be stated in terms of an act of the Lord Jesus ("he arose"), though more usually in terms of an act of God on his behalf ("God raised him" or "he has been raised"), so likewise the ascension can be stated either as an event in which he proceeded into heaven or as an assumption ("he was taken up").

The Ascension as Event

Several things may be gleaned from the records. As to place, the ascension is located at Bethany, on the eastern slope of the mount of Olives (Lk. 24:50; Acts 1:12), the spot where Jesus loved to

---

[5] P. Benoit notes that in the writings of some of the Fathers the same double feature is observable, some statements positing an ascension on the day of resurrection, others by the same individuals citing the event at the end of the forty-day period. "L'Ascension," RB, 56 (Apr. 1949), 171.

[6] That the exaltation is thought of as including the ascension is clear from Acts 2:33-34, where the word "exalted" in one verse is paralleled by "ascend into the heavens" in the next.

linger, a home away from home (Lk. 10:38-42; Mk. 11:11). As to time, it is put at the end of the forty days following the resurrection (Acts 1:2-3), when the Lord had indicated to the disciples the scope of their witness and the divine empowering which would be theirs through the Holy Spirit (Acts 1:8).

Luke notes that just before the parting from the Eleven, Jesus lifted up his hands and blessed them. These were the hands that had held the loaves when they were blessed for the feeding of the multitude (Mk. 6:41) and that held the little children who were brought to him (Mk. 10:16). As they were spread out toward the men he loved and trained and trusted, these who received the blessing could discern the marks of the nails, an unforgettable reminder of the Savior's sacrifice on their behalf. The blessing was an assurance to them that his presence and intercession would never fail them.

Then came the departure, the lifting up from the earth and removal to the higher sphere where he would continue to minister. There was no fanfare, no chariot of fire such as swept Elijah up to glory, but rather a quiet withdrawal such as came to Enoch when God took him. After witnessing it, the disciples could be content with a simple homegoing, devoid of pomp and ceremony, when their time came to depart from this world.

"And a cloud took him out of their sight." This phenomenon is rather frequent in the Old Testament as a token of the divine presence and its mystery, an emphasis that carries over into the Gospels. At the transfiguration it may be said to be an anticipation of the future glory of the Son of God; at the ascension, a token of the realization of that glory; and in the predictions of his return, an accompaniment of the open manifestation of that same glory. The cloud added a distinct touch of majesty to the scene. This was true also of the presence of angels. For them it was a matter of unspeakable privilege to escort the King of glory to his heavenly reception.

The message of comfort left by the angels to the disciples as they stood riveted to the earth, gazing up into the heaven to keep their departing Master in view as long as possible, promised that he would return in person in the same manner as he had departed (Acts 1:11). It follows logically that one who doubts the ascension must reject a personal return of the Lord to earth, but the one who holds to the ascension as a historic reality has a firm ground for confidence concerning the future unveiling of the Son of man.

It may seem strange that the effect of the ascension on the disciples was to fill them with joy rather than with sadness, but surely this event served to seal in their minds the supreme truth that God had sent his Son as the Savior of the world. Their joy at seeing the Lord after his resurrection was not shadowed by the periods of absence between the appearances. Whether the interval between his departure and his return was to be long or short, they were not in a position to say; but this did not greatly matter. Their fellowship with the Son was constant and it brought them great joy (cf. I Jn. 1:4). Beyond lay the joyful reunion he himself had promised them (Jn. 14:3).

THE SIGNIFICANCE OF THE ASCENSION

Much of the meaning of this christological event has to be derived from the teaching of the Acts and the Epistles, a fact that confronts us also in dealing with the death and resurrection of Christ. The event is noted in connection with the history, but the importance of the event dawned on the church only gradually as the Spirit revealed it in its many-sidedness.

(1) As noted above, the ascension forms the boundary between the period of the appearances of the risen Savior and the full resumption of his heavenly life. From this time on, there would be no immediate contact with the earth in a physical sense until the return. The appearances to Stephen (Acts 7:55), to Saul of Tarsus (Acts 9:3-5), and to the seer of Patmos (Rev. 1:12-16) all have a heavenly setting. So it becomes fully clear that the resurrection body of the Lord does not fit into the Pharisaic mold of resuscitation of the flesh, but has a distinctly spiritual nature (cf. I Cor. 15).

(2) The ascension is complementary to the incarnation, for as a union of God with man was effected then, now a union of man with God is brought about. It is entirely wrong to think of the incarnation as merely the assuming of a body in which the Son of God could die for the sins of the world and then return to a pure spirit existence. No, the incarnation persists in the person of the man Christ Jesus. A saying comes to mind, attributed to "Rabbi" Duncan: "The dust of the earth is on the throne of the majesty on high."

(3) The ascension, in a manner even more striking than the resurrection, accents the universal Lordship of the Savior. Sasse notes that Lordship by virtue of resurrection could simply connote

that Jesus has become Lord of those who will live because of his resurrection. God has done more than raise him from the dead; he has exalted him to his own right hand, the place of power and authority. It is this emphasis that explains how Peter, after speaking of this exaltation in terms of Psalm 110, can go on to say, "God has made him both Lord and Christ" (Acts 2:36).[7] His Lordship and Messiahship do not date from this event, for they were his prerogative after the resurrection, and even before it; but they were not fully claimed yet because they had not yet been fully demonstrated.

(4) By the very nature of the case, the ascension is closely connected with the session of Christ at the right hand of the Majesty on high (Heb. 1:3), and therefore contributed by so much to the proclamation of the finished work of purification of sins. This was the task assigned to him in the divine plan, the task into which he entered with all heartiness and dedication. Now that the work is done, nothing can stand in the way of a return to the Father and the rest from his earthly labors to which he is so fully entitled.

(5) By means of the ascension Christ's victory over hostile spiritual powers is advertised. "When he ascended on high he led a host of captives" (Eph. 4:8). The evil one and all his hosts hang at the girdle of the Captain of our salvation. Paul would have us feel the swing and surge of triumph in the words he pens descriptive of this exaltation: "far above all rule and authority and power and dominion, and above every name that is named, not only in this age but also in that which is to come; and he has put all things under his feet and has made him the head over all things for the church" (Eph. 1:21-22). Christ "has gone into heaven and is at the right hand of God, with angels, authorities, and powers subject to him" (I Pet. 3:22). If there are powers that threaten the church, there is something more important, namely, that they have a superior, the founder of the church himself, now the ascended Lord. "Jesus Christ in his death and ascension has become the new Michael, the new defender of the righteous, the new opponent of the Satan before the heavenly tribunal, who in one mighty thrust of agonizing reconciliation forever rid the heavens of the jurisdictional, accusational presence of the Satan."[8]

[7] Hermann Sasse, "Jesus Christ, the Lord," in *Mysterium Christi* (1930), ed. C. K. A. Bell and Adolf Deissmann, p. 105.

[8] Calvin R. Schoonhoven, *The Wrath of Heaven* (1966), p. 141.

(6) As the exalted one, Christ has given gifts to men (Eph. 4:8). Foremost among these is the gift of the Holy Spirit. On the day of Pentecost Peter made capital of this. He was speaking to men who had not seen the risen Lord but who had been amazed by the manifestations of the Spirit on that very day in which Peter addressed them. The gift of the Spirit, so Judaism taught, was a feature of the messianic age. As Peter pointed to the pouring out of the Spirit as the demonstration of the exaltation of Jesus Christ, whom the nation had rejected, it is no wonder that thousands were convicted and put their faith in this Savior.

Included in the gift of the Spirit were men supernaturally equipped by him to minister to the church, whether apostles, prophets, evangelists, pastors and teachers, workers of miracles, speakers in tongues, etc. (Eph. 4:11; I Cor. 12:28). The variety represented here reflects the diversity of needs within the church as well as the richness of the divine provision to meet those needs.

(7) The functioning of Jesus as our great high priest is directly associated with the fact that he passed through the heavens to take his place at the throne of grace, there to give his sympathetic and timely aid to the saints by his ministry of intercession (Heb. 4:14-16), a ministry that assures continuance in salvation for those who draw near to God through him (Heb. 7:25). No other subject gets so much attention in the Epistle to the Hebrews as this one, so the wealth of allusion to the exaltation of Christ is wholly natural. Attention is focused on the entrance of the Savior into the heavenly sanctuary "to appear in the presence of God on our behalf" (Heb. 9:24).

(8) Because Jesus has gone into heaven "as a forerunner on our behalf" within the veil, the Christian hope of a heavenly inheritance is not a wistful bit of speculation but "a sure and steadfast anchor of the soul" (Heb. 6:19-20). The area within the veil in the worship of Israel was forbidden territory to all but the high priest. But after Christ's single efficacious sacrifice of himself, the veil was rent and sinners who trust in him are freely admitted to the eternal presence of a holy God.

(9) The close connection between the ascension and the return of Christ, already noted in Acts 1:9-11, invites that upward look of faith and expectation that has always characterized the church when obedient to Christ. In days of worldliness and loss of vision, Christians can do no better than to remind themselves that the ascended Lord has never abdicated his kingly right over the earth. The nations shall yet become his footstool. And when

he comes again it will not be to deal with sin but to grant a completed salvation to "those who are eagerly waiting for him" (Heb. 9:28).

BIBLIOGRAPHY

A. W. Argyle, "The Ascension," ET, 66:8 (May 1955), 240-242.

P. Benoit, "L'Ascension," RB, 56:2 (Apr. 1949), 161-203.

J. G. Davies. He Ascended into Heaven. London: Lutterworth, 1958.

Victorien Larrañga. L'Ascension de Notre-Seigneur dans le Nouveau Testament. Rome: Institut Biblique Pontifical, 1938.

C. S. Mann, "The New Testament and the Lord's Ascension," CQR, 158:329 (Oct.-Dec. 1957), 452-465.

Philippe Menoud, "Remarques sur les textes de l'ascension dans Luc-Actes," Neutestamentliche Studien für Rudolf Bultmann, ed. W. Eltester. Berlin: A. Töpelmann, 1954.

William Milligan. The Ascension and Heavenly Priesthood of Our Lord. London: Macmillan, 1894.

G. Campbell Morgan. The Crises of the Christ. New York: Revell, 1903. Pp. 386-413.

C. F. D. Moule, "Expository Problems: The Ascension," ET, 68:7 (Apr. 1957), 205-209.

A. M. Ramsey, "What Was the Ascension?" Bulletin of the Studiorum Novi Testamenti Societas, No. 2 (1951), 43-50.

H. B. Swete. The Ascended Christ. London: Macmillan, 1913.

B. F. Westcott. The Revelation of the Risen Lord. London: Macmillan, 1898. Chs. 10 and 11.

Chapter XVIII

"WHAT SORT OF MAN IS THIS?"

> *"It is easy to make a catalog of the qualities which entered into his human character; but the blending and the harmony and the perfection, the delight and the subduing charm, who can express? Yet all this walked on the earth in the flesh, and men and women saw it with their eyes."*
>
> —James Stalker

> *"I am the way, and the truth, and the life; no one comes to the Father, but by me."*
>
> —Jesus of Nazareth

IN OUR BRIEF JOURNEY THROUGH THE GOSPELS, SELECTING EN ROUTE the outstanding events and features of the life of Jesus of Nazareth for consideration, we have not paused to consider his person in any sustained fashion. To this we now turn.

One who looks for an exposition of this subject tucked away somewhere in the Gospel record is doomed to disappointment, for none is to be found. Jesus is always set forth as part of the living scene as it unfolds. There is no detached analysis and evaluation of him by those who have given us his story. As Channing says with reference to the Evangelists, "They have plainly but one aim, to show us their Master; and they manifest the deep veneration which He inspired by leaving Him to reveal Himself, by giving us His actions and sayings without comment, explanation, or eulogy."[1]

[1] W. E. Channing, "The Character of Christ," *The World's Great Sermons*, IV (1908), 30.

Quite naturally the Epistles of the New Testament are taken up to a large extent with the expounding of the risen and exalted Christ, yet the writers show a keen awareness of the epochal nature of his life as it was lived out in the earthly setting. When they urge upon their readers the cultivation of Christian virtues they are not content with stating them in the abstract or with citing Old Testament figures as examples (though they do this to a degree), but point to our Lord in the days of his flesh as providing the supreme example and pattern.

HIS CHARACTER

We should be prepared, then, for the discovery that the fragrance of Christ permeates the Gospel record, to which we are obliged to turn as our primary source. But it is a tantalizing, elusive fragrance, one that cannot be captured and bottled up. One writer has gone so far as to say that the attempt to describe the character of Christ is foredoomed to failure.[2] If the people of Jesus' time were disposed to identify him with men of such diverse temperament as Elijah and Jeremiah (Mt. 16:14), this should serve as a warning that the personality of the Nazarene presents many facets. This very fact may help to explain the fascination Jesus held for men, women, and children, as well as for all sorts of classes and occupations. We are looking at a many-sided individual.

Those who have little or no theological interest in him are nevertheless powerfully affected by the quality of Jesus Christ. They may stumble over his miracles but they stand erect and salute the man, not always appreciating that the very uniqueness of this life cannot be explained completely in terms of our common humanity. As Campbell Morgan was fond of saying, "In the things of his humanity, where he seems to come closest to us, he is actually farthest from us." Then he would add the complementary truth, "In the things of his deity, where he seems to be farthest from us, he actually comes closest to us." The case for Christianity can be made to rest on his character alone, for he is its supreme miracle.

There can be no doubt about his drawing power. Multitudes came to hear him and to benefit from his healing touch. Men were ready to leave their homes and abandon their occupations

2 John A. Broadus, *Jesus of Nazareth* (1962), p. 10.

in order to be with him, even when they were far from knowing very much about him. To be sure, others who heard the call were not ready to follow (Mk. 10:21), but the very unwillingness to do so left them unhappy and at odds with themselves (Mk. 10:22). The men who heeded the call were so gripped by the Master that they were ready to die for him (Mk. 14:31).

Some leaders of men have tried to enhance their status by creating an aura of mystery through detachment from their fellows or by the pursuit of ascetic practices. Jesus remained in touch with people by living a normal, balanced life. He was glad to be among the guests at a wedding (Jn. 2), and he wept unfeignedly when death brought sorrow to his friends (Jn. 11:35). We find him sitting at the table in the house of Pharisees (Lk. 7:36; 11:37), but more often, no doubt, he was seen eating with tax-gatherers and sinners and scandalizing the Pharisees in the process (Lk. 5:30). His presence was meat and drink in itself for those who loved him (Lk. 10:38-42).

Let any who will do so be satisfied with the pious (?) observation that Jesus is never said to have smiled. Some things are so readily assumed that they do not need mention. Certainly enough of the humor of the Master crops out here and there to warrant the feeling that he had a rich vein of it in his nature. What about the sobriquet *Boanerges* which he pinned on the sons of Zebedee (Mk. 3:17), proving he knew them better than they knew themselves (Lk. 9:54)? Can we imagine him uttering his comments about the plank and the speck (Mt. 7:3) with a straight face? He must have managed a sly smile when he pictured the Pharisees straining out a gnat and swallowing a camel (Mt. 23:24).

Impressive also is Jesus' sense of fairness. He rushes to the defense of his disciples when they are wrongly reproached by others (Mk. 2:23-24), but he does not hesitate to upbraid his own when he detects some genuine failing in them, such as lack of faith (Mk. 4:40) or the attempt to turn him from his chosen path of obedience to God's will (Mt. 16:23).

He was not lacking in courtesy. Anticipating the need of an animal for his ride into Jerusalem, he gives instruction to two of his disciples, who then go off to procure the colt. From their words of explanation, "The Lord has need of it and will send it back here immediately," it is apparent that Jesus included this item in his briefing.

Thoughtfulness marked his contacts with others, sometimes in striking ways. Before rousing the daughter of Jairus from her death-sleep, Jesus put a stop to the hubbub of the mourners and allowed only his inner circle of three disciples in addition to the father and mother to go into the chamber when the damsel was called back to life, thus sparing her the trauma that could easily result from noise and confusion. Added to this was his reminder that the maiden could use some food. Similarly we see him stopping a great concourse of moving humanity that had gathered around him as he moved through Jericho, in order to deal with a single man who needed his healing touch (Lk. 18:35-43). Amid the intense drama of his seizure in the garden he restored the detached ear of Malchus (Lk. 22:51), and a short while afterwards, in the midst of his own interrogation by the Jewish authorities, took a moment to turn and look upon Peter when the cock sounded (Lk. 22:61).

His appreciation should not pass unnoticed. He was quick to observe and respond to faith, particularly when it came from unexpected sources such as a Canaanite woman (Mt. 15:28) or a Roman centurion (Lk. 7:9). It might have seemed to some of his contemporaries that Jesus did not do much to thank John the Baptist for his outspoken testimony to "the greater light." Yet such an impression is contradicted by the Master's moving commendation of the forerunner that climaxes in the verdict that among those born of women none is greater than John (Lk. 7:28). Were it not for the cavils of small men, we might not have known how Jesus felt about attention paid to his own person by the anointing of his feet. In defending these women, he expressed his gratitude (Lk. 7:36-50; Mk. 14:1-9)

Consistency is so rare among men that for this reason it has been called a jewel, but it is not too rare to be found as a sparkling element in the character of Jesus. Here is one who talked much about the importance of prayer and also made it central to his own devotional life. When he proclaimed the folly of distracting anxiety, the ring of conviction was in his words, for he had learned to stay his soul with complete abandon upon the goodness and faithfulness of the Father.

Prudence also had its place. Though our Lord met opposition whenever it was necessary to face it, and although he did not hesitate to rebuke his adversaries when their conduct called for it, he nevertheless refused to give needless offense. So he avoided collision with the Pharisees by leaving Judea for Galilee (Jn. 4:1-3), and by departing from the confines of the country itself after a stiff confrontation with local Pharisees aided by a delegation of scribes from Jerusalem (Mk. 7:1, 24). When the Sanhedrin became inflamed over the raising of Lazarus, he and his disciples withdrew from Jerusalem to the edge of the eastern wilderness (Jn. 11:54). Bravado had no place in his being.

Some other things were noticeably lacking also, things that would have to count as blemishes were they detectable in him. Self-pity was foreign to his thought. Presumably we would not have had his saying that the foxes had holes and the birds of the air their nests but the Son of man lacked a place to lay his head, apart from the need of warning a would-be disciple about the lot he must expect to share (Lk. 9:58). When the daughters of Jerusalem thought to commiserate with him as he moved wearily along the Via Dolorosa, he bade them not weep for him but for themselves, in view of the distresses that were in store for their city (Lk. 23:28).

Vindictiveness was absent also. Under frequent mistreatment, he refused to retaliate. The twelve legions of angels were never summoned. Typical is the incident of the snubbing he received from the Samaritans as he journeyed toward Jerusalem. The want of hospitality so roused the sons of Zebedee that they proposed a flame-throwing demolition of the village. All the Master did was to rebuke the pair and pass on (Lk. 9:51-56).

He had no craving for fame. Repeatedly he tried to forestall it by commanding the beneficiaries of his miracles to keep quiet about what had happened to them (Mt. 12:16). When the multitudes thronged him with their sick and received them back sound in body, the usual response was a volume of praise to God for this marvelous gift of healing (Mt. 15:31). Jesus was not ruffled or hurt that the people failed to include him in their praise. He was the Servant of the Lord, in whom notoriety had no place (Mt. 12:18-21).

One could go on detailing the fine points of Jesus' character, for the list is long; but at this juncture it would probably be more helpful to concentrate on a few primary traits.

(1) *Humility.* "I am gentle and lowly in heart" (Mt. 11:29). Familiarity with these words has blunted the force of their message. They were daring words, for they asserted as an asset what the pagan world regarded as weak and despicable. Humility? "No Greek writer employed it before the Christian era, nor, apart from the influence of Christian writers, after."[3] Men thought that

[3] R. C. Trench, *Synonyms of the New Testament*, 12th edition (1894), p. 148.

humility interfered with the full expression of personality. So it was that the ancient world had to suffer the pratings of its great men, especially its rulers, who were insufferably addicted to the cult of self-importance.

The remarkable thing about this declaration of our Lord is that it seems to have been uttered in conjunction with his assertion of a knowledge of the Father that was peculiarly his own (Mt. 11:27). Yet that privilege did not inflate him. Similarly, it was in the light of his realization that all things had been given into his hands by the Father, and that he had come from the Father and was returning to him, that Jesus bent down to wash the disciples' feet and give them a lesson in humility (Jn. 13:3-5). Here we learn what true humility is—not the miserable habit of thinking mean thoughts about oneself, but engaging in self-giving that brings good to others. When James and John requested places of honor for themselves in the kingdom, Jesus gently rebuked them with the observation that, while it was customary among the Gentiles for those who ruled to lord it over their people, the path to any greatness among his followers was quite different. "Whoever would be great among you must be your servant" (Mk. 10:43). Then to burn home the lesson he pointed to himself. "For the Son of man also came not to be served but to serve, and to give his life as a ransom for many" (Mk. 10:45). Humility was the very pulse-beat of the incarnate life of our Lord. In the most regal situation of his career he insisted on presenting himself to Israel as her humble king, as Scripture had foretold (Mt. 21:5).

(2) *Compassion.* "He took our infirmities and bore our diseases" (Mt. 8:17). According to Matthew, who climaxes his report of a day's ministry in Capernaum with these words from Isaiah 53, Jesus willingly took upon himself the burden of humanity's ills. Whether it was to touch the hand of Peter's mother-in-law and banish her fever, or to heal the many who gathered at the door later in the evening, through it all he was taking to himself the troubles of others and being drained accordingly.

There is such a thing as a sentiment of compassion which can move people to tears, but there is no further movement. Robert Law warns against being satisfied with a tender heart. "It may, indeed, only disguise a peculiarly subtle selfishness. For we enjoy feeling simply as such."[4] The same writer goes on to say, "You

4 *The Emotions of Jesus* (1915), p. 53.

cannot effectually help any man unless by taking in some way his burden upon you. You must pay the price; and while for mere pecuniary help the pocket may suffice to pay, and for physical help the body, at the basis of all real help is soul-help, and for it you must pay with your soul."[5] Jesus paid in terms of loss of strength (Lk. 6:19; 8:46), of rest at night (for the day of activity left no time for prayer, hence the necessity of rising before dawn to commune with the Father), of comfort (at times there was no leisure even to eat), and of reputation, for he was criticized for mingling with the outcasts of society (Lk. 15:1). His recompense came in the realization that he was needed and that he was responding to the call, whether it be of the sick or the sinful. He was able to give himself with equal compassion to the individual (Mk. 1:41) and to the crowd that milled about like sheep without a shepherd (Mt. 9:36). The sight of Jerusalem, the citadel of blindly religious men, moved him deeply (Mt. 23:37). Though his love for his people would be spurned, he must love them still and hold out his arms to them, until those arms were held out to the open sky in the final supplication of Calvary. Such love never fails.

(3) *Indignation.* "And he looked around at them with anger" (Mk. 3:5). It happened in the synagogue, on the sabbath, when a man with a withered hand was in attendance. Would Jesus heal him? Some Pharisees who were present hoped he would, that they might have a basis of accusation against him. Sensing this, Jesus asked, "Is it lawful on the sabbath to do good or to do harm, to save life or to kill?" They knew as well as he that with all its restrictions, the sabbath law laid down in the Old Testament did not forbid the doing of good. Here was a case of raw inhumanity, which was all the more inexcusable for its being perpetrated in the name of religion. No wonder the Master burned with indignation.

On another day, when people were bringing children that Jesus might bless them, the disciples sought to intervene and put a stop to it. "But when Jesus saw it he was indignant" (Mk. 10:14). He could not help resisting with all his heart any attempt to shield him from contact with the little ones. The disciples shared the limitations of their age in their attitude toward children; Jesus anticipated the best of modern insights as to their worth and the power of early impressions upon their lives.

5 *Ibid.*, p. 61.

Does the display of indignation spell weakness in the character of Jesus? It should be borne in mind that he did not display it in self-interest or self-defense, even though greater wrongs were heaped on him than those that elicited his anger. Furthermore, there is no ground for supposing that Jesus was ever guilty of passionate rage, that he ever broke out in a fit of temper. If he had failed to have indignation, there might be ground for supposing defect. "If wood does not burn, it is because it is green or rotten. If hearts do not burn with holy fire against wicked men and their wicked deeds, it is because the heart is too undeveloped to feel what manly hearts were meant to feel, or because the core of the heart has been eaten out by the base practices of a godless life."[6]

Any display of anger on Jesus' part is not to be prejudged as a sign of weakness or failure, for after all, God himself is represented as being angry (e.g. Ps. 7:11). To object to anger as such would be to impugn the character of God.[7]

(4) *Courage.* It is nowhere said that Jesus had courage, for it did not need saying; it is implied from beginning to end in his story. This is one virtue that has always drawn the open admiration of the whole world. When Aristotle advanced his famous doctrine of the "mean," he illustrated it by courage, which stands midway between cowardice and recklessness. Gauged by this analysis, the character of Jesus appears in a most favorable light, for in him one detects no wild instability even in the most intense activity, nor does he find supineness in his passivity.

There are men who exhibit courage spasmodically. Peter's courage tended to be of this order until he attained rocklike strength at Pentecost. But Jesus had a constancy of spirit. Like the arms of Moses he was steady till the going down of the sun. It took courage for the son of the carpenter to leave his village and launch out upon his ministry without the help of family or friends. It took courage to accept baptism from John and thus run the risk of being thought of as a needy sinner. It took courage to face the rigors of the temptation alone in the wilderness. It took courage to oppose the traditions of men that obscured or even contradicted the word of God. It took courage to tell men that they were evil, and to expose their sins so relentlessly that they were left without a cloak for those sins. It took courage to

6 Charles E. Jefferson, *The Character of Jesus* (1908), p. 305.

7 J. B. Lightfoot has an illuminating sermon, "The Wrath of the Lamb," in *Cambridge Sermons* (1893), pp. 193-211.

refuse the demand of the people that he consent to be made their king. It took courage to set his face steadfastly to go up to Jerusalem. It took courage to cleanse the temple. It took courage to accept the cup from the Father's hand. It took courage to face the venom of his accusers and the brutality of his crucifiers. It was one long trail of courage from beginning to end—the courage of conviction and consecration. It has the church and all of Christian history as its abiding monument.

Jefferson points out that, by and large, the great people of this world have gained that accolade by reason of some achievement that makes them stand out from their fellows. But again and again these same giants of action have exhibited smallness and compromise of character. They are remembered for what they accomplished but not for what they were.[8] How different with Jesus of Nazareth. The work and the worth are in splendid equipoise.

If we think to detract from the character of Jesus by pointing to some episode in which he seems to us to fall a bit short of perfection, we should reflect that the very presence of such an item in the record is testimony to the fidelity of the Evangelists, a testimony to the fact that they were not manufacturing a character and then slipping it on Jesus as a garment. On such a basis nothing that looked at all like a shortcoming could be permitted to appear. The data obviously rest on real life and reflect truthful reporting. It is in the total picture set before us that we discern the uniqueness of our Lord's character. When the wonder of that portrait is perceived, it will be in order once more to estimate any supposed blemishes and to ask ourselves the question whether that portrait can really tolerate the faults, however minuscule, that we in our first shallow assessment thought we had found. It may turn out that the blemish lies in our own perception and understanding.

> It is not merely that we see in Him an approximation to the moral ideal, nearer and more successful than is to be discerned in any other man; but that we find in Him the moral ideal, once for all realized and incarnated, so that no man can ever go beyond Him, while all men in all ages will find it their strength and joy to grow up toward the measure of His stature.[9]

[8] *Op. cit.*, pp. 340-342.
[9] T. B. Kilpatrick, "Character of Christ," HDCG, I, 295b.

His Claims

The understanding of Jesus acquired by his disciples undoubtedly came first of all through the impact of his character upon them, which prepared the way for the ultimate question of his identity. In this quest they were aided by occasional statements from their Lord and Master about himself. The grander the assertions the greater their reliance had to be upon his proven character, for if his truthfulness and sincerity remained in doubt, his lofty claims could only bring disgust and alienation.

To be sure, the word "claims" labors under a certain disadvantage, since it may suggest an attempt to create an impression that goes beyond the facts. For this reason, plus a certain embarrassment in employing a word that may carry with it rather obvious apologetic overtones, there are those who prefer to speak of Jesus' "self-disclosure." No doubt this term has some advantage from this particular standpoint, but it is weaker than "claims" inasmuch as it may give the impression that there was no attempt on the part of Jesus to gain a verdict for himself in the estimation of men. Both terms are needed, for both elements are present.

In confining the investigation of Jesus' person to his self-revelation, the inquirer faces a problem at the very outset, in that the subject of the inquiry wrote nothing. Consequently, whether we like it or not, we are dependent on what others report as his sayings. A certain type of criticism delights to remind us of this and uses this circumstance as a basis for questioning the reports. After all, we see Jesus, we are told, only through the eyes of the church; we cannot know him as he was in the days of his flesh. Some would go so far as to assert, whether openly or by implication, that he is the product of the church, which has read its own ideas, impressions, and hopes into the picture to such an extent that we cannot be sure what the original was. But as Rawlinson reminds us, "If it was Christianity that created the figure of the Christ of the Gospels, what was it that created Christianity?"[10] The more we exalt the Christian faith, the more inexplicable it is apart from the greatness of its founder. It is quite gratuitous to assume that the church buttressed the figure of Jesus by working up a rather elaborate network of Old Testament predictions regarded as fulfilled in him. Judging from the opaqueness of the

---

[10] A. E. J. Rawlinson, *The New Testament Doctrine of the Christ* (1929), p. 10.

disciples, this achievement cannot be credited to them. It is far more credible that our Lord himself had this concept of his mission and shared it with his own. This happens to be the explanation of the New Testament (Lk. 24:44ff.). We do well to remember that the doctrine of Christ held in the early church was not derived from the Gospels, so that if the Gospel records can somehow be discredited the doctrine will vanish. On the contrary, the doctrine attained its place in the Gospels because such a view of our Lord was present in the church from the beginning and is due to Christ's own impression made on his followers.[11]

We turn now to consider certain specific claims advanced by Jesus the Christ during the course of his ministry.

(1) His *heavenly origin*. Instead of talking about his birth in Bethlehem and his early years in Nazareth, Jesus talked in otherworldly terms. "You are from below, I am from above; you are of this world, I am not of this world" (Jn. 8:23). Consequently, when he says over and over again that the Father sent him into the world, we are not to think of this sending in the same terms as that of the prophets. Our Lord was conscious of a previous existence; he could talk of the glory he had with the Father before the world was (Jn. 17:5). If such assertions suggest boastfulness and on this basis deserve to be dismissed, such an impression is immediately countered by the fact that this very claim of divine origin is accompanied by statements indicating complete dependence on the Father.[12]

(2) His *relation to God*. While all men are the offspring of God (Acts 17:28), the position of Jesus is different, unique. That is the force of the word *monogenēs* (rendered *only begotten* in the KJV) in John 3:16 and other passages. When Jesus said, "My Father is working still, and I am working" (Jn. 5:17), the Jews who were present caught the meaning very well. They understood that he was making himself equal with God, and, in their view, for this reason deserved to die the death of a blasphemer. The people generally seem to have known that Jesus advanced this claim, for they said at the crucifixion, "If you are the Son of God, come down from the cross" (Mt. 27:40). Then they said to one another, "He trusts in God: let God deliver him now, if he desires him; for he said, 'I am the Son of God' " (Mt. 27:43).

In commenting on Jesus' statement, "He who has seen me has

---

[11] J. K. Mozley, *The Doctrine of the Incarnation* (1949), p. 28.

[12] This subject of Christ's dependence is worked out in considerable detail by J. Ernest Davey in *The Jesus of St. John* (1958).

seen the Father" (Jn. 14:9), Robert Law says, "The character of Jesus is the character of Almighty God, the holiness of Jesus the holiness of God, the wrath of Jesus the wrath of God, the compassion of Jesus the compassion of God, the Cross of Jesus the revelation of the sorrow and self-sacrificing love with which the sin of man fills the heart of the Eternal."[13]

Jesus asserted a special knowledge of God. "No one knows the Father except the Son and any one to whom the Son chooses to reveal him" (Mt. 11:27). This is preceded by a statement of the Father's unique knowledge of the Son. A strikingly similar affirmation is made by Jesus when he says, "I am the good shepherd; I know my own and my own know me, as the Father knows me and I know the Father" (Jn. 10:14-15). C. H. Dodd notes that this conception of knowing God, not in abstractions but embodied in a living person, has a "peculiar character of its own, to which no exact parallel can be found."[14]

(3) *Divine prerogatives* present in him. Christ's knowledge of man, as to what was in him, seems to be represented as supernatural in quality (Jn. 2:25). He could identify Nathanael as a man without guile (Jn. 1:47-48) and could spot Judas as a man filled with it (Jn. 6:70).

His claim to authority goes far beyond that which is common to man. "All authority in heaven and on earth has been given to me" (Mt. 28:18). There is no usurpation here; the authority has been given. Rome, the mighty conqueror and all but universal ruler, could claim the devotion of its subjects as a religious act, for Rome had proved its prowess. Jesus, though he had wrought some mighty works, was restricted to a small land and a despised people. Only in prospect could he speak of exercising worldwide authority. His claim left room for faith.

It lay within his power, according to Jesus, to forgive sins (Mk. 2:10). Dalman writes, "The meaning is that He does so here on earth just in the same way as is done by God in heaven."[15] Men may forgive each other, but that forgiveness touches only human relations and the manward effects of sin, whereas Christ's forgiveness bears on the individual's relation to God.

The power to quicken the dead (Jn. 5:28), which Jesus demonstrated in the case of Lazarus, is a corollary of the creative work of the Son (Jn. 1:3), for the same power that creates is surely

13 *Op. cit.*, p. 11.
14 *The Interpretation of the Fourth Gospel* (1953), p. 168.
15 G. Dalman, *The Words of Jesus* (1909), p. 213.

able to restore life. In the same context Jesus indicated that the function of universal judgment belonged to him (Jn. 5:22). Men judge one another, but that judgment makes no pretense of fixing eternal destiny as his judgment does.

A function which necessarily brackets the Son with the Father is the sending of the Holy Spirit, "whom I shall send to you from the Father" (Jn. 15:26; cf. 16:7). In the Old Testament the outpouring of the Spirit is clearly connected with the realization of the messianic hope. The coming of the Messiah would mean the gift of the Spirit (cf. Acts 2:33). Not to be overlooked is Jesus' assertion that when the Spirit comes, "He will glorify me" (Jn. 16:14).

(4) *Oneness with the Father.* "I and the Father are one" (Jn. 10:30). This is the final statement in a series of comments made by our Lord to the Jews who demand an answer to the problem of his identity. "If you are the Christ, tell us plainly" (Jn. 10:24). There is nothing here or elsewhere to suggest that what our Lord had in mind was an elevation of his humanity by contemplation and devotion to the point where he had attained a union with the divine. Rather, in himself the unity with the Father "is original and perfect."[16] In the confidence of full equality with the Father, Jesus could promise to those who love him and keep his word, "My Father will love him, and we will come to him and make our home with him" (Jn. 14:23).

(5) *The way to God.* "I am the way, and the truth, and the life; no one comes to the Father, but by me" (Jn. 14:6). As noted at an earlier point, the language here is significant—no one *comes,* not "goes." This is not mere quibbling about words. When Jesus talks about going to the Father, he uses a different word. In this claim of John 14:6 he is clearly taking his stand on the side of God, where he knows he belongs. It is only because of that prior relationship that he is able by his mediatorial work to bring men to God. Once again we hear him declare how indispensable he is to those who would find acceptance with God. "So every one who acknowledges me before men, I also will acknowledge before my Father who is in heaven; but whoever denies me before men, I also will deny before my Father who is in heaven" (Mt. 10:32-33).

(6) *Sinlessness.* Christ could throw out the challenge, "Which of you convicts me of sin?" (Jn. 8:46) and have it go unanswered.

16 Dodd, *op. cit.,* p. 197.

It is a truism that the greatest awareness of sin and grieved sensibility to its presence in life is found among the saintliest of men. On this basis it follows that if Jesus, with all his moral excellence, had any awareness of sin whatsoever, he would have given expression to it. But there is not a whisper of any such thing. Our Lord was apparently conscious of a vast difference between himself and all others at this crucial point. What makes it impossible to explain this difference in terms of a "holy man" or "saint" framework is his filial consciousness, his awareness of perfect rapport with the Father based on a full community of life with him. This does not fit into the category of human experience, whether normal or extraordinary.

(7) *Lordship over the spirit world.* Jesus proclaimed himself Master of the hosts of heaven. Angels were at his beck and call (he calls them *his* angels in Mt. 13:41; 16:27); and evil spirits, the hosts of darkness, were subject to him (Lk. 11:20).

(8) *The value of his life when given for others.* "For the Son of man also came not to be served but to serve, and to give his life as a ransom for many" (Mk. 10:45). As the psalmist says, "No man can ransom himself or give to God the price of his life" (Ps. 49:7); but here is one who is able to ransom the "many" who need redemption. Jesus knew his unique value in the sight of God as the mediator between God and men. "The suddenness of the Church's faith in an atoning, redeeming, glorified, eternal Christ is quite unintelligible unless there was that in Jesus which made it inevitable as soon as the whole range of his work was finished, and the total scope of his person realized."[17] The same writer has remarked somewhere that, "No half-God could redeem the soul which it took the whole God to create."

(9) *The demand that his followers sacrifice for him* and not simply with him for God. This is an important aspect of Jesus' self-awareness and ought to be considered along with the claims that he made Godward.[18] "You will be dragged before governors and kings for my sake" (Mt. 10:18). "He who loves son or daughter more than me is not worthy of me" (Mt. 10:37). "He who loses his life for my sake will find it" (Mt. 10:39). "He who receives you receives me, and he who receives me receives him who sent me" (Mt. 10:40).

(10) He offers *eternal life* as his own gift. "And I give them

[17] P. T. Forsyth, *The Person and Place of Jesus Christ* (1910), p. 46.
[18] It is well handled by James Denney in *Jesus and the Gospel* (1913), pp. 215-240.

eternal life, and they shall never perish, and no one shall snatch them out of my hand" (Jn. 10:28). In this he acts jointly with the Father (v. 29).

(11) He offers *rest*. "Come to me, all who labor and are heavy-laden, and I will give you rest" (Mt. 11:28). What mortal would dare to invite the whole world to cast its entire load of weariness and abuse upon himself, or even dream of doing so?

(12) The claim of *Godhood* is implied in Jesus' acceptance of worship. We are not basing anything on the mere fact that at times people came and prostrated themselves before him. This could be done before any Oriental monarch or personage of importance. A problem of translation is involved here, as to whether "worship" or "bow down" is the appropriate expression. It is well to limit our attention to two incidents that included teaching by Jesus or the imparting of definite knowledge about himself. One has to do with the blind man (Jn. 9:38) and the other with the apostle Thomas (Jn. 20:28). If Christ had been less than the Son of God in the absolute sense, it would have been morally wrong for him to accept this adoration (cf. Acts 14:13-15).

Looking back over the various items enumerated here, it is noticeable that they are grounded, in a majority of instances, on testimony contained in the Fourth Gospel. No apology need be made for this. Clearly this Gospel has a more sustained christological interest than the others, but to say that it stands completely apart and gives an entirely different picture of Christ's person than the Synoptics is to revive a dogma of the criticism of yesteryear. Today men of various schools of thought are agreed that it is vain to try to establish a lower Christology-from the Synoptics than is taught in the Fourth Gospel. Jesus' sermon in the synagogue at Nazareth is reported by Luke, not by John. The Scripture reading (from Isaiah 61) was followed, as usual, by the interpretation: "Today this Scripture has been fulfilled in your hearing" (Lk. 4:21). What minister of the gospel, apostle or otherwise, would think of reading that passage and then announcing to the congregation that the Scripture had been fulfilled in his own person? The old liberalism, in denying that Jesus was a part of his gospel, yes, indispensable to it, only revealed its spiritual blindness. Jesus called for faith in himself (Jn. 6:29; 14:1). To preach Christ and to preach the gospel are synonymous terms (Acts 8:5, 12, 14).

In all fairness it behooves us to look at certain items that seem to present the Lord Jesus in a lesser light than deity, and by his own confession. One such utterance touches the scope of his knowledge. Speaking of his return, he said, "But of that day or that hour no one knows, not even the angels in heaven, nor the Son, but only the Father" (Mk. 13:32). It is worthy of note that despite the limitation that Jesus acknowledges, he still puts himself above men and even above angels. All one can say is that this one area of self-limitation belongs to the state of humiliation he had voluntarily assumed.

Another case involves Jesus' disavowal of the epithet "good" when it was applied to him by one who came asking what he must do to inherit eternal life (Mk. 10:17, 18). It is not certain that Jesus would have responded thus if one of his followers had used this term. Likely it was used with a certain flippancy, which grated on him. He reminded the inquirer that God alone could properly be so described. One notes a certain hesitancy about using the term "God" for Jesus, even though the divine prerogatives belong to him. The reason lies in the history of the Jews, who had been taught that God was one. "For 'the Jews' 'God' meant the heavenly Father; and until a wider understanding of the term was reached, it could not be readily applied to Jesus. This is reflected in Mark 10:18, where Jesus refuses to be called good because only God is good." [19]

A third instance has to do with Jesus' subordination to the Father in the area of greatness or power. "My Father, who has given them [the sheep] to me, is greater than all" (Jn. 10:29). Still more specific is the admission, "The Father is greater than I" (Jn. 14:28). Consider this last statement carefully. How preposterous it would be for any other member of the human race to say this! It presupposes a unique relation to the Father. A son should defer to his father, and Jesus is no exception. Especially is it suitable in the state of humiliation the Son assumed for purposes of redemption.

Those who exalt Jesus as the great teacher do not always realize the awkwardness of their position when they go on to refuse to him the rank of deity. Is it logical to accept his teaching on God, on man, on the ethical life, and then refuse to accept his teaching about himself? The words of Geerhardus Vos need to be weighed with care. "In the religious sphere all spiritual powers acquire a heightened sensitiveness and develop a desire for absolute posses-

[19] Raymond E. Brown, *The Gospel According to John* (Anchor Bible), I (1966), 24.

sion and interpenetration. How halting and inwardly disrupted a religious approach to Jesus must be which feels bound to stop short of accepting and receiving Him at the face-value of his central self-estimate!"[20] He goes on, "No one can take a Savior to his heart in that absolute unqualified sense which constitutes the glory of religious trust, if there persists in the background of his mind the thought that this Savior failed to understand Himself."

If Jesus were only a man as we know men, or even only a very great man, could those who knew him best have presented him as more than this? "If, as is asserted, that age had a bias towards crowning great men with the *aureole* of the supernatural, why should this superstitious tendency have concentrated itself upon Jesus, and Jesus only?"[21]

On the assumption that Jesus really made the claims attributed to him in the Gospels, is it psychologically possible for a person to project such claims, which lie so far outside the realm of human attainment, and be otherwise completely normal; and could the record of these claims as they stand in the Gospels have created such profound reception and faith as it has created, apart from having solid truth behind them? After listing some of the lofty assertions of Jesus concerning himself, Bushnell throws out the challenge, "Take on all these transcendent assumptions, and see how soon your glory will be sifted out of you by the detective gaze, and darkened by the contempt of mankind!"[22]

Actually, if we confine ourselves simply to the teaching of Jesus and abstract the element of self-testimony in it to his own person, it is quite impossible to view what is left without instinctively feeling that there is something here that goes beyond man. Commenting on the words of our Lord, "Heaven and earth will pass away, but my words will not pass away" (Mt. 24:35), Alfred Noyes feels bound to say, "The values of that utterance—subjected to the coldest standards of literary criticism—are not human. The voice of the Eternal is in it, before whom even the suns and universes dissolve like a shadow, and all the ages of Time are but a moment."[23]

But the truly significant thing is that the followers of Jesus, who had sat under his instruction for three years, did not go

20 *The Self-Disclosure of Jesus* (1926), p. 14.
21 F. Godet, *Lectures in Defence of the Christian Faith* (1881), p. 185.
22 Horace Bushnell, *The Character of Jesus* (1860), p. 49.
23 *The Unknown God* (1934), p. 354.

forth primarily to transmit his teaching to others, but to be witnesses to him, to his person. They sensed that he stood alone and apart from all others. It was this uniqueness that their burning hearts constrained them to communicate to the world.

BIBLIOGRAPHY

Otto Borchert. *The Original Jesus.* London: Lutterworth, 1933. Pp. 159-393.

John A. Broadus. *Jesus of Nazareth.* Grand Rapids: Baker, 1962. Pp. 9-36.

Horace Bushnell. *The Character of Jesus.* New York: Scribners, 1860.

W. E. Channing, "The Character of Christ," in *The World's Great Sermons,* compiled by Grenville Kleiser. New York: Funk and Wagnalls, 1908. Vol. IV, pp. 29-52.

G. K. Chesterton. *The Everlasting Man.* London: Hodder and Stoughton, 1947. Pp. 215-247.

F. Bertram Clogg. *The Christian Character in the Early Church.* London: Epworth, 1944. Pp. 15-56.

James Denney. *Jesus and the Gospel.* London: Hodder and Stoughton, 1913. Pp. 198-371.

————. *Studies in Theology.* New York: Doran, n.d. Pp. 24-46.

P. T. Forsyth. *The Person and Place of Jesus Christ.* Philadelphia: Westminster, 1910. Pp. 101-133.

F. Godet. *Lectures in Defence of the Christian Faith.* Edinburgh: T. & T. Clark, 1881. Pp. 165-260.

C. E. Jefferson. *The Character of Jesus.* New York: Crowell, 1908.

T. B. Kilpatrick, "Character of Christ," HDCG. Vol. I, pp. 281-297.

Robert Law. *The Emotions of Jesus.* New York: Scribners, 1915.

C. H. Robinson. *Studies in the Character of Christ.* London: Longmans, Green, 1920.

E. Stauffer. *Jesus and His Story.* New York: Knopf, 1960. Pp. 154-195.

G. Vos. *The Self-Disclosure of Jesus.* New York: Doran, 1926.

B. B. Warfield. *Christology and Criticism.* New York: Oxford, 1929.

Alexander Whyte. *The Walk, Conversation and Character of Jesus Christ Our Lord.* New York: Revell, 1905.

INDEX OF AUTHORS

275

INDEX OF SUBJECTS

278

INDEX OF SCRIPTURE REFERENCES

NON-CANONICAL LITERATURE

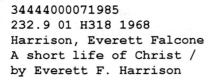